by:
Publications
icago Rd, Coldwater, MI.

 or Angels
ion published 2013

arol Geisinger
itor: Debi Tesser
y: Tabatha D. Mattzela

d by:
C Ministries
588
OR 97119

 printed in the USA
© 2012 by
orres

9703553-8-6
KJV (Primary Version) | NKJV | RSV | NASB | TLB | ASV
NCV (The New Century Version)

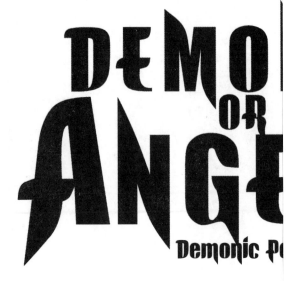

DEMO

OR

ANGE

Demonic Po

BY
LOUIS R. TOR

Printe
Remna
649 E.

Demo
This e

Edior:
Copy-
Desigr

Publis
Torres
PO Bc
Gasto

ISBN

TABLE OF CONTENTS

FOREWORD

In February 2002, while I was ministering in a church in Brisbane, Australia, a distressed mother brought a young girl, and she asked me to determine if demon possession was her ailment. What a pitiful sight! The girl was 18 years old but carried herself as if she were only eight. She gazed and stared with almost no recognition of my presence. The guardian suspected possession because of the girl's frequent self-abuse; the unprovoked blood-curdling screams were another indication. At the conclusion of my interview with the girl and surrogate mother, the church pastor approached me.

"Can you give a talk to the area pastors?" he had asked. "Most of us don't have a clue what to look for. And if we did, we wouldn't know where to begin to help the victim."

Because of the widespread ignorance concerning this enigma, strange ideas and practices have arisen. There are those who claim to be "exorcists." They prowl for candidates in order to declare someone "possessed." Then they undertake the task to free the supposed victim. Hence, organizations called "Deliverance Ministries," or "Spiritual Warfare Ministries," claim to provide exorcism services.

"Exorcism" is the term used to describe an expulsion from a person of a supernatural being called a demon, devil, evil spirit, or Satan. Though often considered primitive in the Western world, this practice is now in vogue in many metropolitan areas and among the elite.

There are different approaches to the problem of demonic possession. Hence, the rise of Deliverance Ministries; and while many with good intentions undertake this challenge, a lack of careful scrutiny has led to seriously flawed outcomes.

Take the case of the late Pope John Paul II's attempts on September 11, 2000, to exorcise a young woman. The outcome was disastrous, resulting in the girl's death. Exorcists have pronounced people to be possessed when the person was suffering from a medical condition only. Exorcisms have also left victims with an additional spiritual stigmatization that exacerbated their medical conditions.

This book will, I hope, clear up some misconceptions, and help the sincere sufferer find relief while, at the same time, help avoid mislabeling those who are suffering from medical maladies, and not possession.

BALDY'S TAKEOVER

One Sunday afternoon we gathered in our basement clubhouse, on Miller Avenue near the corner of Belmont Street. I was a gang member and war lord of the Latin Lovers, who were in the East New York neighborhood of Brooklyn, New York City. Like in the famous movie, West Side Story, we were a Puerto Rican gang warring against our Italian neighbors. Several gang members longed to get going with the planned drinking spree. Baldy (a nickname given to him because he shaved his hair) was the chosen one to do the "escape-and-evade" tactic. To accomplish the feat, he would have to walk through the enemy's turf (the Liberty Tots, an Italian gang), get to the liquor store, buy the alcohol, and return to the waiting sponges with the purchased goods in hand.

We threw in our contributions, and off he went. We all knew how far it was, and how much time it would take—about two-and-one-half city street blocks, and no more than twenty minutes. The appointed time came and went with no sign of Baldy. Concerned that he had been caught, we sent a search and, if need be, rescue party. The rest of us waited anxiously. About an hour and a half later, we heard the shuffling of feet and the huffing and puffing sound similar to men struggling with a heavy load coming down the staircase.

They were carrying Baldy: limp and apparently lifeless. He looked as if the street had been mopped up with his body. Torn shirt, gutter-soiled slacks, and unconscious, Baldy was placed in a chair centered in the middle of the room.

"What happened?" someone asked. "We don't know. We found him in the street out cold. Looks like the Tots caught him!" explained another.

"Get some water," Jimmy commanded. "Let's revive him." Someone then splashed water onto his face.

"Baldy, Baldy, wake up," Joe shouted as he slapped him; no response came.

All of a sudden, Baldy's body began to tremble and shake. We jumped back, moving as rapidly as possible. Falling off the chair, he crashed onto the floor writhing, moaning, and foaming at the mouth. His body seemed to be lifted, then yanked, and smacked against the concrete basement floor. His eyes rolled back and seemed to disappear into his head. We all made a hasty flight up the stairs and outside the building. We were terrified. There seemed to be an evil presence, and it frightened us. We were tough enough to handle a street fight, but this—who could fight it? Once outside, we tried to gain our composure. No one said a word. We just glanced back and forth at each other bewildered.

"We better go down and see what's happened to him," I said after awhile.

We hesitantly slipped back down the stairs to our club. Curious and suspicious, we wanted to know what was going on. As we made the descent, we spotted Baldy lying on the basement floor. He was motionless.

"Is he dead?" questioned one of the members. "No, look, he is breathing," Tito said.

Once again, we picked him up, sat him on the chair, and attempted to revive him. With similar tremors and convulsions, his body began repeating the same strange behavior. We all began our mad dash for the staircase.

Our feet did not seem to carry us fast enough in the wild stampede; thus, this time, before we had the opportunity to escape, a woman's voice arrested our flight. Stopping to see where the woman's voice was coming from, we looked right at Baldy. Still sitting on the chair, and with the absence of the erratic behavior, he stared with eyes wide open. Baldy was addressing us. With a strange look, almost as if there was an evil foe peering through his glassed eyes, he was speaking. A dense atmosphere prevailed—eerie, thick, and mysterious. *It wasn't his voice, though it was obvious the sound was coming from his moving lips.* It was like someone else had possession of his mind and voice.

"It's his mother!" whispered Marianne, Baldy's Gypsy girlfriend.

"Baldy's mother was dead. How could that be?" I thought.

Without delay the voice began to question us. With his right arm outstretched and index finger pointing to each one of us as we stood on the particular ascending step, the voice from the being within questioned, "Do you believe in God?" Almost trembling the first gang member stammered, "Ye-yess."

Pointing to the next in line, the same question was repeated. The second answered with the same affirmation, but reluctantly like the first. The ascending, but detained, would-be escapees continued to be queried. When I was asked, I affirmed the same thing that the others had. Finally, the searching, penetrating eyes of Baldy rested on Jimmy, the gang president.

"Do you believe in God?" the voice demanded.

"Yes!" Jimmy replied confidently.

"You don't even believe in your own mother!" the voice retorted immediately.

At this, there was a rapid mad dash up the steps and onto the sidewalk. This time we waited a long while before any of us dared to venture back down to the clubhouse. Finally, not scared sufficiently enough, we let our curiosity get the best of us. Baldy was not coming out, so we decided to go and see what was happening. Slowly we stole down the stairwell. Upon our descent, we found Baldy standing and awake.

"What happened?" he questioned. "How did I get here?"

The latter question we could answer, but to the first we had no answer. The mysterious erratic convulsions and the eerie woman's voice we heard coming out of Baldy's mouth, coupled with whatever being was peering through his eyes, were a mystery.

Later on, I wondered why the voice signaled out Jimmy as it did. What was it that the inner being knew that I didn't know? Why was his mother mentioned with such cynicism? All of us knew that his life was far from pious, and certainly at that time God was not part of my life or any of the others' lives. Neither did we have any scruples. So, for me to lie was as natural as a Puerto Rican eating rice and beans. Yet, no reference was made concerning our fibs. Why, then was Jimmy selected? Who or what had enough intelligence to speak through the mouth of Baldy like a ventriloquist? Who had apparent inside knowledge to controvert Jimmy's statement of faith?

Looking back and understanding what I now know, I was witnessing a manifestation of a demonic takeover of a human being. This experience left no doubt in my thinking that what the Bible calls "demonic possession" still occurs. It is more frequent and more overt in third-world countries, where the level of Bible education is low and superstition is high. In countries such as Thailand, the worshipers don special attire and then wait to be possessed by an unseen power that will enable them to walk on red hot coals untouched by the heat, or to walk on a bed of nails and not feel the sharp barbs penetrating their flesh. There are countries like India and Haiti, where these occurrences are commonplace, even encouraged. More and more, spiritualism and involvement in the occult are on the rise in sophisticated high-tech American societies.

Growing up, I was surrounded by a mesh of atheism and raw superstition. Dualism of religions coexisted with my mother's too often (as far as I was concerned) visits to séances. I had many encounters with possessed people, even though I never paid much attention to them. As long as one didn't dabble in it, there was safety. "You leave it alone, and it left you alone," was the notion.

When I became spiritually converted and biblically informed, I awakened to the seriousness of the matter: I was not dealing merely with a queer happenstance occurring and affecting strange individuals' bizarre manners. As my spiritual eyesight was opened through the biblical revelations, I saw that a cosmic war was unfolding. Every person is the battleground, and the object of the struggle is the mastery of the mind—one is either exercising one's own volition or being made a puppet.

This strange biblical phenomenon called "possession" became more familiar as I entered the Christian ministry. By virtue of my calling, I have, at times, been cast into the "boxing ring" (as it were) to help individuals with the problem. Because of these encounters, I have some experience (though no expertise) in these things. I know enough to know that this is something that only Divinity can controvert and conquer.

The questions that most people have relative to this topic vary. However, here are some of the general concerns:

- How can one tell who is possessed?
- If a person is possessed, at what level is the possession?
- How can a person be freed if possessed?
- Is it even possible to free one's self, or is it essential to enlist the aid of an "exorcist?"

While these are important questions, a caution: great care should be exercised in not allowing a hasty conclusion relative to this subject until we can cover the topic.

In the following chapters, examples of varying degrees of encounters will help to address the questions already presented and raise other questions.

THE DEMON
OF EGG OMELETS

In the fall of 1977, I had just been called to a new church district. Not long after my arrival I attended a pastors' meeting. At the meeting, that evening a pastor was asked to share his testimony with the rest of the workers present. He told of his wife having severe emotional problems. One day he came across a book dealing with what he called "demonic oppression." As he read, he came to the conclusion that his wife was a sufferer from what the book described.

He then followed the steps prescribed in the book. According to his presentation, he set an appointment with the demons. Then at the appointed hour, he said, "I began to talk as I was facing my wife, believing that there were demons oppressing her." He then stated that he began to command the demons to depart from his wife. "There were seven demons in her," he declared. "It was an exhausting ordeal, but one by one they left."

The outgoing pastor, whose position I was filling, was also in the audience listening to the strange occurrence. When the meetings were over, we both returned to our respective homes. He was still living in the area because he had not been able to sell his house.

A few days later we happened to run into each other. He appeared excited by this coincidental meeting, and seemed most anxious to talk with me. "Can we talk?" He asked. "I have something very exciting to share with you."

"My wife had a terrible allergy to egg omelets," he began. "But at our workers' meeting I was intrigued by the testimony of the pastor whose wife had allergies to other things. I got a copy of the book the presenter mentioned and read it." Like the other pastor, after reading the book he felt convinced that his wife's allergy was 'devil harassment', referred to by the book as 'oppression.' This volume provided the remedy to the problem. He continued, "The book recommended that an appointment be set. At the scheduled time the one initiating the session was to confront the devil, or devils should there be more than one. Then, in the name of Jesus, demand it, or them, to identify themselves and leave.[1]

---

[1] Theoretically, by the demon revealing its identity, it would disclose the secret means by which the person was possessed.

"My colleague followed the instructions and he said that seven devils identified themselves, and he commanded them to get out of her. Remember, he shared this with all of us at the worker's meeting," the pastor quipped, his long eyebrows hinting that he had stumbled onto something. His next revelation was like an episode stemming from the television series *The Twilight Zone*.

"I determined to try it on my own wife," he mused. "I set a time, and then at the appointed moment, I began to demand that the devil reveal himself and depart from my wife. I lost consciousness in the process. When I came to, I was delighted to discover that my wife could eat omelets without any problem," he exclaimed with glee.

I did not dare respond. Frankly, I was highly surprised. "Strange, bizarre!" was all that I could think. What made him assume that the devil or devils would be so amiable, pliant, and gentlemanly enough to keep an appointment? To say the least, I was doubtful and uneasy about his revelation. I had hoped that the matter would remain there with a satisfied husband whose wife could relish eating egg omelets, even though the achievement, as far as I was concerned, was accomplished through very questionable and weird means.

Then, what I was hoping would not happen, came to pass. At the conclusion of the next worship service a church member approached me.

"I have hay fever," she began, "and Pastor Tom wrote us a letter sharing his encounter and resulting release of his wife from the demon. Can you do the same for me, so that I can be delivered from the demon of hay fever?"

She paused, expectantly awaiting an affirmative answer. I gave no assurance. Rather, I simply told her I would discuss it with her later.

As the parishioners exited the church, several did not greet me in the usual manner. As they did so, it became quite obvious from the comments that the lady was not singular. The lady with the hay fever was not the last person to make comments along these lines. Several other members sought me out to help them get rid of the demon of chocolate, anger, lust, etc. Needless to say, the matter had to be dealt with immediately.

"How did my members know about the situation with their former pastor and his wife?" I wondered. At the fellowship dinner following the church service, I cautiously inquired and found out that he had written a letter to all the members about his wife's problem and how he found the cure for it. He mentioned several maladies, such as allergies of various sorts and other problems, and he told them the steps he took to cure his wife. Then he recommended that they ask me to do for them what he had done for his wife.

My church members, I felt, were being influenced into a wrong course, and the need to study into this subject became urgent. There had to be a more sane approach than to set an appointment with such powerful beings, thinking them to be mere puppets and wimps to be ordered to an appointment, and succumbing, without out a duel.

These episodes did not match up with anything biblical that I was acquainted with. Even the use of the word "oppression" was odd. This new phrase "demonic oppression," was a conundrum. The Bible referred to Jesus as being "oppressed," I recalled. In prophetic vision Isaiah wrote about the Messiah: "He was *oppressed*, and he was afflicted, yet he opened not his mouth: he is brought as a lamb to the slaughter, and as a sheep before her shearers is dumb, so he openeth not his mouth" (Isaiah 53:7, emphasis added). From this text I could see that Jesus was oppressed, but never was there any suggestion (except as an attempt by the religious leaders to unsuccessfully cast a shadow on His work) that a demon was in possession of Him and, therefore, had to be exorcised.

Oppression, as expressed in the Bible, can take place in different ways. It may be in the sense of a taskmaster laying on more work than one can bear. People can feel crushed, which can lead to physical or mental anguish. A prime biblical example is Job. He suffered not only material loss, but he also experienced physical maladies, which led to mental anguish.

"There was a man in the land of Uz, whose name was Job; and that man was perfect and upright, and one that feared God, and eschewed evil" (Job 1:1). He had ten children: seven sons, and three daughters. Besides this, he was a wealthy man. "His substance also was seven thousand sheep, and three thousand camels, and five hundred yoke of oxen, and five hundred she asses, and a very great household; so that this man was the greatest of all the men of the east" (verse 2).

Job's children decided to throw a feast that would last 10 days (see Job 1:4). They all took turns hosting the festivities. Apparently, when Job got wind of their activities, he became concerned and decided to intercede in their behalf by rising "up early in the morning," and offering "burnt offerings *according* to the number of them all: for Job said, It may be that my sons have sinned, and cursed God in their hearts" (Job 1:5). Then the Bible writer draws back the curtain, and ushers the reader into the cosmic realm.

> Now there was a day when the sons of God came to present themselves before the Lord, and Satan came also among them. And the Lord said unto Satan, Whence comest thou? Then Satan answered the Lord, and said, From going to and fro in the earth, and from walking up and down in it. And the Lord said unto Satan, Hast thou considered my servant Job, that there is none like him in the earth, a perfect and an upright man, one that feareth God, and escheweth evil? Then Satan answered the Lord, and said, Doth Job fear God for nought? Hast not thou made an hedge about him, and about his house, and about all that he hath on every side? thou hast blessed the work of his hands, and his substance is increased in the land. But put forth thine hand now, and touch all that he hath, and he will curse thee to thy face. And

the Lord said unto Satan, Behold, all that he hath is in thy power;
only upon himself put not forth thine hand. So Satan went forth
from the presence of the Lord. (Job 1:6–12)

Then it happened. "There was a day when his sons and his daughters were
eating and drinking wine in their eldest brother's house" (verse 13). Afterwards,
a messenger ran to Job with troubling news.

The oxen were plowing, and the asses feeding beside them: And
the Sabeans fell upon them, and took them away; yea, they have
slain the servants with the edge of the sword; and I only am escaped alone to tell thee. While he was yet speaking, there came
also another, and said, The fire of God is fallen from heaven,
and hath burned up the sheep, and the servants, and consumed
them; and I only am escaped alone to tell thee. While he was
yet speaking, there came also another, and said, The Chaldeans
made out three bands, and fell upon the camels, and have carried them away, yea, and slain the servants with the edge of the
sword; and I only am escaped alone to tell thee. While he was
yet speaking, there came also another, and said, Thy sons and
thy daughters were eating and drinking wine in their eldest
brother's house: And, behold, there came a great wind from the
wilderness, and smote the four corners of the house, and it fell
upon the young men, and they are dead; and I only am escaped
alone to tell thee. (Job 1:14–19)

Job's response to the astonishing news is noble.

"Then Job arose, and rent his mantle, and shaved his head, and
fell down upon the ground, and worshipped, And said, Naked came I out of my mother's womb, and naked shall I return
thither: the Lord gave, and the Lord hath taken away; blessed be
the name of the Lord. In all this Job sinned not, nor charged God
foolishly" (Job 1:21, 22).

In the true biblical sense, this is oppression.

There is another case. It is of a woman in Jesus' day who, likewise, had been
struck with sickness. "He [Jesus] was teaching in one of the synagogues on
the sabbath," Luke recorded. "Behold, there was a woman which had a spirit
of infirmity eighteen years, and was bowed together, and could in no wise lift
up herself. And when Jesus saw her, he called her to him, and said unto her,
Woman, thou art loosed from thine infirmity. And he laid his hands on her: and
immediately she was made straight, and glorified God" (Luke 13:10–13).

When the ruler of the synagogue protested with indignation that the work
of healing should not be done on the Sabbath, Jesus said, "Thou hypocrite, doth
not each one of you on the sabbath loose his ox or his ass from the stall, and

lead him away to watering? And ought not this woman, being a daughter of Abraham, whom Satan hath bound, lo, these eighteen years, be loosed from this bond on the sabbath day" (Luke 12:15, 16)?

In both cases, physical illness resulted from satanic affliction. In Job's case, his persistent trust and faith in God got him the victory. In the case of the woman, she was physically healed, not exorcised. While no date was set, or a need to address devils, neither malady was just an irritant as in the case of the omelet. Both Job and the woman had their mental capacities intact, although they suffered physically and felt mental oppression. The biblical definition of "oppressed" is to "press, drive, oppress, exact, and exert demanding pressure."[2] In other words, they were sorely tempted with physical and mental anguish. Thus, from my readings, I concluded that the encounters of the pastor were not in concert with these scriptural examples.

It was needful, I believed, to invalidate this dangerous charade. These experiences with the pastors' wives struck a chord reminiscent of past experiences—both with my mother's occult practices and the encounters in the early part of my ministry. Though the pastors were sincere, they were playing with fire, and by their encouragement they were leading others to do the same and to get seriously burned.

Initially, there was reluctance on my part to address this too aggressively because of the offices held by both men. Nevertheless, these happenings sent up red flags. In fact, this use of the term "oppressed" was reminiscent of a young lady's horrific terrifying experience in my first pastoral district. For the sake of protecting the person, the name has been changed, but the next chapter provides the story.

---

2   Enhanced Strong's Lexicon, s.v. "oppressed" (Strong's number H5065).

OPPRESSED?

As I picked up the phone, there was a frantic voice on the other end.

"Pastor Torres, I need your help!"

"Who is this?" I asked.

"It's Connie," replied the troubled caller.

"Connie, where have you been?" I questioned.

"Well, that's a long story, but I desperately need to meet with you and talk with you right now! May I?" she asked.

Although I was having lunch with my family, they immediately sensed the urgency of the call, and encouraged me to invite her to the house. "Sure, come on over," I said.

As it turned out, Connie had been through a hair-raising experience. She was a young Italian lady of the Catholic faith to whom I had been giving Bible studies. We had studied for several months; she then decided to stop. As we had progressed with the study of the Bible , we entered into areas of study that conflicted with her lifestyle.

The religion I was portraying, as far as she was concerned, was too restrictive or too boring. This was her response after attending a few church services that I had conducted, and finding out the conditions Christ placed before his hearers in order to follow Him. She did not want to join a church that in her estimation was too "strait-laced."

"I am going to find a church that is 'spirit-filled,' a church with more freedom" she concluded.

The Bible studies came to a halt. Connie determined she could do much better for herself someplace else. A couple of months passed before the abrupt phone call—then she was back. Frightened, pale, and with trembling voice, she revealed what had transpired in her church-seeking escapade.

"My sister invited me to her church when she discovered my interest in spiritual things," Connie began. "She told me that her church was a spirit-filled church. Anxious to discover what that meant, I went with her."

The rest of the story was quite intriguing.

"When I arrived, things looked quite normal. The people appeared normal and friendly. When the services began, the atmosphere seemed to be filled with an air of exuberance. Then something unusual took place. People began praising God. Some began to speak in some form of sounds they called 'speaking in tongues.' Others got out of their seats and began to twirl and jump.

"The church service exploded into an ecstatic convergence of sounds and motions. I felt left out. I was the only one not having this kind of experience. At first I was tense," she continued. "These unusual manifestations were alarming to me, but the people seemed to be reveling in a euphoria that I had never seen or experienced in any of my church life. Then my fear turned into chagrin. My impressions changed."

Feeling cheated and the obvious one out of place, Connie decided to do something about it. She approached the pastor of the church to make her complaint.

"Everyone is having this wonderful experience but me. Why am I left out?"

"You need to receive the gift of the spirit," replied the pastor.

"What do I need to do to get it?"

"I have to lay hands on you," the pastor responded to this enquiry. Upon her request and permission, the pastor requested that she kneel and then hit her with his palm on her forehead.

"As I fell backwards, I began to feel something come over me. There seemed to be a thrill come surging through my body—it was like electricity tingling through my entire being. Then I was driven to the floor and began to roll around. As I uncontrollably rolled, I couldn't keep my dress down. I was conscious through this weird and unusual takeover of my body. I tried to stop it, but I couldn't. Then I became frightened. Finally, it stopped."

In the midst of the uproar, Connie, struck with fear, approached the pastor. "I am scared to death," she explained. "I can't control what has come over me."

"You will be okay," encouraged the pastor. "You are being *oppressed*. The devil is trying to scare you so that you'll reject the gift.

"Remember," he continued citing the following Scripture verse, "God has not given you the spirit of fear, but of love and of a sound mind. So, we need to take you to the back room have prayer over you, and get rid of the spirit that's harassing you" (2 Timothy 1:7). Connie went with him to a back room where there assembled several of the church's leaders.

"They made a circle around me," she remembered, "and began to perform their ritual. I was kneeling while they were doing this. Then, somehow, I felt uncomfortably eerie, so I opened my eyes to see what was going on. My hairs stood up on the nape of my neck. As I looked around, I was gripped with horror. Rather than seeing human beings surrounding me, I saw demons."

She screamed, vaulted to her feet, and ran out of the church and went back home.

When she reached her home, she quickly got inside. With the door bolted behind her, she felt secure. After a little while, she began to feel hungry. Going to her refrigerator, she gathered some food and sat at her dining table. When she began eating, and while still sitting, she felt a shove by unseen hands that pushed her off her seat. Now frightened, and not knowing what to do, she went to her bedroom to lie down on her bed. While lying down, she felt something grabbing her feet and pulling at her legs. This prompted her to quickly spring off her bed and sink to her knees to pray. Here she thought there would be safety. But while she was on her knees, she experienced being pushed off her knees. Now in a state of horror, she reached for the telephone, dialed my number, and begged for an immediate audience.

"What's happening to me? Am I going crazy? They told me I was being oppressed!" Connie frightfully inquired, experiencing an indefinable dread.

"No, you are not going crazy. What is taking place is that a demon has taken possession of your body," I cautiously told her.

"What? No, it can't be! What can I do?" Connie was visibly shaken.

"If you are going to free yourself of this, you must accept the reality and deal with it."

"Please tell me what to do. I am terrified."

After I gave her some biblical advice, Connie immediately put into practice the counsel and overcame her predicament. Eighteen years later she was still going strong in her faith, with no reoccurring problems. What was my counsel to her? This will be discussed in the chapter entitled "How Deliverance Comes," but until then we must continue with this matter of "oppression."

THE MISSOURI EXORCIST

Our tenure in Oregon was short lived, —about six months. Having received a request to relocate, we moved to Kansas City, Missouri, and, I began to focus on our new assignment. Time slipped quickly by, and before we knew it, we were in full swing with the summer activities. Camp meeting was a few days ahead, and all the ministers were on site in advance, preparing the camp for the arrival of the parishioners and attendees. During one of our breaks, I happened to notice the conference president.

"John, how is it going?" I asked.

Pulling me aside, he said, "I just had the weirdest experience. I was invited by one of the camp meeting speakers to witness an exorcism. It was the strangest thing I ever saw!" he exclaimed.

"What happened?" I asked.

"We went to exorcise a young girl. The speaker began his efforts to cast out the demon. The girl rose up and punched him squarely on the head. The struggle continued for a while. Man, I felt eerie! How thankful I was to get out of that situation," he ended. Unfortunately, we were interrupted, and I was never able to get any more information than that.

That evening the same speaker was to address the audience at the main auditorium. Though I determined to be present and hear what he had to say, I was apprehensive. Sitting in the back of the auditorium with my ears perked and eyes vigilant, I listened. I was acquainted with the speaker. During my first year of college, I attended a church service where this man and two others with him were being introduced. He testified that they had just abandoned the occult practice of witchcraft, but their look and demeanor seemed to betray his words.

Notwithstanding, I decided to put a check on my judgment. My wife and I invited them to visit with us in our home for lunch. We felt that if they were sincere, they would be willing to get some counsel concerning the type of music they were performing—a carry-over from their former practices and lifestyle.

The meeting was cordial, but our counsel did not appear to make its mark. Even though they verbally agreed, I sensed resistance. They left, and though our paths crossed twice after that, these two encounters were not congenial.

Later, I heard that they joined up with a popular itinerant preacher and began to gain notoriety. At this camp meeting, the leader of the threesome was no longer with the team. Instead, he was now a circuit preacher with a special focus on "deliverance ministry." This was his subject that particular evening. At the conclusion of the presentation on "oppression," he passed out a "warfare prayer" sheet. When I read the content on the sheet, I was alarmed.

My concern was heightened when, on the day following his presentation, one of my good, solid members—a young certified public accountant—came to ask if there was a possibility that she was suffering and being victimized from what the speaker had described. This young professional woman was as stable mentally and emotionally as a gyroscope, but she had been going over and over the warfare prayer without relief. I couldn't believe my ears.

How could this intelligent, stable person be so easily caught up with this superstition? Without showing my shock, I carefully cautioned her to throw the paper away and rely not on praying with "vain repetitions, as the heathen" (Matthew 6:7), but as Jesus taught.

"There is no inherent power in a written prayer," I told her. "The power is in God and this power comes by an exercise of faith in Him. Spiritists, heathens, and those who practice mysticism place their confidence in objects, conveying to them some sort of magical powers or abilities. But God has not counseled us in his Word to trust in written-out prayers, trust in magic charms, or place our confidence in objects such as the heathens do. He wants to hear the simple prayer from the hearts of his children. He is the One who can bring freedom and relief."

She took my advice, and found peace. Sometimes the most effective agents Satan uses to lead believers into presumptuous sins against God are other human beings who claim like faith.

Spiritists make preposterous claims. They generally do not accept Christ as the Son of God; in fact, some claim superiority over Christ. Through my experience I have observed that those who boast of their superiority, demonstrate in language and actions the sins of a revolting character. Others, I've noticed, have taken the exalted name of Christ on their lips and have attempted to ally Him with their own vileness and corrupt characters.

Generally speaking, spiritist mediums make their means by professing to communicate with the dead, cast spells, and remove spells. They convene séances, and declare they have abilities foretell the future. Those involved in the occult, such as self-proclaimed witches and devil worshippers, are more involved with direct worship of the devi. They have been known to offer human sacrifices, and make no pretention of alliances with Christ. While some of the beliefs may be similar concerning the supernatural, there are marked differences in their practices.

Prior to the evening meeting that same night, I went into the men's shower building at the camp meeting to comb my hair and shave. While I was shaving, the speaker walked in and began shaving next to me. Without any encouragement, he began to extol the fact that he was bald and stated that hair was a result of sin.

"In the kingdom," he said, "no one will have hair."

As he was speaking, I noticed him looking into the large mirror we were both facing to see what my reaction would be. He could not help but tell my utter surprise at his statement. Just a few days prior I had read:

> Some have put forth the theory that the redeemed will not have gray hair—as if this were a matter of any importance. I am instructed to say that these theories are the production of minds unlearned in the first principles of the gospel. By such theories the enemy strives to eclipse the great truths for this time.[3]

Turning to him, I stared for a moment. His usual look of dignified command gave way to an expression of one expecting a severe rebuke. Vacillating, he attempted to backtrack from his boastful theological quip. I was surprised at his cowering. With halted speech, he stammered his way to another subject. I felt it was time to confront him concerning his involvement with this bizarre, I felt, practice.

"You have veered off the right course and turned to sensationalism," I said. "This is leading a host of people into spiritualism under the ploy of deliverance."

With obvious nervousness, he abruptly departed. I never saw him again, for I absented myself from his last presentation. When camp meeting ended, I heard that he went back on the road. It was later confirmed that a few years after, he was committed to a mental institution. He ultimately committed suicide.

Upon returning home, I faced a difficult task. Several members had given heed to the whole idea of demonic oppression and were desperately seeking for deliverance. They were certain a devil was in everything. Fortunately, the experience in Oregon had prepared the way to deal with the issue. Using the biblical examples from my studies, and the written counsels for the church, I was able though the power of the Lord to bring peace to the disheartened and fearful.

---

3   E. G. White, Gospel Workers, 313.

CHOKING THE DEMON TO IDENTIFY HIMSELF

Once again we were on the move. This time, the call came to pastor in Jacksonville, Florida. After much prayer, we accepted the invitation and relocated to our new district. While there, several phone calls came from former parishioners in Missouri. Among other subjects, one seemed to be repeated—an itinerant lay preacher who had visited my former church. "He sounds just like you—straight down the line," stated the caller. I was happy to know there were others preaching the message, or so I thought.

Several months later an announcement was made that the same circuit preacher would be in my town. Since many of my members had planned to attend his lectures, I decided to be present also. No question, he was a dynamic and charismatic speaker. In fact, I found myself saying "Amen" to many of his statements. Then suddenly an apprehension came over me. There flashed in my mind the experience of Paul being harassed by a demon-possessed girl who admonished all present to pay attention to his teachings. Paul rebuked the spirit. This biblical scenario caused me to take precaution. Keeping my silence, I now felt the need to squelch my confirmation of the speaker until there was an assurance that he was straight. No sooner was the decision made, than the speaker abruptly changed his subject matter from "last-day events" to the topic of "deliverance ministry."

"You ought to have been with me," he began. "I met this godly man who runs a deliverance ministry. It was astounding! He took me with him to exorcise a woman with a smoking problem." He continued, "He commanded the demon to reveal himself and expose the method he used to take possession of the woman. When the demon refused to speak, he commanded the good angels to choke the evil spirit, and force him to talk."

I couldn't believe my ears—another one preaching the same demonic heresy. Fearing for my people, I felt a grave responsibility to challenge the speaker, something I very seldom do. My "Amens" had given my stamp of approval to him, now I must remove the affirmation.

My wife made a beeline for the restroom to pray. She felt it coming. I stood to my feet and remonstrated with him. "Mister," I said, "I would advise you to return back to your subject and leave this one alone."

"You must be a minister!" he smartly retorted. Then he asked, "What is your commission?"

"I know quite well what my commission is," I responded.

He interrupted with an air of sarcasm and said, "Doesn't it say, 'Cleanse the leper, cast out demons!'"

"Mister," I admonished, "you do not know who I am or what experiences I have had. Again, I am encouraging you to move away from this subject. You are leading people in the wrong direction."

There was no apparent reason for his stopping the detour, but he took my advice, and returned to his original subject. When the meeting finished, I joined up with my waiting wife at the foyer. Before I left, the man in charge of recording the presenter's lectures, verbally accosted me because "his recording had been ruined."

"How could you do that as a minister?" he demanded.

"As a minister," I responded, "it would have been criminal and a denial of my responsibility to remain silent and thus leave my sheep vulnerable. Your speaker got way off course presenting unbiblical teachings, and somebody had to bring him back in line."

A year later, I ran across the same man doing the recording at another convocation. He said he would like to have a word with me after the meeting. When the opportunity presented itself, he confessed that my concerns had been well-founded. Unfortunately, he did not catch on in time enough to avert his financial losses resulting from the speaker's embezzlement.

The need arose to give my congregation information and education on the subject. Hours had to be spent reassuring those affected by the presentation that they were not suffering from demonic harassment. Education was the key to enable the sincere, yet vulnerable, to meet the challenge.

Unarguably, there was a need to deal with the issue. After putting together what I thought were the issues and the corresponding answers, I placed in the hands of those who had been victimized resources that clarified in lay terms the falsehoods that entangled so many in this deception of "oppression." Biblically speaking, if an individual experiences what Baldy, Connie, and the aforementioned pastors' wives experienced, what some are calling oppression must really be called "possession." An acknowledgement of the fact can lead to a successful biblical approach and thus a scriptural outcome.

Nevertheless, the challenge of getting a person who has the obvious symptoms of possession to recognize it is fraught with several challenges.

First, if people are truly possessed, and they have no knowledge or understanding of this phenomenon, then most of the time they are incapable of recognizing it. They may sense there is something wrong, but often they are bewildered as to the cause. Their minds being controlled; their thinking becomes cloudy.

Second, if they still possess their senses to a limited degree, it would be considered an embarrassment tainted with a stigma should they be a person of reputation, e.g. pastor, pastor's wife, etc. It would suggest or mean that the person has, at some point, voluntarily subjected himself or herself to the control by either practicing a known sin or seeking to dabble, knowingly or naively, in some form of spiritualism.

In the case where a person may be a professed Christian, it would appear to be too humiliating for that individual, even one of good repute, to acknowledge the cause. Hence, it is easier to cast the blame on a devil with "the devil made me do it" cliché. This leaves the individual free of any personal guilt or responsibility or any burden of admitting sin. Hence, the scapegoat used is "oppression."

However, a danger lurks here. The person, who is exorcised under the guise of oppression, finds a supposed escape by removing the causative agent—the demon. Consequently, the individual is alleviated from making confession or righting any wrong, an essential step in the process of victory over sin—the usual cause of possession. The victim is also cheated since the problem is relegated to a supposed demonic harassment.

The outcome is that an acknowledgement of the true cause can be bypassed, thus leaving the victim in a delusion. As a result, the remedy provided by the Lord for true deliverance—that of repentance, confession and forgiveness—is circumvented. Therefore, not only did "the devil make me do it," but he also removed the solution. This causes the duped sufferer to be dependent upon the exorcist for relief from harassment, rather than to be expiated by the blood and power of Christ from sin, an act that cannot be accomplished by proxy. Another outcome is that, rather than distancing the person from demons, it actually places him under their control through the exorcist agent!

Another grave danger for people who have physiological and psychological disorders is that their symptoms may appear to be similar to those of a possessed person. Seizures can bring about convulsions, foaming at the mouth, and erratic body movements. Persons who suffer from bi-polar disorder can easily become victimized. Their up-and-down emotional rollercoaster experience may produce a great sense of being stigmatized, resulting in a low self-esteem. Consequently, they have a feeling of guilt, which develops from taking medicine. To add to their already guilt-ridden conscience, the supposition that their problem stems from a direct association with a demon may push the sufferer over the brink of despair.

Take, for instance, a young man who was suffering from bipolar disorder. He decided to volunteer at a Christian school, thinking that by doing so he would draw closer to God. Rather than being a positive atmosphere, the school became a damaging situation for him. Being around other spiritually healthy young people, who were very active, made him feel spiritually inferior because of his condition. Since they did not need to depend on medicine, he perceived in them a spiritual superiority, which contributed to his belief that using his medicine showed a lack of faith. Besides this, he didn't fully understand that the medicine kept him in a cloudy mental state.

He determined that his taking medicine and depending on it interfered with, and circumvented, God being able to heal him. He was going to quit using his pills and, instead, depend upon God. For the first two days he seemed normal. Then it happened. His behavior became erratic. In his room he was found naked and acting strangely. He was finally convinced to get dressed and have a visit with me.

We met in the cafeteria and sat at one of the tables across from each other. I noticed that he was quite apprehensive. He acted paranoid. His eyes looked somewhat glassy and filled with apprehension. He could hold a conversation, but his reasoning was off. Because there were flies around us, I grabbed a fly swatter. When I lifted the swatter, he raised his arms in defense, with a look of terror. His actions could well have been attributed to demonic possession.

Looking out for his well being, I summoned the police. Upon arrival, they made a quick assessment and concurred with my conclusion. They put him in the patrol car, and took him to the mental hospital for observation. Onlookers questioned my spirituality, evidenced (as far as they were concerned) by my going to humans rather than to God.

One of the onlookers was a nurse. She and her husband decided to undo the evil I had done. They went to the hospital and signed him out, taking full responsibility for him. They were certain that prayer would heal him. However, a couple of days later, when they returned home from work, they found him in their bathroom dressed with the wife's underclothing. This brought them to their senses, and they immediately sent him back to the hospital. About two weeks later he was released, and he returned to his hometown.

Nearly a year later, he made a surprise visit. He returned to thank me for what I did, informing me that the physicians discovered the problem. The drug formerly prescribed to him for his treatment was determined to be the wrong one for his particular diagnosis. Once this was discovered, they administered the appropriate medication, resulting in him being able to function and feel normal. At the time he visited, he shared with me that he was able to keep a regular job as an aviation mechanic. He was also happily married. Who knows where this young man would be if he had fallen into the hands of one of those individuals looking for a demon behind every problem?

What if, in reality, the problem is not oppression but actual possession? What are the indicators that truly identify possession? Another question: are there real invisible beings that live on Earth along with human beings? If this is true, then who are they? Where have they come from? Why would they even want to take possession of an inferior being? Have they ability to do a "coup d'état" over the human frame? If they do, to what extent have they this power? How is it possible to detect it? What can and should be done to overcome the takeover? But more importantly, what precautions should be taken to avoid a mutiny of our minds and a manipulation of our bodies?

SUPERSTITION: A PRECURSOR

While I was in Romania presenting a series of Bible lectures, a Gypsy family who attended the meetings requested that I pray for their very sick daughter. When I arrived at the home, the man was elated. He obviously held a prominent position among the Gypsies in that area. He bade the women to take me to his sick daughter's beside. I was quickly escorted to where the young woman lay.

Many family members were in the home. Their facial expressions gave evidence of the grave concern. The daughter's father requested that I pray for her so that her illness would depart.

"Somebody has placed a curse on her, and if you pray for her she will be well," my interpreter translated.

Given my former training as a medic in the military, I did not suspect anything more than physical illness. After a quick surface evaluation, I said, "I do not believe this has anything to do with a spell, she looks very sick and should be taken to the hospital."

"No!" he demanded. "It is a spell, and you must pray for her so she can be healed."

"I will pray for her," I said. "But if she does not recover quickly, you need to get her to medical help."

I then knelt and prayed. As I was leaving the home, the father displayed a look of satisfaction.

A few days later my translator told me the sequel. Upon my departure, the young woman arose from her bed, walked around the room to kiss each of her loved ones, and went back to bed. However, her condition worsened. Her father, feeling that my prayer did not have the power to accomplish his aim, went to an Orthodox priest. In Romania the priests claim to have power to cast spells and remove them, all for a price. He paid the priest the equivalent of $200 in US currency for the task.

Before he returned home, he had an automobile accident and landed in the hospital with a broken leg. While this was transpiring, the young woman's condition became so critical that the family rushed her to the hospital.

Unfortunately, they waited too long. She had spinal meningitis, and the delayed treatment caused her death. She left behind a widowed husband and two children.

Her life was a huge price to pay for that superstitious father. The financial loss was insignificant in comparison to the loss of his daughter. However, the terrible loss could have been averted if only he had relied on his Christian faith, and Bible knowledge, and not yielded to his cultural superstitious beliefs. I am troubled when I encounter tragic outcomes that could have been prevented. I recalled thinking, as I walked in the procession behind the horse-driven cart carrying the bier: "This could have been avoided if only the father had not embraced superstition and the occult."

The phobia afflicting people with a morbid, irrational fear of Friday the 13th is called *paraskevidekatriaphobia*. In 1993 the *British Medical Journal* published the results of a study entitled "Is Friday the 13th Bad for Your Health?" The findings reached the following conclusion:

Incredibly, they found that in the region sampled, while consistently fewer people chose to drive their cars on Friday the 13th, the number of hospital admissions due to vehicular accidents was significantly higher than on "normal" Fridays. Their conclusion:

> "Friday 13th is unlucky for some. The risk of hospital admission as a result of a transport accident may be increased by as much as 52 percent. Staying at home is recommended." . . . I suspect these statistics have more to teach us about human psychology than the ill-fated date on a calendar.[4]

Other superstitious phobias include breaking a mirror, walking under a ladder, spilling the salt, and spying a black cat crossing one's path. Breaking a mirror in and of itself has no intrinsic power, and spilling salt does nothing more than direct the potential savor-lifter to the realm of insipidity. However, superstition provides an avenue whereby the mind can be held captive to the workings of evil powers. If the mind thinks it, then demons can perform the expected results, just to keep the naive open to their manipulations.

What is superstition? It is an excessively trusting belief in and almost blind reverence for supernatural things or beings. Generally speaking, it can also include a widely held but unjustified belief in supernatural causation, leading to certain consequences of an action, event, or practice based on such a belief. The example of the Gypsy man's superstition of spells, and his belief in the priest's ability to perform supernatural acts, demonstrates the point. Another example is the magnetic pull of scores of people stampeding to sites announcing to have been visited by supposed apparitions of deceased personages.

Let me share another example of blind, misled faith. While I was living in Dover, Delaware, two young men of Puerto Rican descent moved into town. Since they could not find housing, I took them in to stay with us in the basement

4   David Emery, "Why Friday the 13th Is Unlucky," About.com Urban Legends, http://urbanlegends.about.com/cs/historical/a/friday_the_13th.htm (accessed August 21, 2012).

apartment of our home. One day I overheard them having a heated argument. Wondering what issue might have such great import that would cause the heated debate raised my curiosity.

"Boys, what are you arguing about?" I inquired.

"I am glad you asked, pastor," one responded. "Isn't it true that if a person is gravely ill, one can take a pigeon, split it open in the breast, then place it on the chest of the sufferer, and the infusion of the great amount of vitamins absorbed through the chest would cause the sufferer to immediately die, thus releasing them from their suffering. Now, isn't that true pastor?"

Amused at what the false notion espoused, I told them, "Physiologically speaking, it is impossible for that to happen. It is true that the skin is able to absorb substances at different rates, depending on the substance and area of application. However, to suppose that a person dies sooner because of a split bird placed on the chest is nothing more than mere superstition."[5]

Ignorance leading to superstition provoked people in the Dark Ages to declare someone a witch, and then, in order to prove the fact, that individual was burned at the stake in the hope that the skin would burn differently or some supernatural happening would occur. Fabricated stories stirred up suspicion and paranoia. People were obsessed with the witch-hunt and assumed that maladies could be cured simply by destroying the witch, who was subject to the suspicion of being connected to the devil or the mysterious world of the occult.

A notable case was of Joseph Merrick, born in Leicester, England in 1862. "He appeared to be a normal, healthy child, until the age of five when deformities began to appear."[6] They called him "The Elephant Man." He suffered from a strange abnormality and was subjected to wild frenzies from the people's paranoia. Scientists today "believe Joseph Merrick, who lived in Britain more than 100 years ago, could have suffered from type 1 neurofibromatosis (NF1) and Proteus syndrome."[7]

Superstitious paranoia has led people to place ugly looking idols to ward off evil spirits or to place magic charms on their bodies for protection. Images, icons, or small statues on car visors are placed to protect from accidents or dangers while traveling. Magic charms, like a rabbit's foot or other emulates placed in homes, were supposed to pour out a blessing while at the same time other charms were endowed with power to ward off evil. Nevertheless, the Scriptures emphatically state:

> Thus saith the Lord, Learn not the way of the heathen, and be not
> dismayed at the signs of heaven; for the heathen are dismayed

---

5   "Percutaneous absorption varies depending on the concentration and nature of the substance, the composition of the vehicle, the properties and state of the stratum corneum, the anatomical region, its integrity and skin occlusion, and the area of exposure." ("Dermal Absorption as an Exposure Route" [side column reference], Children's Environmental Health Project, www.cape. ca/children/derm2.html). Through this means companies attempt to help people quit smoking using a stop-smoking patch.

6   "Curse of the Elephant Man" (video), Science Channel Presents, http://science.discovery.com/tv-shows/science-channel-presents/videos/curse-of-the-elephant-man-joining-the-circus.htm (accessed October 3, 2012).

7   "Elephant man mystery unraveled," BBC News, http://news.bbc.co.uk/2/hi/health/3084483.stm. (Accessed October 3, 2012).

at them. For the customs of the people are vain: for one cutteth a tree out of the forest, the work of the hands of the workman, with the axe. They deck it with silver and with gold; they fasten it with nails and with hammers, that it move not. They are upright as the palm tree, but speak not: they must needs be borne, because they cannot go. Be not afraid of them; for they cannot do evil, neither also is it in them to do good. (Jeremiah 10:2–5)

My mother bought certain plants from witch doctors or spiritists that were supposed to contain evil fighting power when she boiled the noxious weeds and then sprinkled the water around the apartment. The intent was that the procedure would ward off or deflect any spell sent by her enemies. Unfortunately, it did not stop a drunken woman who, with a knife in hand, attempted to attack her in our own apartment. Fortunately, her six boys went to her rescue.

Demonic possession is a delusive bent still well and alive today. Those declaring themselves to be exorcists tend to the same subjective mentality. The root of superstition causes them to form a checklist of indicators, and once the exorcists conclude that this "evidence" is present, they declare the subject a "victim" and proceed with their incantations and practices, hoping to get some manifestation that would prove the accuracy of their findings. Unfortunately, the devil is ever too anxious to grant them their request.

Therefore, separating fact from fiction is imperative. People do not inherently possess supernatural or magical powers. If there are individuals demonstrating these extraordinary abilities, it is simply that supernatural or extraterrestrial beings (either good or evil) are using the humans as conduits or instruments. Or they may, on behalf of humans, perform miraculous acts. For example, Samson had superhuman strength, but the source of this power was revealed. When a lion approached him, the Bible says, "The Spirit of the Lord came mightily upon him, and he rent him as he would have rent a kid, and he had nothing in his hand" (Judges 14:6).

It is God that gives spiritual gifts to His believers. The fact that they are called "gifts" makes obvious the source. Paul wrote:

Now there are diversities of gifts, [Paul writes] but the same Spirit. And there are differences of administrations, but the same Lord. And there are diversities of operations, but it is the same God which worketh all in all. But the manifestation of the Spirit is given to every man to profit withal. For to one is given by the Spirit the word of wisdom; to another the word of knowledge by the same Spirit; To another faith by the same Spirit; to another the gifts of healing by the same Spirit; To another the working of miracles; to another prophecy; to another discerning of spirits; to another divers kinds of tongues; to another the interpretation of tongues. (1 Corinthians 12:4–10)

Likewise, Satan and his devils enable strange things to happen, or provide the behind-the-scenes power to make his servants appear to have superhuman abilities. The understanding that evil is involved will lead souls away from fanaticism or from imputing to images, statues, or inanimate objects attributes or powers not inherent in themselves. Knowing this will also prevent assessments or tendencies of demon-searchers from finding a demon in every corner, from finding a demon responsible for every unusual occurrence, or from finding a demon behind every abnormal human divergence, either physical or mental. It can also aid in distancing from, or avoiding and shunning, people who claim to have deluding, self-proclaiming magical powers.

BEINGS FROM
OUTER SPACE?

Obviously, the previous stories show that there must be supernatural beings who are in control of people's minds and/or bodies. Where do they come from? Who are they? What are their desired goals?

In spite of the many verifiable cases of demonic activity, many deny the existence and agency of the devil and his angels. None are in greater danger from the influence of evil spirits than those who, in spite of the testimony of the Scriptures and modern-day exhibitions, are in denial about this evil. Also, because of ignorance relative to their wiles, these demons have an almost inconceivable advantage; many give heed to their suggestions while they suppose themselves to be following the dictates of their own astuteness.

To the web-surfing, postmodern society, this spiritual takeover appears to be only a figment of the imagination generated by some zany wiz on a star-track trek. Film producers have cranked out several sensational films such as the hand wringing, nail-biting, suspense-charged *The Exorcist*; on the opposite side, there are films that mock the issue as being merely humorous or ridiculous. One side drives one to have nightmares, thus prompting the victim to be scared of his own shadow; the other side places this serious and dangerous spiritual epidemic on the level of entertainment, nothing more. In order to defeat or resist this invasion, there must first be recognition of its veracity.

One day while speaking to the disciples, Jesus said, "I saw Satan fall like lightning from heaven" (Luke10:18). He made this statement upon the return of the seventy disciples from their first missionary tour.

> Then the seventy returned with joy, saying, "Lord, even the demons are subject to us in your name." He said to them, "I saw Satan fall like lightning from heaven. Behold, I give you the authority to trample on serpents and scorpions, and over all the power of the enemy, and nothing shall by any means hurt you. Nevertheless do not rejoice in this, that the spirits are subject to you, but rather rejoice because your names are written in heaven." (Luke 10:17–20NKJV)

Christ made a candid declaration—He "saw Satan fall from heaven." The revelator revealed this fall in more detail.

> There was war in heaven: Michael and his angels fought against the dragon; and the dragon fought and his angels, and prevailed not; neither was their place found any more in heaven. And the great dragon was cast out, that old serpent, called the Devil, and Satan, which deceiveth the whole world: he was cast out into the earth, and his angels were cast out with him. (Revelation 12:7–9)

Both Isaiah and the prophet Ezekiel pull back the prophetic veil. Ezekiel, using a human personage of the King of Tyre, revealed who this fallen being is as well as the reasons for his and his cohorts' presence on earth.

> Moreover the word of the Lord came to me, saying, "Son of man, take up a lamentation for the king of Tyre, and say to him, 'Thus says the Lord God:
>
> "You were the seal of perfection, full of wisdom and perfect in beauty. You were in Eden, the garden of God; every precious stone was your covering: the sardius, topaz, and diamond, beryl, onyx, and jasper, sapphire, turquoise, and emerald with gold. The workmanship of your timbrels and pipes was prepared for you on the day you were created.
>
> "You were the anointed cherub who covers; I established you; you were on the holy mountain of God; you walked back and forth in the midst of fiery stones. You were perfect in your ways from the day you were created, till iniquity was found in you. "By the abundance of your trading you became filled with violence within, and you sinned; therefore I cast you as a profane thing out of the mountain of God; and I destroyed you, O covering cherub, from the midst of the fiery stones. "Your heart was lifted up because of your beauty; you corrupted your wisdom for the sake of your splendor; I cast you to the ground, I laid you before kings, that they might gaze at you.

Isaiah contributed to the profile as well.

> "How you are fallen from heaven, O Lucifer, son of the morning! How you are cut down to the ground, you who weakened the nations! For you have said in your heart: 'I will ascend into heaven, I will exalt my throne above the stars of God; I will also sit on the mount of the congregation on the farthest sides of the north; I will ascend above the heights of the clouds, I will be like the Most High." (Isaiah 14:12–14)

Several clues from these passages contribute to unraveling the mysterious takeover of the aforementioned victims. Jesus calls the arch-rebel, "Satan." The

NAMES of ENEMY!

Scriptures give him several names, including Apollyon, deceiver, murderer, prince of the power of the air, the spirit who now works in the sons of disobedience, Abaddon, accuser of our brethren, your adversary, Beelzebub, Belial, the power of darkness, the serpent, son of perdition, the tempter, the god of this world, the wicked one, Satan, the dragon, and the Devil.

Satan's Angels

Along with this cosmic mutineer, there are others that the Scriptures refer to as demons, familiar spirits, unclean spirits, etc. The Bible unfolds their true identity. They are fallen angels. These fallen extraterrestrial beings tallied up to be one-third of the untold number of angels who were together before the great rebellion in heaven. "His tail [the dragon's] drew a third of the stars of heaven and threw them to the earth" (Revelation 12:4), the apostle John records. Stars in the apocalyptic book symbolize angels: "the seven stars are the angels of the seven churches" (Revelation 1:20).

These cosmic pirates are innumerable. Just to have an idea concerning the numbers, let's look at the biblical example of the demoniacs. The Bible records that there was a legion of evil angels controlling this man. In the encounter between Jesus and the possessed man, Jesus asked, "'What is your name?' And he answered, saying, 'My name is Legion; for we are many'" (Mark 5:9 NKJV).

So what is a legion? Legion "was a Latin term denoting a group of about 6,000 Roman soldiers."[8] It is hard to determine the precise number controlling this man. However, there were at least 2,000.

> The devils besought him, saying, Send us into the swine, that we may enter into them. And forthwith Jesus gave them leave. And the unclean spirits went out, and entered into the swine: and the herd ran violently down a steep place into the sea, (they were about two thousand;) and were choked in the sea. (Mark 5:12, 13)

The mass of demons controlling the man explains why he "had his dwelling among the tombs; and no man could bind him, no, not with chains: because that he had been often bound with fetters and chains, and the chains had been plucked asunder by him, and the fetters broken in pieces: neither could any man tame him" (Mark 5:3, 4). Superhuman strength was afforded this man through the demons.

Think of it! At least 2,000 demons inhabited this man. By the same token, seven demons were enough to possess Mary Magdalene (see Luke 8:2). Also, the Gospels mention a host of others: "When the even was come, they brought unto him many that were possessed with devils: and he cast out the spirits with his word, and healed all that were sick" (Matthew 8:16).

Of course, this is not to point out the unnumbered myriad of agents

8   Walvoord, John F., and Zuck, Roy B., *The Bible Knowledge Commentary* (Wheaton, Illinois: Scripture Press Publications, Inc., 1983, 1985), ___.

supplied to harass or tempt every single individual alive at that time. This is why the apostle Paul wrote, "For we wrestle not against flesh and blood, but against principalities, against powers, against the rulers of the darkness of this world, against spiritual wickedness in high places" (Ephesians 6:12).

When it serves their purpose, these beings perform good acts but do so in order to deceive. Again, the apostle Paul noted, "No wonder! For Satan himself transforms himself into an angel of light. Therefore it is no great thing if his ministers also transform themselves into ministers of righteousness, whose end will be according to their works" (2 Corinthians 11:14, 15 NKJV). In other words, when it serves their purpose, they appear angelic in nature. By giving apparently correct counsel, as in the case of King Saul's experience (which we will discuss later), they gain devotees. Nevertheless, their usual preoccupation is that of performing evil. This they carry out by deception, violence, sickness, destruction, calamities, harassment, mental agony and confusion, physical pain, and/or mental illnesses, etc. *work of the enemy.*

In the case of the demoniac, the demons' subtle purpose was to destroy the herd of swine and have the blame cast on Jesus. In response to the extraordinary turn of events, "they that fed the swine fled, and told it in the city, and in the country. And they went out to see what it was that was done. And they come to Jesus, and see him that was possessed with the devil, and had the legion, sitting, and clothed, and in his right mind: and they were afraid. And they that saw it told them how it befell to him that was possessed with the devil, and also concerning the swine" (Mark 5:14–16).

Assuming that Jesus was the culprit for bringing their financial ruin, "they began to pray him to depart out of their coasts" (Mark 5:17). These devils wanted to hedge up the way so that Jesus would not even have an opportunity to influence the dwellers of this region, but He who is all wise had an unsuspected strategy.

> When he was come into the ship, he that had been possessed with the devil prayed him that he might be with him. Howbeit Jesus suffered him not, but saith unto him, Go home to thy friends, and tell them how great things the Lord hath done for thee, and hath had compassion on thee. And he departed, and began to publish in Decapolis how great things Jesus had done for him: and all men did marvel" (Mark 5:16–20).

What the Lord could not accomplish directly, He purposed to do through the converted, delivered man. When He returned to the area, the record states: "So it was, when Jesus returned, that the multitude welcomed Him, for they were all waiting for Him" (Luke 8:40 NKJV).

Another instance is the story of Job. In the biblical record, somewhere in the cosmic beyond, there was a meeting of supernatural beings. The only self-proclaimed representative that attended was Satan; the other rightful dignitaries were not named.

Now there was a day when the sons of God came to present themselves before the Lord, and Satan came also among them. And the Lord said unto Satan, Whence comest thou? Then Satan answered the Lord, and said, From going to and fro in the earth, and from walking up and down in it. And the Lord said unto Satan, Hast thou considered my servant Job, that [there is] none like him in the earth, a perfect and an upright man, one that feareth God, and escheweth evil? (Job 1:6–8).

Satan then charged Job with a fickle loyalty based purely on a sweetheart deal. He acknowledged that God dispensed only good to Job. Then he cynically charged, "Hast not thou made an hedge about him, and about his house, and about all that he hath on every side" (Job 1:10). Then Satan turned it around and said: "put forth your hand now and touch all that he has, and he will curse you to your face" (verse 11). But God set the record straight by saying, "Behold, all that he hath is in thy power; only upon himself put not forth thine hand" (verse 12). In other words, God would not intervene; He told Satan to do what he wanted in order to see if what he said was true. But one thing He did not permit—touch Job physically. "So Satan went forth from the presence of the Lord" (ibid).

God overlooked Satan's claim as the rightful ruler of Planet Earth. Instead, He pointed to one inferior in strength, genius, talent, and power. This infuriated the devil. So in order to prove his point, he lashed out his animosity and completely devastated the innocent. The result of Satan's envy was cruelty, murder, and mental harassment through Job's friends and exasperated wife. Job's demeanor and loyalty are admirable and worthy of emulation.

There was a day when his [Job's] sons and his daughters were eating and drinking wine in their eldest brother's house: And there came a messenger unto Job, and said, The oxen were plowing, and the asses feeding beside them: And the Sabeans fell upon them, and took them away; yea, they have slain the servants with the edge of the sword; and I only am escaped alone to tell thee. While he was yet speaking, there came also another, and said, The fire of God is fallen from heaven, and hath burned up the sheep, and the servants, and consumed them; and I only am escaped alone to tell thee. While he was yet speaking, there came also another, and said, The Chaldeans made out three bands, and fell upon the camels, and have carried them away, yea, and slain the servants with the edge of the sword; and I only am escaped alone to tell thee. While he was yet speaking, there came also another, and said, Thy sons and thy daughters were eating and drinking wine in their eldest brother's house:

And, behold, there came a great wind from the wilderness, and smote the four corners of the house, and it fell upon the young men, and they are dead; and I only am escaped alone to tell thee. (Job 1:13–19)

Notice the decoys Satan used as avenues to deploy his secret vengeance. First, he used human instruments, the Sabeans. Then fire was unleashed to burn up the sheep and the servants. The escapee, of course, blamed God.

Though we have no idea, one cannot help but wonder what advanced technology Satan used to accomplish these deeds. That his high-tech knowledge far exceeds even the most ingenious science fiction star wars gadget and stunts is clear from the fact that he was able to travel to the dwelling place of God, heaven. The New Testament shows that he has the ability to transport people through the air without the aid of any conveyance: he took Jesus to the top of the temple and asked him to cast himself down (see Matthew 4:5). Then in verses 8 and 9, he projected into thin air all the finest of the world's empires. (Perhaps, if time lasts, science may catch up with him.) This he did to entice Christ to give up the struggle of saving the world; He could have it by a simple act of bowing down and rendering worship to Satan.

Back to the story of Job: Satan continued his acts of violence using another human instrument to perform another inhumane crime, the Chaldeans. Finally, he invested his power over the air to annihilate Job's children. This may serve as a clue to unravel the mystery of the increased number of intensified killer tornados and storms of our day. It may also serve to explain why the medical profession, at times, finds itself in a quandary trying to resolve a physical malady, using conventional methods without due consideration of the supernatural.

Evil angels? They are here! Can man in his frail state match the supernatural and sharp cunning of these spirits? Is there safety for those who must deal with the unseen, yet powerful, aliens?

DECEPTION:
THE PREFERED WEAPON

Jesus once declared, "You [the religious leaders] are of your father the devil, and the desires of your father you want to do. He was a murderer from the beginning, and does not stand in the truth, because there is no truth in him. When he speaks a lie, he speaks from his own resources, for he is a liar and the father of it (John 8:44NKJV)."

In the creation story, Adam and Eve were forewarned concerning the danger lurking about. "Then the LORD God took the man and put him in the Garden of Eden to tend and keep it. And the LORD God commanded the man, saying, "Of every tree of the garden you may freely eat; but of the tree of the knowledge of good and evil you shall not eat, for in the day that you eat of it you shall surely die (Genesis 2:15–17 NKJV)."

Satan was determined to conquer the decreed stewards of this planet. In order to achieve this he disguised himself, using a serpent as a vehicle to attempt his act of delusion. Using the artful technique of a ventriloquist, the woman was captivated by the speaking snake. As the dialogue ensued, Satan insinuated doubt concerning the words of God.

> He said to the woman, "Has God indeed said, 'You shall not eat of every tree of the garden'?" And the woman said to the serpent, "We may eat the fruit of the trees of the garden; but of the fruit of the tree which is in the midst of the garden, God has said, 'You shall not eat it, nor shall you touch it, lest you die.'" Then the serpent said to the woman, "You will not surely die. For God knows that in the day you eat of it your eyes will be opened and you will be like God, knowing good and evil"
> (Genesis 3:1–5 NKJV).

Satan implanted the suspicion, and Eve followed his train of thought. Unsuspecting of his devices, she pondered the suggestions. Her musing gave the enemy hope and, seeing that she took the bait—he enticed her to partake. He intensified his temptation with another suggestion. "God doth know that in the day ye eat thereof, then your eyes shall be opened, and ye shall be as gods, knowing good and evil" (Genesis 3:5). "So when the woman saw that the tree was good for food, that it was pleasant to the eyes, and a tree desirable to make one wise, she took of its fruit and ate. She also gave to her husband with her, and he ate. Then the eyes of both of them were opened" (Genesis 3:6, 7).

Satan beguiled them with deception. By his uncanny ability to implant suspicion, doubt, lust, impure thoughts, pride, and a variety of other provocative thoughts, he often succeeds in directing the mind. It is obvious from this encounter of Adam (who had been created with a mental acuity unsurpassed by any succeeding human being) with the arch-deceiver that only God can converse with Satan and win.

He succeeded with the first recorded lie, "thou shalt not surely die," to gain his object. God said they would die, but Satan disputed it. He stated that their eyes would be opened. In this, he told part truth—their eyes would be opened—but not to what had been promised them. "Every dying leaf," every shiver, and every death of a human being was an eye-opener. Yes, their eyes were opened to see the untold woe and misery that would engulf the human family until the Deliverer should appear. Adam and Eve did, in fact, die—contrary to the false assurance.

The devil's labors are incessant. Yet, like a deadly adder, his movements are undetectable, his efforts often unperceivable. As silent as a stealth bomber, his approach is detected only once the strike is made. The victim is usually left with the self-condemning inquiry, "Why did I do that?" For this reason, the Christian must avail himself of the insights given in the Scriptures concerning the manner and ways of the enemy's approaches and how to withstand and quench his fiery darts.

It is this level of defense that Satan fears. The devil knows the limit of his power when he attempts to allure one who is knowledgeable of his ways. He is also keen as to the assistance available to resist his temptations. Through the divine strength amply provided, the weakest believer is more than a match for Satan and his hosts. It is for this very reason that the Lord admonishes His saints to be on constant watch. The enemy knows that if he is detected, his prey will flee to God for power to resist through prayer. Hence, Satan recognizes that his defeat is sure. It is, therefore, no wonder that his steps are imperceptible, hoping to ensnare his victim before he or she has a chance to find refuge in God.

The enemy is preparing for his last campaign. The Bible warns, "Woe to the inhabiters of the earth and the sea for the devil is come down unto you, having great wrath, because he knoweth that he hath but a short time" (Revelation 12:12). In order to carry out his desired global conquest, he has so concealed himself that many can hardly believe that he exists—much less be convinced of his amazing activity and power.

---

9   E. G. White, *The Great Controversy*, 647.

Under his bewitching influence he is able to covertly manipulate their minds to carry out his suggestions, while leading the puppet to assume that the vile impulses are original; that is, their own. In some cases the delusion is perfected to the extent that the deluded actually believe they are carrying out the will of God. So was the case of the unconverted apostle Paul.

When his eyes were spiritually opened, he discovered that the liberty he thought he had was in reality the manacle that the devil had fastened on his deluded mind. About his former state of delusion he wrote, "I thank Christ Jesus our Lord, who hath enabled me . . . who was before a blasphemer, and a persecutor, and injurious: but I obtained mercy, because I did it ignorantly in unbelief" (1 Timothy 1:12, 13). So was the case of those led by David Koresh, Jim Jones, and others, who while boasting of their freedom and independence, led the sheep to their ruin.

The unconverted man is Satan's captive; he is naturally inclined to follow Satan's suggestions and do his bidding. Being inbred with evil, man has no power, in himself, to resist evil. The only antidote against man's natural evil propensity is to have Christ dwelling in him. A mere agreement or intellectual concurrence will not suffice. The only instance in which man can venture to face so cunning a foe is when he receives, and persistently keeps, his Savior in the heart by living faith. The apostle Paul wrote: "I have been crucified with Christ; it is no longer I who live, but Christ who lives in me; and the life I now live in the flesh I live by faith in the Son of God, who loved me and gave himself for me" (Galatians 2:20 RSV). Once he gained the first step, then he wrote, "I die daily" (1 Corinthians 15:31). Paul was cognizant of the urgent need to keep a vigilant watch over his carnal desires; to keep them daily surrendered to a personal indwelling Lord.

Every other defense is futile. Only through Christ is Satan's power held in check. This is a crucial truth that all should be aware of and comprehend. Well do the Scriptures warn that the devil is busy every moment; going to and fro, walking up and down in the earth (see Job 1:7), "seeking whom he may devour" (1 Peter 5:8). One word of encouragement: the earnest prayer of faith will baffle Satan's strongest efforts. So, take "the shield of faith, wherewith ye shall be able to quench all the fiery darts of the wicked" (Ephesians 6:16).

With the fusion of divine and human powers, Christ came from heaven to empower fallen humanity, because Adam's progeny could not overcome the devil with only their human strength or acuity. In Eden God had equipped Adam with the mental capacity to withstand the temptations and conquer the arch foe. But once man was placed outside the protected environment of Eden with his compromised will; and having lost his direct attachment to God, he rendered himself, in his own strength, incapable of resisting the devil.

Thus, in order to help and rescue mankind, the divine Christ condescended to take on human nature. The Holy Scriptures calls this a mystery. "Without controversy great is the mystery of godliness: God was manifest in the flesh, justified in the Spirit, seen of angels, preached unto the Gentiles, believed on in the world, received up into glory" (1 Timothy 3:16).

Not only did he meld the two natures together, but He also descended with that combination down to the earth where frail man dwelt. Man needed the strength to conquer his captor, but, by virtue of Satan's conquest, mankind lost the original inherent power to do so. Thus, man was held a hopeless captive. It was for this reason that this combination was brought down to where man could have access to it.

"Whereby are given unto us exceeding great and precious promises that by these ye might become partakers of the divine nature, having escaped the corruption that is in the word through lust" (2 Peter 1:4). Through this mysterious blend, He provided for the fallen race the strength necessary to resist temptation—a power no longer inherent in man. By His incarnation He obtained for the fallen race power that it is impossible for them to gain for themselves. In His name they are made "more than conquerors through him that loved us" (Romans 8:37) and are able to overcome the temptations of Satan.

Let none suppose that without serious effort on their part, they can obtain the assurance of God's salvation. There's good reason for this caution. When the mind has been long permitted to dwell only on secular and carnal things, such as war, violence, immorality, dishonesty, etc., it is a difficult matter to change the current of thought. That which the eye sees and the ear hears too often attracts the attention and absorbs the interest, but if we would enter into a sweet, abiding communion with God, and have a reality of His presence in our hearts and minds, we would become accustomed to beholding Him with the eye of faith. The words and the character of Christ recorded in Holy Writ must be often the subject of our thoughts and of our conversation.

Oftentimes, when we commence down this avenue of walking with Christ, great effort must be exerted to keep the mind from drifting or getting distracted. It is well to meditate on the Word in the morning and repeat it throughout the day. As one persists in the effort, at first it will appear to be a losing battle. Especially will this be true for those whose minds have become like sponges, absorbing all the grit and grime of life, or been debilitated with drugs, alcohol, or any other mind-altering substances.

I can testify to this. Before I became a Christian, and even in the initial stages of my newfound experience, I suffered from a terrible memory shortage. Oftentimes, I could not even remember what I had said the day before. This was very frustrating to my wife, who has a computer-like memory. She would tell me that I had said something, and I would dispute her. But as my mind began to clear up, it became apparent that she was right. All this was due to my former substance abuse. So, I know what it is like to struggle with the apparent inability to remember. If effort is perseveringly continued, gaining ever so little day by day, the mind will be retrained to focus on that which is holy, just, good, pure, true, and noble. Each day some time should be especially devoted to prayerful meditation upon these sacred themes.

The need to guard the affections and the passions with a firm purpose is a lifelong struggle. The reason is not ambiguous. An inward corruption in us responds to the outward temptation, and it is as natural as the magnetic north being attracted to the magnetic south. Because of this natural reality, the devil arranges circumstances so that temptations come with overpowering force. Therefore, the only way that we can be secure in God is to rely moment by moment on Him.

In some Christians' thinking, the practice of meditation is linked to New Age, Buddhism, etc.—something antagonistic to Christianity—but a love for thought reflection and cherishing a spirit of devotion is a habit that every believer should cultivate. Moments spent concentrating on the pure, noble, and faithful life of Christ, and moments spent in the searching of the Scriptures, coupled with prayer, are not time wasted. On the contrary, by disciplining the mind and thoughts to dwell upon heavenly things, new life with increasing fortitude will be received.

The Scriptures admonishes to "keep thy heart with all diligence; for out of it are the issues of life" (Proverbs 4:23). As a man "thinketh in his heart, so is he" (Proverbs 23:7). It is with this understanding that David prayed, "Create in me a clean heart, O God; and renew a right spirit within me" (Psalm 51:10). His prayer should be the supplication of every soul. He knew by experience that his heart had to be renewed by divine grace, without which purity of life would be impossible. Consequently, anyone who tries to develop an upright, righteous character without the power of Christ, is doomed to fail.

Is your faith small? Jesus recognized this when He said, "If ye have faith as a grain of mustard seed" (Matthew 17:20). The grain of mustard seed is very tiny. Yet it contains the same mysterious life principle that produces growth in lofty trees. When the mustard seed is thrown into the ground, the tiny kernel takes hold of every ingredient that God has provided for its sustenance, and it incrementally begins a strapping growth. If your faith is this minuscule, you must take hold upon God's Word, and upon all the helpful agencies He has provided. Your faith will then increase, bringing to your aid heaven's power. The obstacles and illusions of iron barriers that the devil piled across your way, though seemingly insurmountable, will disintegrate before the demand of faith. "Nothing shall be impossible unto you. As you partake of his strength, you will be "kept by the power of God through faith" (1 Peter 1:5).[10]

---

10   E. G. White, *The Desire of Ages*, 431, author's paraphrase.

THE ROOT OF THE MODERN-DAY PARAPSYCHOLOGY

Because possession is a reality, what is the root of these demonic successes? In order to perpetuate and establish his lie concerning the true condition of mankind in death, the devil has sought to create what would appear to be concrete evidence of his speculation. Using humans as channels, he has for centuries employed psychics, spiritists, clairvoyants, astro-travelers, rebirthers, or channelers. These people make it appear as if the dead are still alive, living in some spirit world. In the Bible, these human channels are referred to with disparaging language. God warned:

> When thou art come into the land which the Lord thy God giveth thee, thou shalt not learn to do after the abominations of those nations. There shall not be found among you any one that maketh his son or his daughter to pass through the fire, or that useth divination, or an observer of times, or an enchanter, or a witch. Or a charmer, or a consulter with familiar spirits, or a wizard, or a necromancer. For all that do these things are an abomination unto the Lord: and because of these abominations the Lord thy God doth drive them out from before thee. Thou shalt be perfect with the Lord thy God. For these nations, which thou shalt possess, hearkened unto observers of times, and unto diviners: but as for thee, the Lord thy God hath not suffered thee so to do. (Deuteronomy 18:9–14)

Though the Babylonians were steeped in the occult, and their leaders staked their future on the guidance of sorcery, God revealed the futility in trusting it. Mockingly, He said to them, "Stand now with thine enchantments, and with the multitude of thy sorceries, wherein thou hast laboured from thy youth; if so be thou shalt be able to profit, if so be thou mayest prevail. Thou art wearied in the multitude of thy counsels. Let now the astrologers, the stargazers, the monthly prognosticators, stand up, and save thee from these things that shall come upon thee" (Isaiah 47:12, 13).

Years before, after the Lord had established Israel in the Holy Land, they desired a man as king instead of Jehovah. Though dismayed with their desire, God gave them their choice. Things apparently started out well. The king was humble in his own estimation. In considering his need for such a lofty position, God endowed him with spiritual powers. "God gave him another heart . . . and the Spirit of God came upon him, and he prophesied among them" (1 Samuel 10:9, 10).

It was not long before his position went to his head. Rather than follow the counsel of his God, he relentlessly pursued his own course. Things went from bad to worse. The decline was so steep that God had to reject him.

> Now the Lord said to Samuel, "How long will you mourn for
> Saul, seeing I have rejected him from reigning over Israel? Fill
> your horn with oil, and go; I am sending you to Jesse the Beth-
> lehemite. For I have provided Myself a king among his sons.
> But the Spirit of the Lord departed from Saul, and a distressing
> spirit from the LORD troubled him. (1 Samuel 16:1, 14 NKJV)

Hardening his heart against the Holy Spirit and unwilling to follow His leading, Saul gave way for another spirit to possess him. The text says "an evil spirit from God" (verse 14 KJV). When a person is blessed by God to be raised to the level of prominence, privilege, and responsibility, it is an awful thing to turn God's blessing into personal, selfish gain or heighten prideful arrogance. The Scriptures warn concerning the spurning of His Spirit. "Quench not the Spirit" (1 Thessalonians 5:19) is the admonition. Jesus himself warned:

> Wherefore I say unto you, All manner of sin and blasphemy
> shall be forgiven unto men: but the blasphemy against the Holy
> Ghost shall not be forgiven unto men. And whosoever speaketh
> a word against the Son of man, it shall be forgiven him: but
> whosoever speaketh against the Holy Ghost, it shall not be for-
> given him, neither in this world, neither in the world to come.
> (Matthew 12:31, 32)

Turning one's back to the Spirit of God creates a vacuum to be filled with possessive and seducing spirits. Giving insight to these phenomena, Jesus said:

> When the unclean spirit is gone out of a man, he walketh
> through dry places, seeking rest; and finding none, he saith, I
> will return unto my house whence I came out. And when he
> cometh, he findeth it swept and garnished. Then goeth he, and
> taketh to him seven other spirits more wicked than himself; and
> they enter in, and dwell there: and the last state of that man is
> worse than the first. (Luke 11:24–26)

Saul found himself devoid of counsel. He was fearful of the future and, having premonitions of some evil omen, became anxious to discover the future. Because he could no longer go to the late prophet Samuel and obviously felt forsaken by God, he sought another forbidden avenue.

> Then said Saul unto his servants, Seek me a woman that hath a familiar spirit, that I may go to her, and inquire of her. And his servants said to him, Behold, there is a woman that hath a familiar spirit at Endor. And Saul disguised himself, and put on other raiment, and went, he and two men with him, and they came to the woman by night: and he said, Divine unto me, I pray thee, by the familiar spirit, and bring me up whomsoever I shall name unto thee. And the woman said unto him, Behold, thou knowest what Saul hath done, how he hath cut off those that have familiar spirits, and the wizards, out of the land: wherefore then layest thou a snare for my life, to cause me to die? And Saul sware to her by Jehovah, saying, As Jehovah liveth, there shall no punishment happen to thee for this thing. Then said the woman, Whom shall I bring up unto thee? And he said, Bring me up Samuel. And when the woman saw Samuel, she cried with a loud voice; and the woman spake to Saul, saying, Why hast thou deceived me? for thou art Saul. And the king said unto her, Be not afraid: for what seest thou? And the woman said unto Saul, I see a god coming up out of the earth. And he said unto her, What form is he of? And she said, An old man cometh up; and he is covered with a robe. And Saul perceived that it was Samuel, and he bowed with his face to the ground, and did obeisance. And Samuel said to Saul, Why hast thou disquieted me, to bring me up? And Saul answered, I am sore distressed; for the Philistines make war against me, and God is departed from me, and answereth me no more, neither by prophets, nor by dreams: therefore I have called thee, that thou mayest make known unto me what I shall do. And Samuel said, Wherefore then dost thou ask of me, seeing Jehovah is departed from thee, and is become thine adversary? And Jehovah hath done unto thee, as he spake by me: and Jehovah hath rent the kingdom out of thy hand, and given it to thy neighbor, even to David. Because thou obeyedst not the voice of Jehovah, and didst not execute his fierce wrath upon Amalek, therefore hath Jehovah done this thing unto thee this day. Moreover Jehovah will deliver Israel also with thee into the hand of the Philistines; and to-morrow shalt thou and thy sons be with me: Jehovah will deliver the host of Israel also into the hand of the Philistines. (1 Samuel 28:7–19)

This encounter underscores the biblical fact that people in ancient times not only sought out those of familiar spirits (today called mediums) but also secretly practiced communicating with the supposed spirits of the dead. This same kind of means is still used by Satan to make concrete the practice of demonic interchange with humans. This encounter can be so real that it defies the senses, which is why so many become deluded. The senses are bewitched. The inexplicable only leads to its embrace. So cunning is this arch-deceiver that he successfully convinced this ancient, deluded king to believe the lie.

From the language in these verses, some have misconstrued the meaning. They have concluded that here is biblical proof of a dead person communicating with the living, through a medium. That this being was not really Samuel, but an apparition, is obvious because of the following reasons:

1. The record states that Saul requested a person with a "familiar spirit." The term in the singular or plural is found in 15 verses in the Old Testament. All these terms deal with humans who consort with spirits, and the spirits are fallen angels, not humans. In the New Testament, this practice is associated with witchcraft (Galatians 5:20) or the spirit of divination (Acts 16:16). These spiritists are connected with devils (Revelation 16:14).

2. Necromancers had been sentenced to death and banned from the land (1 Samuel 28:3; Leviticus 20:27).

3. God had departed from Saul and would not communicate with him (1 Samuel 28:15). If God would not communicate with Saul through Samuel, while he was yet alive, why would he allow Samuel to communicate with him after his demise?

4. God would not grant a necromancer, an agent of his archenemy, divine authority to summon Samuel from his resting place. To think that God, who had condemned the practice of witchcraft (Deuteronomy 18:10–12), would acquiesce to the request of a medium and allow a righteous man to be manipulated by an agent of Satan would be wholly inconceivable.

5. Samuel was supposedly "brought up." Other expressions: "ascending out of the earth," "cometh up," and "bring . . . up." Is this the habitation of the righteous dead, in the earth? Is that where they reside after death? Not according to those who believe in and teach the immortality of the soul. They teach that the righteous go up to heaven, not down.

6. The apparition of Samuel told Saul, "Tomorrow shalt thou and thy sons be with me." Saul had departed from God and committed suicide on the following day. If Saul was to be with Samuel, then the question must be raised as to the whereabouts of the righteous—that is if they are alive in the so-called "spirit world." Do the wicked and the righteous then dwell together? The obvious answer is, no! But the truth of the matter is that the prophecy came true. All who die go to the grave. So, in this sense, Saul went to the same place—death—as did Samuel.

7. The record never says that Saul saw Samuel. He only "perceived" that it was Samuel, based on the information he received from the witch, and only

concluded it was the old prophet from the description. The truth is that the devil deceived the dissolute old woman, and she deceived Saul. It was nothing more than a devil-generated séance.

The enormity of Saul's sin is revealed in these words: "So Saul died for his trespass which he committed against Jehovah, because of the word of Jehovah, which he kept not; and also for that he asked counsel of one that had a familiar spirit, to inquire *thereby*, and inquired not of Jehovah: therefore he slew him, and turned the kingdom unto David the son of Jesse" (1 Chronicles 10:13, 14 ASV).

Why Christianity perpetuates this dangerous monstrous doctrine today is an enigma. God declares that the living will "return to the earth from which thou was taken" (Genesis 3:19). Yet his professed ministers contradict Him by declaring that people go immediately to heaven or hell at death. In doing this, they leave open a wide gate for the devil to perpetuate his lie and, thus, deceive and destroy.

The irony is that while preachers preach that the dead go to hell, no one seems to go there, at least that's what is assumed at the funeral. Have you ever heard a minister or priest in a funeral service pronounce, "Poor soul, he/she is in hell now burning forever." They are either pronounced to be in heaven, as Billy Graham, during his homily at the memorial service, declared of those who died in the Twin Towers in 9/11, or they are resting in peace. Pastor Graham said, "Many of those people who died this past week are in heaven right now and they wouldn't want to come back."[11] The other option was to declare them to be in hell, suffering excruciating pain throughout eternity.

Frankly, I have not seen one tombstone in a cemetery (and I have been to a good number all over the world) with the words etched, "Burning forever." Usually, the epitaph has them resting in peace.

---

11   Billy Graham, sermon delivered on September 14, 2001, Washington National Cathedral, http://www.nationalcathedral.org/worship/sermonTexts/bg010914.shtml (accessed: June15, 2012).

DEMONIC APPARITIONS

Modern-day spiritualism has been given a boost by the doctrine of Natural Immortality, which is held in common by most Christians. In this teaching, those who have died are supposed to immediately be transported to the presence of the holy angels and God. Their imaginary admittance into heaven entitles them to knowledge and insights previously denied them. They then purport that these departed dead make frequent visits to their loved ones and friends, hovering over them and imparting counsels and warnings suited to protect them.

Clearly, this erroneous teaching places the believer in a gullible posture. This channel, created by the mastermind himself and passed on to adherents of trusted theologians, has proven successful all too well. Satan's messengers of darkness transform themselves into channels of light materialize, acting the part of connecting the living with the supposed dead. At this point Satan exercises his bewitching spell upon their minds.

He exercises his power to put before men supposed replicas or decoys of their departed friends and loved ones. The counterfeit is made perfect. With marvelous distinctness, they see the familiar expressive look, the mode of speech, and even the tone of voice that all contribute to give undeniable evidence to the bewildered that their loved ones are alive. Many feel comforted with the assurance that their deceased relatives are enjoying heavenly bliss; thus, without suspicion, they give ear to seducing spirits and doctrines of devils. Not a few have invited these presumed departed spirits to take possession of them in order to enjoy, they hoped, powers and privileges afforded by this takeover.

I well remember the many stories told by neighbors in Brooklyn who believed that they saw their dead family members appear to them. As a boy, I knew some of these "visitants," and if there was a heaven, their lifestyles would have prevented them from going there. Yet reports were given from those who claimed to have happiness in heaven. Those who went into their graves unprepared seemed to be placed on a par with the righteous, as far as where they went after death.

Thus, the error was widely believed that, at death, everyone was placed into the same batch, making no difference between the righteous and the wicked.

Sometimes the pretending visitors from the spirit world declare truths (as in the case of King Saul's experience with the apparition), or they give warnings (as in my experience with the possessed girl) that proved correct. Once the person's confidence was gained, these demons presented teachings calculated to undermine confidence in the Bible. People's faith is then riveted in the sayings of devils rather than in the teachings of the Word of God.

It is not beyond their ability to foretell the future; neither is it uncharacteristic for them to make truthful statements. This is done with the intention of giving their teachings credibility, resulting in millions of adherents tenaciously grasping and holding unto these errors as sacred truth. Through this channel, Satan has forged his way into the teachings of many professed Christian faiths. The principals of God's holy law are trodden underfoot and, as the Bible states, they deny the divine nature of Christ. (See 1 John 4:2, 3.)

Many endeavor to account for spiritual manifestations by attributing them wholly to fraud and sleight of hand. Though the results of trickery have often been misrepresented as genuine manifestations, there have also been marked exhibitions of supernatural power. "In 1848 mysterious rappings were heard in the home of the Fox family at Hydesville, a community about thirty-five miles east of the city of Rochester, New York."[12] These mysterious rappings, with which modern spiritualism began, were not the result of human trickery or cunning, but the direct work of evil angels, who thus introduced one of the most successful of soul-destroying delusions. Many will be ensnared through the belief that Spiritualism is merely a human imposture. However, when brought face to face with manifestations that they must regard as supernatural, they will be deceived and led to accept them as the great power of God.

These persons overlook the testimony of the Scriptures concerning the wonders wrought by Satan and his agents and its explicit and plain truth concerning the dead. It was by satanic aid that Pharaoh's magicians were enabled to counterfeit the work of God. (See Exodus 7:10–12.) The apostle John described the miracle-working power that will be manifested in the last days. He declared, "He doeth great wonders, so that he maketh fire come down from heaven on the earth in the sight of men, and deceiveth them that dwell on the earth by the means of those miracles which he had power to do" (Revelation 13:13, 14). No mere impostures are here brought to view. Men are deceived by the miracles that Satan's agents have power to do, not which they pretend to do. By rejecting the plain biblical statements regarding those who are dead, people are easily deceived. God's servant wrote:

> For the living know that they shall die: but the dead know not
> any thing, neither have they any more a reward; for the memory
> of them is forgotten. Also their love, and their hatred, and their

12   E.G. White, *Early Writings*, 300.

envy, is now perished; neither have they any more a portion for ever in any thing that is done under the sun. (Ecclesiastes 9:5, 6)

For in death there is no remembrance of thee [God]: in the grave who shall give thee thanks? (Psalm 6:5)

Put not your trust in princes, nor in the son of man, in whom there is no help. His breath goeth forth, he returneth to his earth; in that very day his thoughts perish. (Psalm 146:3, 4)

After King Hezekiah was told that he would die, and upon receiving word that his repentance and plea had been acknowledged, with the sign of the sun dial going backward ten degrees given as a guarantee, he wrote, "For the grave cannot praise thee, death cannot celebrate thee: they that go down into the pit cannot hope for thy truth. The living, the living, he shall praise thee, as I do this day: the father to the children shall make known thy truth" (Isaiah 38:18, 19).

The One who inspired the Scriptures and directed His prophets to write down the instructions certainly knew the true condition of man in death. Jesus' own revelator recorded:

Fear not; I am the first and the last: I *am* he that liveth, and was dead; and, behold, I am alive for evermore, Amen; and have the keys of hell [meaning the "grave"] and of death. Write the things which thou hast seen, and the things which are, and the things which shall be hereafter. (Revelation 1:18, 19)

The question of the hereafter is declared to be in the hands of Him who is the "resurrection and the life" (John 11:25). The sentence, declared by God upon Adam and Eve resulting from their transgression, was not heaven or hell. It was the dust. "In the sweat of thy face shalt thou eat bread, till thou return unto the ground; for out of it wast thou taken: for dust thou art, and unto dust shalt thou return" (Genesis 3:19). Dust is the biblically declared habitat for the dead. The writer of the book of Job wrote, "Why dost thou not pardon my transgression, and take away mine iniquity? for now shall I sleep in the dust; and thou shalt seek me in the morning, but I shall not be" (Job 7:21). This fact is reiterated throughout Holy Writ. (See Job 10:9; 17:16; 20:11; 21:26; 34:15; Psalm 30:9; 104:29; Ecclesiastes 3:20; Isaiah 26:19; Ezekiel 37:12, 13; Daniel 12:2; Matthew 27:52, 53; John 5:28, 29; 6:39, 40, 44, 54; 12:17; Acts 2:29; 1 Corinthians 15:55.)

Addressing this issue, the Lord left no shadow of doubt concerning the state of those who have died. Speaking of Lazarus, a close associate and friend, and after receiving a message from his sisters concerning Lazarus's death, He said to His disciples:

Our friend Lazarus sleepeth; but I go, that I may awake him out of sleep. Then said his disciples, Lord, if he sleep, he shall do well. Howbeit Jesus spake of his death: but they thought that he had spoken of taking of rest in sleep. Then said Jesus unto them plainly, Lazarus is dead. (John 11:12–14)

Here, Jesus called death a sleep. Four days later after Lazarus' body was already in a state of decomposition, Jesus awoke him out of the sleep of death.

This teaching and practice of Christ was consistent with the posture taken by the prophets relative to the dead. The following references and quotes verify this fact. "The Lord said unto Moses, Behold, thou shalt sleep with thy fathers" (Deuteronomy 31:12). King David had the same fate. "When thy days be fulfilled, and thou shalt sleep with thy fathers, I will set up thy seed after thee, which shall proceed out of thy bowels, and I will establish his kingdom" (2 Samuel 7:12). David himself wrote, "Consider and hear me, O Lord my God: lighten mine eyes, lest I sleep the sleep of death" (Psalms 131:3). Daniel recorded, "Many of them that sleep in the dust of the earth shall awake, some to everlasting life, and some to shame and everlasting contempt" (Daniel 12:2).

Regarding Stephen, the first Christian martyr, the apostle Luke wrote, "They stoned Stephen, calling upon God, and saying, Lord Jesus, receive my spirit. And he kneeled down, and cried with a loud voice, Lord, lay not this sin to their charge. And when he had said this, he fell asleep" (Acts 7:60).

He who is the Creator, who gave life to mankind and finally walked among men, certainly knows their state in death. It is He who declared: "I am the resurrection, and the life" (John 11:25); He who has the keys of death and the grave; the One who spoke life into the decaying body of Lazarus; He who promised:

> This is the Father's will which hath sent me, that of all which he
> hath given me I should lose nothing, but should raise it up again at
> the last day. And this is the will of him that sent me, that every one
> which seeth the Son, and believeth on him, may have everlasting
> life: and I will raise him up at the last day. (John 6:39, 40)

Even his beloved disciples—the men who had the most prominent positions with the Savior—are resting, awaiting the glorious moment when they will be awakened out the their graves. For the Savior promised them:

> Let not your heart be troubled: ye believe in God, believe also in
> me. In my Father's house are many mansions: if it were not so, I
> would have told you. I go to prepare a place for you. And if I go and
> prepare a place for you, I will come again, and receive you unto
> myself; that where I am, there ye may be also. (John 14:1–3)

These honored men are not in heaven, else Jesus would not have told them that he would return to receive them unto Himself. It is He, the One who has promised who should know their whereabouts, and He has spoken unequivocally—the dead are asleep! That is why He is returning.

If the saved were already with Him, he would make a wasted trip back to earth to gather what He already has. This is why Paul encouraged the bereft with the assurance:

> But I would not have you to be ignorant, brethren, concerning
> them which are asleep, that ye sorrow not, even as others which

have no hope. For if we believe that Jesus died and rose again, even so *them also which sleep in Jesus* will God bring with him. For this we say unto you by the word of the Lord, that we which are alive and remain unto the coming of the Lord shall not prevent them which are asleep. For the Lord himself shall descend from heaven with a shout, with the voice of the archangel, and with the trump of God: and the dead in Christ shall rise first: Then we which are alive and remain shall be caught up together with them in the clouds, to meet the Lord in the air: and so shall we ever be with the Lord. (1 Thessalonians 4:13–17, (emphasis added).

On one occasion, while Jesus was ministering, there came to him a ruler anxious to usher Jesus to his home. His daughter was ill, and he desired Jesus to heal her. While on the way, the sad news came.

While he yet spake, there cometh one from the ruler of the synagogue's house, saying to him, Thy daughter is dead; trouble not the Master. But when Jesus heard it, he answered him, saying, Fear not: believe only, and she shall be made whole. And when he came into the house, he suffered no man to go in, save Peter, and James, and John, and the father and the mother of the maiden. And all wept, and bewailed her: but he said, Weep not; she is not dead, but sleepeth. And they laughed him to scorn, knowing that she was dead. And he put them all out, and took her by the hand, and called, saying, Maid, arise. And her spirit came again, and she arose straightway: and he commanded to give her meat. And her parents were astonished: but he charged them that they should tell no man what was done. (Luke 9:49–56)

Yes, death is but a pause in the path of life. It is a resting time until the Lifegiver awakens all to receive, according to their works, their just destiny or fate. Jesus said:

Marvel not at this: for the hour is coming, in the which all that are in the graves shall hear his voice, and shall come forth; they that have done good, unto the resurrection of life; and they that have done evil, unto the resurrection of damnation. (John 5:28, 29) He that is unjust, let him be unjust still: and he which is filthy, let him be filthy still: and he that is righteous, let him be righteous still: and he that is holy, let him be holy still. And, behold, I come quickly; and my reward is with me, to give every man according as his work shall be. (Revelation 22:11, 12)

For those who die in Christ, the Scriptures pronounce it a rest. "I heard a voice from heaven saying unto me, Write, blessed are the dead which die in the Lord from henceforth: Yea, saith the Spirit, that they may rest from their labours; and their works do follow them" (Revelation 14:13). This "*rest*" will terminate in the day of the Lord at the second coming. The apostle Paul wrote:

> But now is Christ risen from the dead, and become the first-fruits of them that slept. For since by man came death, by man came also the resurrection of the dead. For as in Adam all die, even so in Christ shall all be made alive. But every man in his own order: Christ the firstfruits; afterward they that are Christ's *at his coming*" (1 Corinthians 15:20–23, emphasis added).

Sleep = Rest in Christ's work.

COMMUNICATING WITH THE DEAD

The belief and teaching that the spirits of the dead are among us, and accessible to us, lead to dangerous practices. Those who are anxious for fame, wealth, or success will invite these supposed spirits, with envious skills or talents, to possess them in order to receive those gifts themselves. The knowledge or powers that appear with supernatural ability are real. There's a limit to human strength and foresight ability, but when it is obvious that the demonstrations are beyond the human, it is evidence that supernatural agencies are at work.

Demonic possessions have been described as people experiencing erased memories or changes in personality. There can be convulsions, "fits," and fainting as if one were dying. Other displays can include *gnosis* (access to hidden knowledge and ecstatic utterances), which some claim to be foreign languages. There can be drastic changes in vocal intonation and facial structure. In a recent conversation, a friend shared with me that a man, an expert in martial arts, wanted to demonstrate a new development in his energies. He began to make strange facial contortions and sweat profusely. Then he lifted up his shirt, and there were strange scratches that appeared on his chest, evidence that some unseen hands had scratched him. These sudden appearances of injuries (scratches, bite marks, or lesions) are demonstrations of demonic presence.

Spiritualism or witchcraft was once held in contempt—as it was associated with callous evil and shrouded with superstition and mystery, thus subjecting the apprehended practitioner to public shame and disgrace, stocks, and death. Yet, the same practices have gone through a metamorphosis and have surfaced in our modern age with new contemporary titles. The claim that men can hold discourses with spirits is no longer regarded as a fable of the Dark Ages. Spiritualism—which has gone through an apparent transmutation and which numbers its converts by hundreds of thousands, yea, by millions—has made its way into scientific circles. It is a well-known fact that even heads of state like former Presidents Abraham Lincoln with Mary his wife, and Ronald Reagan and his wife Nancy, for a time turned to the séance.[13]

13   Mr. Lincoln's White House, "Red Room," The Gilder Lehrman Institute of American History, www.

States the *Online Opinion* of Australia: "Where does the role of the psychic lie in policing? The secular, rationalist follower of hard facts and evidentiary reason might well question their very existence, let alone value. But moments of crisis can increase the emphasis on faith and desires to communicate with the world of the dead. As far back as October 1987, the American magazine *McCall's* published an article entitled "Clairvoyant Crime Busters" featuring the feats of such "psychics" as Dorothy Allison and John Catchings. In recent times, a global audience has reveled in the predictive powers of Octopus Paul, predicting sea creature *par excellence* who managed a near perfect record for the football world cup in South Africa."[14]

In Newnan, Georgia, Channel News 11 Alive reported, "Newnan police are crediting a clairvoyant with helping them identify and catch a man suspected of assaulting women.

"They say the clairvoyant's information was so helpful, they're now consulting with her to help crack a couple of other cases.

"Her work is an unconventional police weapon—and an unprecedented one for the Newnan Police Department.

"Detective Sergeant Rick Mires was skeptical about it, at first.

"When the clairvoyant came forward, she gave Mires information about an unsolved sexual attack last year on a 90 year old Newnan woman, inside the woman's home. The victim had not been able to give police a description of the man who attacked her. . . .

"Mires said Cadore's [the clairvoyant] description of the attacker, and the other information she provided, were crucial tips that helped detectives come up with hard evidence that led them to a suspect."[15]

This renewed Dark Ages practice has invaded churches and has found favor in legislative bodies, even in the courts of kings—this mammoth deception is but a revival in a new disguise of the witchcraft condemned and prohibited in days of old. The Holy Writ says, "The idols have spoken vanity, and the diviners have seen a lie, and have told false dreams; they comfort in vain" (Zechariah 10:2).

By exciting the desire for power or special knowledge, Satan beguiles mankind today. He uses the suggestions of, "ye shall be as gods" and "knowing good and evil" (Genesis 3:5) to entice, and many who are allured by desire of grandeur fall prey. Those who yield to the supposed wisdom of spiritualism yield to that which "descendeth not from above, but is earthly, sensual, devilish" (James 3:15).

The devil works "with all deceivableness of unrighteousness" (2 Thessalonians

mrlincolnswhitehouse.org/inside.asp?ID=71&subjectID=3 (accessed, October 3, 2012).

14   Binoy Kammark, "'Clairvoyant crime busters': using psychic powers in policing," ON LINE opinion: Australia's e-journal of social and political debate, August 23, 2010, http://www.onlineopinion.com.au/view.asp?article=10869, (accessed, October 3, 2012).

15   Jon Shirek, "Newnan Police Credit Clairvoyant with Helping Suspect," News 11 Alive, Atlanta, July 6, 2010, http://www.11alive.com/news/local/story.aspx?storyid=146004 (accessed, June 6, 2012).

2:10) to gain control of whomever turns an interested eye in the least bit toward his sophistry, but his object can only be gained when there is a willingness to yield to his temptation. Like Judas, who yielded to the devil, those who indulge their evil propensities place themselves in his power. They will find themselves helplessly in the strong current of evil being plunged into their ruin, and at the same time they will be employed to ruin others.

Nearly all forms of ancient sorcery and witchcraft were founded upon a belief in communion with the dead. Those who practiced the arts of necromancy claimed to have contact with departed spirits and obtain through them knowledge of the future. This custom of consulting the dead was prohibited by the Bible: "Regard not them that have familiar spirits, neither seek after wizards, to be defiled by them: I am the Lord your God" (Leviticus 19:31).

That humans could hold communion with the dead was the belief that formed the cornerstone of heathen idolatry. They held to the idea that their gods were deified spirits of departed heroes. This resulted in a religion that rendered worship of the dead. The Scriptures give examples of this. In the account of the debacle of Israel at Bethpeor, it is stated:

> Israel abode in Shittim, and the people began to commit whore-
> dom with the daughters of Moab. And they called the people
> unto the sacrifices of their gods: and the people did eat, and
> bowed down to their gods. And Israel joined himself unto
> Baalpeor" (Numbers 25:1–3).

The psalmist further described what kind of gods these sacrifices were offered to. Speaking of the same apostasy of the Israelites, he said, "They joined themselves also unto Baalpeor, and ate the sacrifices of the dead" (Psalm 106:28). That is, sacrifices that had been offered to the dead.

In warning the Christians against participating in any manner in the idolatry of their heathen neighbors, the apostle Paul said, "The things which the Gentiles sacrifice, they sacrifice to devils, and not to God, and I would not that ye should have fellowship with devils" (1 Corinthians 10:20). Speaking of the nations that surrounded Israel, God warned, "They sacrificed unto devils, not to God; to gods whom they knew not, to new gods that came newly up, whom your fathers feared not" (Deuteronomy 32:17). The psalmist, speaking of Israel, said that "they sacrificed their sons and their daughters unto devils," and in the next verse he explained that they sacrificed them "unto the idols of Canaan" (Psalm 106:37, 38).

> In their supposed worship of dead men they were in reality wor-
> shiping demons. The deification of the dead has held a promi-
> nent place in nearly every system of heathenism, as has also the
> supposed communion with the dead. The gods were believed
> to communicate their will to men, and also, when consulted, to

give them counsel. Of this character were the famous oracles of Greece and Rome.[16]

The thought that the living can communicate with the dead is still held, even in professedly Christian countries. The practice of communicating with beings claiming to be the spirits of the departed comes under different favorable titles or names and has become more widespread. Hence, it takes hold of the sympathies of those who have buried their loved ones. Spirits sometimes manifest themselves to persons in the form of their departed friends, relate incidents connected with their lives, or do activities that they particularly did while living.

This is done so convincingly that men are led to believe that their dead friends are still alive, or are angels, hovering over them and communicating with them. Those who assume these spirits to be their dearly departed loved ones revere and regard them with a certain reverence. The deceived, thus, take their counsel and word above the implicit and unambiguous Word of God.

Many Christian faiths teach that the dead go directly to heaven at death. Hence, they can be communicated with after their physical demise. This teaching directly contradicts the Word of God, which declares, "In the sweat of thy face shalt thou eat bread, till thou return unto the ground; for out of it wast thou taken: for dust thou art, and *unto dust shalt thou return*" (Genesis 3:19, emphasis added).

Many, however, regard spiritualism as a mere imposture. At one time, I did too. On one occasion, one of my brothers had committed a crime and was sentenced to prison. My mother, anxious to get him released, or at least lessen his time, went to a spiritualistic medium. She took me along. When we arrived, a black man dressed like a wizard holding a large sword by his side came to the door.

We went inside and passed a room that was painted black and filled with witchcraft paraphernalia. My mother went into that room with him and shut the door. I was upset. When my mother finally came out of the room I discovered that she had paid him $200 to cast a spell on the judge. I was incensed.

"You are a fake!" I said.

"You better be careful what you say, or I will make you go crazy," he threatened.

"Here, go ahead," I demanded, taking out a handkerchief from my back pocket and offering it to him. I knew spiritists claimed they could cast a spell on the owner of some article.

"Please don't listen to him," my mother interrupted.

"Oh, mom!" I said, "He is just stealing your money. He can't do a single thing!"

Then grabbing me by my arm for fear that the man would cast a spell on me, she rushed me out. Unfortunately, my brother was sentenced to more time in prison than anticipated, and my poor mother had been taken for a costly ride.

---

16   E.G. White, *Patriarchs and Prophets*, 684.

Others suggest that the manifestations by which these occult practices support their claims to be supernatural characters are simply accomplished fraudulently on the part of the medium. Truly, trickery has often been palmed off as being genuine. This does not negate that there have also been marked evidences of supernatural power. Consequently, those who reject spiritualism as the mere result of human craftiness, great knowledge, or sleight of hand, when confronted with manifestations that they cannot account for, will be led to concede to its claims.

The "familiar spirits" mentioned in the Bible were not the spirits of the dead but evil angels, the messengers of Satan. Ancient idolatry, which, as we have seen, comprises both worship of the dead and pretended communion with them, is declared by the Bible to have been demon worship. In their purported worship of the dead, people were in reality worshiping demons.

Modern spiritualism, resting upon the same foundation, is but a revival in a new form of the antiquated witchcraft and demon worship that God condemned and prohibited. The Scriptures foretell that "in the latter times some shall depart from the faith, giving heed to seducing spirits, and doctrines of devils" (1 Timothy 4:1). Paul, in his second letter to the Thessalonians, pointed to the special working of Satan in spiritualism as an event to take place immediately before the second advent of Christ. Speaking of Christ's second coming, he declared that we can expect "the working of Satan with all power and signs and lying wonders" (2 Thessalonians 2:9).

Peter, in describing the dangers to which the church was to be exposed in the last days, said that as there were false prophets who led Israel into sin, so there will be false teachers, "who privily shall bring in damnable heresies, even denying the Lord that bought them . . . and many shall follow their pernicious ways" (2 Peter 2:1, 2). Here the apostle pointed out one of the marked characteristics of spiritualist teachers—they refuse to acknowledge Christ as the divine Son of God. Concerning such teachers, the beloved John declared, "Who is a liar but he that denieth that Jesus is the Christ? He is antichrist, that denieth the Father and the Son. Whosoever denieth the Son, the same hath not the Father" (1 John 2:22, 23). Spiritualism, in denying Christ's divinity, denies both the Father and the Son, and the Bible pronounces it the manifestation of antichrist.

It was Satan's plan to ensnare the people of Israel by, through the woman of Endor, predicting Saul's doom. Because Saul was under his control, Satan could dictate with accuracy the deluded king's fate. By the fulfillment of this prediction he hoped that the Jews would be inspired with confidence in the sorceress and be led to consult her. This would result in turning them from God as their counselor and place them under the control of Satan.

The lure by which spiritualists and fortunetellers attract large numbers is their pretended power to draw aside the veil from the future. God has in His Word opened, to all who would search, the great events of the future. In the Word, he has placed all that is essential for us to know. He declares, "The secret things belong unto the Lord our God: but those things which are revealed belong unto us and to our children for ever, that we may do all the words of this law" (Deuteronomy 29:29). On the other hand, the subtle purpose of the enemy is to destroy men's faith in God and His Word. Satan leads people to seek knowledge of that which God has wisely hidden from them.

Many, because of some anticipated evil, are driven into a great apprehension. They become restless because they cannot know the precise outcome of future affairs. In their impatience they refuse to wait on the unfolding of divine providence. This results in giving way to their feelings, causing them to run here and there in their passionate grief. They make effort to gain intelligence regarding what has not been revealed. Anxiety pushes them into unsafe paths of the same error committed by King Saul which, were they to "wait upon the Lord," they would escape. Demanding forbidden knowledge, they fall a prey into the bewitching charm of the archenemy.

God's great displeasure is revealed in the Scriptures relative to this inclination. Because of this anxiousness to remove the veil from the future, man's soul is left open to the suggestions of the wily foe. By experience acquired through his longevity in the earth, he can, by reasoning from cause to effect, forecast to some degree of accuracy future events. This is especially true when the unwary place themselves inadvertently into his hands. He can thus orchestrate matters in such a way as to bring about his prediction to fulfillment. By these means he is able to inspire confidence in his power to foretell the future and, thus, at his will lead captive those who are deluded. His devices should not deceive us. Through the prophet Isaiah God warned:

> When they shall say unto you, Seek unto them that have familiar spirits, and unto wizards that peep and that mutter: should not a people seek unto their God? for the living to the dead? To the law and to the testimony: if they speak not according to this word, it is because there is no light in them. (Isaiah 8:19, 20)

Many reject the great principle, which is the foundation of true Christianity, that the Word of God is the all-sufficient rule of faith and practice. Instead, they put their trust in the unpredictable, doubtful standard of their own feelings and impressions. By setting aside the great detector of error and falsehood—the Holy Scriptures—Satan is given an advantage to control minds as best pleases him.

Why should those who are acquainted with an all-knowing, all-powerful God settle for erring man with a supposed connection with the "Force"? It is like depending on a mere flashlight with weakened batteries, emitting faintly its light rather than on the bright beams of light blazing from the sun. Why trust in one who can, by reasoning, make an educated guess as compared with One who holds the future in His hand—the One who has the power to set up kingdoms and take them down. Daniel exalted:

> Blessed be the name of God for ever and ever: for wisdom and might are his: And he changeth the times and the seasons: he removeth kings, and setteth up kings: he giveth wisdom unto the wise, and knowledge to them that know understanding: He revealeth the deep and secret things: he knoweth what is in the darkness, and the light dwelleth with him. (Daniel 2:20–22)

> Remember the former things of old: for I am God, and there is none else; I am God, and there is none like me, Declaring the end from the beginning, and from ancient times the things that are not yet done, saying, My counsel shall stand, and I will do all my pleasure. (Isaiah 46:9)

God declares, "The secret things belong unto the Lord our God: but those things which are revealed belong unto us and to our children for ever, that we may do all the words of this law" (Deuteronomy 29:29). All that we need to know about the future is revealed in the Scriptures. All other insights concerning our own personal destiny can be sought for and He promises:

> If any of you lack wisdom, let him ask of God, that giveth to all *men* liberally, and upbraideth not; and it shall be given him. But let him ask in faith, nothing wavering. For he that wavereth is like a wave of the sea driven with the wind and tossed. [7]For let not that man think that he shall receive any thing of the Lord. A double minded man *is* unstable in all his ways. (James 1:5)

The reason why people seek after prognosticators usually stems from an unwillingness to defer gratification. The anxiety "to know now," while providing the wanted immediate experience, usually ends up in a gratified, yet delusive, attachment ultimately ending in devastation and ruin.

> The demon's message to Saul, although it was a denunciation of sin and a prophecy of retribution, was not meant to reform him, but to goad him to despair and ruin. Oftener, however, it serves the tempter's purpose best to lure men to destruction by flattery. The teaching of the demon gods in ancient times fostered the vilest license. The divine precepts condemning sin and enforcing righteousness were set aside; truth was lightly regarded, and impurity was not only permitted but also enjoined. Spiritualism declares that there is no death, no sin, no judgment, no retribution; that "men are unfallen demigods;" that desire is the highest law; and that man is accountable only to himself. The barriers that God has erected to guard truth, purity, and reverence are broken down, and many are thus emboldened in sin. Does not such teaching suggest an origin similar to that of demon worship?[17]

---

17   *Patriarchs and Prophets*, 688

God had vehemently warned the children of Israel concerning the results of holding communion with evil spirits, using the example of the abominations of the Canaanites. These people had become greatly depraved. They were without natural affection, idolaters, adulterers, murderers, and abominable by every corrupt thought and revolting practice (see Leviticus 18:22–25). Understanding the tendencies of the depraved nature of man, God in love revealed the pitfalls of venturing down that path. Men do not know their own hearts: for "the heart is deceitful above all things, and desperately wicked" (Jeremiah 17:9). It was Satan's aim, through this avenue, to make the people of Israel as abhorrent to God as were the Canaanites. *NB* *Clue!* *KEY*

Spiritism always brings about conditions favorable to rebellion. This fact the prophet Samuel sought to indelibly sink into the mind of King Saul when he told him that "rebellion is as the sin of witchcraft, and stubbornness as idolatry" (1 Samuel 15:23). This warning was recorded for all future generations to take special care concerning the outcome of this child of the devil. By alluring mankind into this avenue of spiritualism, Satan desires that God will condemn man, leaving him hopeless and ultimately meeting his eternal ruin. As in the past, today the enemy of souls is still ever on the watch to open up spiritualistic whirlpools whose suction drags the victim into an unrestrained flow of evil.

Prior to the Israelites' entry into the land of Canaan, Satan had a stronghold on the inhabitants of that land. When God, with the ultimate goal of ridding the devil of his influence, interjected the children of Israel into Canaan, Satan determined to keep his hold on the land. Knowing that he was no match to physically withstand such an intrusion, Satan resorted to a strategy of enticing God's people to violate heaven's safeguards. Evil angels implanted the same bewitching allurement which was used on Eve in the garden, into the minds of God's people. Strange gods, made to have a magical charm, invited the Israelites to their adoration. By this means, the children of Israel fell into the same trap into which Eve and Adam fell, resulting in the transgression that overthrew and ruined them. Using the same practice of spiritualism, with its resulting degradation that provoked God to frown on the former inhabitants of the land and caused their demise, Satan succeeded in attracting the Jews into its practice. Thus, the chosen people were finally scattered from the Land of Promise.

By throwing the curtain open in prophetic language, God warned that history would be repeated. "The devil is come down unto you, having great wrath, because he knoweth that he hath but a short time" (Revelation 12:10). Satan is striving today to repeat what he successfully accomplished in the past, but in the midst of this modern societal malaise, God is also working to accomplish His aim. In spite of the devil's relentless efforts, those seeking God are being led away from the delusive abominations of the world. God is awakening many, who inwardly suspect the practice of the occult to be evil, to its dangers and leading them into an obedient relationship with him. This enrages of "the accuser of our brethren" (Revelation 12:10) who knows no bounds.

The Word of the Lord to ancient Israel is addressed also to His people in this age: "Regard not them that have familiar spirits, neither seek after wizards, to be defiled by them" "for all that do these things are an abomination unto the Lord" (Leviticus 19:31; Deuteronomy 18:12).

DEADLY MIXTURE

Possessed people are not always easy to detect. They can make today's high-tech espionage look like child's play. Some are so clothed with a garb of goodness and truth that they become successful agents used to allure and deceive. To the person without spiritual discernment, detection is impossible. It takes spiritual eyesight, for the Scriptures declare:

Now we have received, not the spirit of the world, but the spirit which is of God, that we might know the things that are freely given to us of God. Which things also we speak, not in the words which man's wisdom teacheth, but which the Holy Ghost teacheth; comparing spiritual things with spiritual. But the natural man receiveth not the things of the Spirit of God: for they are foolishness unto him: neither can he know them, because they are spiritually discerned. (1 Corinthians 2:12–14)

By wearing the garb of religion to win the confidence of the unwary, occultists oftentimes have an air of innocence. Too often Satan leads them to combine God's truth with his errors. Thus, he succeeds in confusing the masses. He leads the unsuspecting to accept his poison while beguiling them to believe they are accepting Biblical truth from agents of light. Paul experienced this tactic while in Thyatira. Dr. Luke wrote:

It came to pass, as we went to prayer, a certain damsel possessed with a spirit of divination met us, which brought her masters much gain by soothsaying: the same followed Paul and us, and cried, saying, These men are the servants of the most high God, which shew unto us the way of salvation. And this did she many days. But Paul, being grieved, turned and said to the spirit, I command thee in the name of Jesus Christ to come out of her. And he came out the same hour" (Acts 16:16–18).

Paul could see through the farce of apparent support from this psychic, for he could see the enemy's artful sophistry. Satan sought to identify the work of Paul with this clairvoyant, but God's spirit moved Paul to exorcise the damsel and bring to light the truth—there was no association between truth and what this psychic had to say.

Christ had no problem seeing through Satan's masquerades. Upon one occasion Peter, when he thought that Christ was placing Himself in harm's way, rebuked Him. Christ, seeing behind the intruder using the human agent, said, "Get behind Me, Satan! You are an offense to Me, for you are not mindful of the things of God, but the things of men" (Matthew 16:23 NKJV). Jesus had no problem penetrating with his spiritual eyesight through the garb. Oftentimes, He could see fiends in possession of the bodies and minds of men.

The use of this strategy has been all too successful. The most apparently innocuous poison is the intentionally mislabeled one. The packaging may appear alluring and attractive, familiar, even harmless. Yet, its content stings like the deadly adder's bite. It is like the brain-destroying hallucinations experienced by naive young trick-or-treaters during Halloween's cache. They unknowingly ingest candy laced with LSD, often resulting in unalterable brain damage. Hence, this blending of truth with error, the holy with the common, the pure with the profane, has allured many into an insipid and ritualistic religious experience. The Scripture declares that they are "having a form of godliness, but denying the power thereof: from such turn away" (2 Timothy 3:5).

The culmination of the cosmic battle—the struggle between good and evil, righteousness and unrighteousness—will be decided on the basis of truth or error. Babylon is the term used to describe the foe's vehicle and strategy for deceiving the entire world and leading it into apostasy against God. Jesus warned: "For many shall come in my name, saying, I am Christ; and shall deceive many" (Matthew 24:5). Notice that the anticipated deception will come in the guise of "Jesus." The semblance will be so close to the true that even a forensic scientist would find it nearly impossible to separate the genuine from the fake. His warning continued:

> Then if any man shall say unto you, Lo, here *is* Christ, or there; believe *it* not. For there shall arise false Christs, and false prophets, and shall shew great signs and wonders; insomuch that, if *it were* possible, they shall deceive the very elect. Behold, I have told you before. Wherefore if they shall say unto you, Behold, he is in the desert; go not forth: behold, *he is* in the secret chambers; believe *it* not. (Matthew 24:23–26)

In the book of Revelation the name "Babylon" (chapters 17 and 18) is used to describe the highest level of successful decoying. The Biblical term comes from the Tower of Babel story where there was an attempt to defy God in the vale of Shinar (see Genesis 10:8–10).[18] Here God changed the languages (Genesis 11:1–9) and confused the people's plot, turning them away from their self-destructive attempt at self-salvation. In this same plain, centuries later, idolatry took a stronghold and, thus, became the progenitor of contemporary

---

18   Paul J. Achtemier, Th.D., *Harper's Bible Dictionary* (San Francisco: Harper and Row Publishers, Inc., 1985), 86, 87.

idol worship, which was substituting God by venerating the dead.

This dichotomy of beliefs from the worship of the Creator God to the creature god became viral. The entrenchment of which has become so pandemic that heaven has sounded the alarm for the inhabitants of the earth living in the last days to arouse to their danger.

> He [the angel] cried mightily with a strong voice, saying, Babylon the great is fallen, is fallen, and is become the habitation of devils, and the hold of every foul spirit, and a cage of every unclean and hateful bird. For all nations have drunk of the wine of the wrath of her fornication, and the kings of the earth have committed fornication with her, and the merchants of the earth are waxed rich through the abundance of her delicacies. And I heard another voice from heaven, saying, Come out of her, my people, that ye be not partakers of her sins, and that ye receive not of her plagues. For her sins have reached unto heaven, and God hath remembered her iniquities. (Revelation 18:1–5).

The desire on the part of the devil to win allegiance is desperate. So much so that he is creating a spiritual amalgamation. Due to the fear he is spreading through demonically inspired catastrophes and disasters, he is forging multitudes into a false state of religious revival. This false system of religion will be the galvanizing element. This trend was evinced immediately after the September 11, 2001 attack on the Twin Towers. One act of terrorism brought about and coerced Americans to unite in prayer irrespective of personal religious persuasions.

If fear can compel people to become instant religionists, then what is ahead will become more potent. Note that the overwhelming delusion will be executed by means of devils performing miracles.

> He doeth great wonders, so that he maketh fire come down from heaven on the earth in the sight of men, And deceiveth them that dwell on the earth by *the means of* those miracles which he had power to do in the sight of the beast; saying to them that dwell on the earth, that they should make an image to the beast, which had the wound by a sword, and did live. (Revelation 13:13, 14)
>
> Now the Spirit speaketh expressly, that in the latter times some shall depart from the faith, giving heed to seducing spirits, and doctrines of devils; Speaking lies in hypocrisy; having their conscience seared with a hot iron. (1 Timothy 4:1, 2)

The most effective means the devil uses to turn people against God, as well as leading the masses into a false experience with God, is *religion.* Satan has ascribed to God all the evils to which flesh is heir. Satan has represented Him as a God who delights in the sufferings of his creatures, who is revengeful and implacable. Satan originated the doctrine of eternal torment as a punishment for sin because in this way he could lead men into infidelity and rebellion, distract souls, and dethrone the human reason.

The attack on the United States and the subsequent destruction of the Twin Towers, along with more than 3,000 innocent victims, is a prime example of spirits controlling the minds of men through religion and leading them to think they are working on behalf of God. Satan, and men actuated by his spirit, seek to compel the conscience. Under a pretense of zeal for righteousness, men who have confederated with evil angels bring suffering upon others. This is done in order to convert them to their ideas of religion. There can be no more conclusive evidence that people possess the spirit of Satan than the disposition to hurt and destroy those who do not believe as they do, or who act contrary to their ideas. Of this class Jesus cast the verdict. He denounced them by declaring:

> Many will say to me in that day, Lord, Lord, have we not proph-
> esied in thy name? and in thy name have cast out devils? and in
> thy name done many wonderful works? And then will I profess
> unto them, I never knew you: depart from me, ye that work
> iniquity. (Matthew 7:22, 23)

Angels
Strength = do & hear his word.
Angels — protect us when we do the same as they are doing
— those that fear God.

MESSENGERS OF MERCY— GOD'S ANGELS

The Scriptures pull back the veil and enable us to see the unseen world. Apart from the fallen angels, there are many holy loyal angels. They number two-thirds, in comparison to the one-third who rebelled. Jacob was given a vision of their ascent and descent from heaven. While traveling from Beersheba to Haran one night, he had a dream. "Then he dreamed, and behold, a ladder was set up on the earth, and its top reached to heaven; and there the angels of God were ascending and descending on it" (Genesis 28:12).

Several years later Jacob had the joy of seeing an actual appearance of some of these heavenly visitors. "Jacob went on his way, and the angels of God met him. And Jacob said when he saw them, This is God's host: and he called the name of that place Mahanaim" (Genesis 32:1, 2). Later Moses wrote, "He said, The Lord came from Sinai, and rose up from Seir unto them; he shined forth from mount Paran, and he came with ten thousands of saints: from his right hand [went] a fiery law for them" (Deuteronomy 33:2).

These angels "are mighty in strength, that fulfill His word, hearkening unto the voice of His word. Bless Jehovah, all ye his hosts, Ye ministers of his, that do his pleasure" (Psalm 103:20). They are those "who excel in strength, Who do His word, heeding the voice of His word" (Psalms 103:21). These holy beings delight to take part in the rescue mission of mankind. They are set as guardian angels over the ransom of the Lord, but unlike the fallen angels, these regard with sacredness the free-will choice of God's creation. They protect, not possess mankind. "For He [God] shall give His angels charge over you, to keep you in all your ways" (Psalm 91:11 NKJV). Another revelation of their watchful activity is cited in Psalm 34:7: "The angel of the Lord encampeth round about them that fear him, and delivereth them."

Concerning their watch care over children, Jesus said, "Take heed that you do not despise one of these little ones, for I say to you that in heaven their angels always see the face of My Father who is in heaven" (Matthew 18:10 NKJV). Even Jesus Himself was the recipient of their care. After being severely tempted, when "the devil left Him, . . . angels came and ministered to Him" (Matthew

Will help you to carry out your engaged will—not theirs!

4:11 NKJV). On the night of His betrayal, He resisted the attempted rescue effort of His disciples by saying, "Or do you think that I cannot now pray to My Father, and He will provide Me with more than twelve legions of angels?" (Matthew 26:53 NKJV).

These heavenly beings are agents of mercy to mankind. Their role is to minister. "Who makes His angels spirits, His ministers a flame of fire" (Psalm 104:4 NKJV). "And of the angels He says, *Who makes His angels spirits and His ministers a flame of fire.* Are they not all ministering spirits sent forth to minister for those who will inherit salvation?" (Hebrews 1:7, 14NKJV, emphasis added). The Scriptures give generous accounts of angels' interplay and interaction in the human experience. Sent to be comforters, guides, protectors, and rescuers, they carry their mission of love for lost mankind.

They have the ability to materialize and appear as human beings. One of the earliest biblical recordings is found in the book of Genesis. Their charged assignment on this particular mission was to deliver Lot and his family from the impending doom awaiting Sodom and Gomorrah.

> Now the two angels came to Sodom in the evening, and Lot was sitting in the gate of Sodom. When Lot saw *them,* he rose to meet them, and he bowed himself with his face toward the ground. And he said, "Here now, my lords, please turn in to your servant's house and spend the night, and wash your feet; then you may rise early and go on your way." And they said, "No, but we will spend the night in the open square." But he insisted strongly; so they turned in to him and entered his house. Then he made them a feast, and baked unleavened bread, and they ate" (Genesis 19:1–3 NKJV).

These angels were on their usual task of mercy and were at this time on a surveillance mission. Also, they neither made their true identity known nor their errand transparent until later.

As far as Lot was concerned, he was being hospitable to wayfaring strangers, but when the moment came, they unveiled their purpose to Lot and his family. Though discovering the danger, Lot loathed to flee. The angels then sprang into action.

> While he lingered, the men laid hold upon his hand, and upon the hand of his wife, and upon the hand of his two daughters; the Lord being merciful unto him: and they brought him forth, and set him without the city. And it came to pass, when they had brought them forth abroad, that he said, Escape for thy life; look not behind thee, neither stay thou in all the plain; escape to the mountain, lest thou be consumed. (Genesis 19:16, 17)

The angels of heaven are sent forth to minister to those who shall be "heirs of salvation" (Hebrews 1:14). They have an intense interest in the salvation of mankind. "Likewise," Jesus said, "there is joy in the presence of the angels of God over one sinner that repenteth" (Luke 15:10). They are passing throughout the length and breadth of the earth, seeking to comfort the sorrowing, to protect the imperiled, to win the hearts of men to Christ. Though unseen, they are oftentimes being welcomed when a helping hand is given to Christ's needy and suffering ones. By acts of kindness unperceived by us, we are inviting the companionship of heavenly beings. A sacred atmosphere of joy and peace accompanies them.

Throughout all the ages, God has intervened via holy angels for the support and deliverance of His people. They took an active part in people's affairs (see Numbers 22:22–35). They materialized in garments of light (see Judges 13:3–21) or appeared to be as men who had traveled on a long journey (see Genesis 19:1–26). Angels rested, as if weary, under the oaks from the noonday sun (see Judges 6:11–21). They became visible to draw attention to God's will concerning what was about to occur (see Judges 13:3, 10; Daniel 9:20–23; Luke 1:11).

Unknown to their hosts, the angels accepted the hospitalities of human homes. They guided lost travelers. As in the apostle Peter's case, they opened prison doors and set the servants of the Lord free. Arrayed with the splendor of heaven, they rolled away the stone from the Savior's tomb.

As in the story of Sodom and Gomorrah, angels in the form of men visited the gatherings of the wicked in order to register their activities. They weighed their intents as suggested by their acts and deeds to determine if they crossed the line of God's forbearance. Angels have been spokesmen in the councils of rulers of this world, yet the people knew it not. People have spoken with them; they have heard them speak; they have seen them. Some have taken their counsels while others have spitefully opposed their offer of help or admonishment.

These heavenly visitants have not resisted the insult and abuse heaped upon them by human hands. In trials of court proceedings, heaven's messengers have attended and, in their participation, demonstrated an intimate knowledge of human interaction and history. Their eloquence has silenced those who have attempted to oppress the helpless innocent. As the "the angel of the Lord encampeth round about them that fear Him, and delivereth them" (Psalm 34:7), they have assisted those who were in distress and peril.

When I was drafted into the army at the height of the Viet Nam war, I was first sent to Fort Jackson, South Carolina, an infantry training camp. I was surprised and concerned because I went in as a non-weapon carrying conscientious objector. Seeing the ruthlessness of the drill sergeants, I determined to make sure I complied with everything and thus avoid the maltreatment given to those who, for the least infractions, suffered.

Being successful in avoiding any harassment, I was able to keep at a safe distance due to insubordinate individuals who had the attention of the sergeants.

As time passed, I became more apprehensive. Why have they not transferred me to the camp that trained conscientious objectors?, I prayed earnestly that the Lord would deliver me from the camp, but Monday turned to Tuesday, and Tuesday to Wednesday, until it was Friday. As a Sabbath-keeper I had the hunch that if soldiers in this boot camp were not permitted the least amount of time to themselves, due to the incessant activity, they would probably be unmerciful to me if I made known my convictions.

My hopes of being transferred before the Sabbath were dashed. Having no other recourse, I decided to disclose my beliefs. There were Jews among us, but they had not requested to have the Sabbath off. When I shared with the drill sergeant that I requested to take off on the Sabbath, I was met with ridicule, intimidation, and harassment. Sensing that I would not get any where with him, I requested an audience with the first sergeant. That was arranged; to my surprise, the room was filled with several drill sergeants. Undauntedly, I shared with them my convictions, even though I felt they were strangers to divine influences.

Once more, citing military code, I requested to see the chaplain. That request was granted, and I appeared before him. After I presented my convictions, he interrogated me concerning my faith. Once convinced that I was genuine, he granted my request. I was grateful that God delivered me.

Saturday morning, I arose and headed away front the training activities so I could observe the Sabbath. However, I had no clue where I was, neither did I know if there was even a Sabbath-keeping congregation in town. As I was walking through the base, I noticed the chapel. Walking across its parking lot, I was abruptly interrupted in my thoughts by a black man calling out to me.

"Are you a Seventh-day Adventist?" he called, being a little distance from me.

Surprised, I responded, "Yes!"

"Come on over here," he said as he motioned with his hand.

I then turned and walked toward him as he stood beside his car with the driver's door opened. As I approached the car, he said, "Hop in."

I opened the door and slipped onto the seat. Things happened so fast that I did not get a chance to think about how he knew to what faith I belonged, inasmuch as I was dressed with army fatigues and a cap.

"Are you going to church?" he asked.

"Yes," I said.

"Then I will take you there."

With that, he started the car and headed out. I still, to this day, do not remember in which direction he went. All I know is that we arrived at a small church. When we entered, it was obvious that I was the only white person.

Though a complete stranger, I felt at home as I listened to the same familiar hymns, and the service took the normal course I was used to back at my church in Brooklyn. I felt at home. When the services were over, we got back into his car and headed back to the base. It is strange that I did not sense any apprehension going with the man. When we arrived back at the base, he parked the car in the same spot from where he had called me. Once he came to a stop, he began to coach me concerning the future problems I might be confronting. One thing that stuck with me was his advice as to how to respond when being ordered. He coached, "Never say, 'I won't.' Always say, 'I can't.'" We then had prayer, and I left.

To this day, I do not know where he came from, where he went, or even his name. All I remember is the peace that came over me while in his presence, and I was so grateful for his counsel. It delivered me from many a confrontation that I encountered while in the military service. Looking back, I am certain that I was comforted and guided by a heavenly messenger.

Another experience occurred in New York City a few years ago. It took place while I was presenting a series of biblical topics at a church in Queens. On the last night of my evening presentations, I made an appeal and requested that those who wanted to respond approach the altar. Several people came, including a man who was in attendance for the first time. He was obviously stirred about something, but my attention was focused on those who had been attending on a regular basis. He wanted to talk with me, but I explained that I needed to take care of the others. So I told him to return in the morning, and I would be able to address his needs. He consented and left.

The following morning he returned. He sat through the entire program, and as soon as the program was over, he immediately approached me, urgently requesting my attention. Once more I begged him to give me a little time to care for the needs of all who had been attending on a regular basis. He patiently waited until I was done.

At last, the others departed, and I could then give him my full attention. Without delay he began with the most unusual story.

"I was working security on the lower eastside of Manhattan on the night shift. Where I work, I've seen a dead body floating down the river, young thirteen-year-old girls walking the streets as prostitutes, drug pushers looking for their customers or new prey. In seeing all this wickedness, I began to wonder what in the world is happening? Is the world coming to an end? The whole scene of things just made me very anxious. The more I thought about the increase of immorality, crime, and violence, the more disturbed I became. I wondered if there was an answer to all this. 'What is going on?' I thought. I then stepped outside of my building, and while I was deep in thought, a police car drove up.

"'You looked troubled about something,' the policeman said.

"'Yes,' I responded. 'I have been terribly troubled over all the wicked things that are going on.'

"He told me that these were signs of the times. Then he asked me about myself, and as he was talking, he did something strange. He said, 'If you believe in Jesus shake my hand,' while extending his arm out of his squad car window.

"I stood there for a moment almost spellbound. I felt a warm calm feeling come over me. Then without hesitation, I took his hand. We shook hands, and somehow I felt that everything was going to be alright.

"Then without a moment's notice, he pulled his hand inside, bade me farewell, and drove off. Being so profoundly impressed by a policeman who spoke of Jesus, I quickly took out a pen and paper and jotted down his license plate number just in case I wanted to talk with him again. I felt peace come over me. Then I worked until my shift ended, and the new security guard arrived. I told him about the bizarre happenings I had just experienced and asked him if he knew anything about the increase of crime and all. He told me there was a book entitled The Great Controversy and strongly suggested that I should get it, and it would explain everything that was going on and why.

"When I got off at 5:00 a.m. in the morning," he continued, "I thought I would look up the policeman and thank him for coming and talking with me. I made my way to the local station and walked up to the counter. After the usual greetings, I told the officer that I would like to talk with the policeman on the beat last night. I told him I did not even think of asking his name, but I wrote down his license plate number.

"'Let me see it,' requested the officer, and I handed him the piece of paper where I had written the number.

"'Mister, are you alright? We don't have any such number or anything that resembles it,' he stated.

"'But I took care to make sure I wrote down the exact number,' I said.

"'I am sorry! I don't know what you saw, or whom you think you talked with. That license plate does not exist,' he retorted while looking at me like I was some sort of a kook.

"Bewildered, I walked out of the precinct, wondering if I was really losing my mind. Then I remembered the book that the security guard had mentioned. So jumping into my car, I drove off and went to my neighborhood. Rather than going home, I went to the library instead, but it was closed. I determined that I was not going to leave until it opened. As soon as it did, I quickly went in.

"I reached the librarian, and soliciting her help, I inquired if there was any such book. The librarian looked at the files and found one title. She pointed me in the direction of the religious section. Anxiously, I quickly went to the area where the book was supposed to be. Sure enough, there it was. I immediately took it and began devouring it. I became so engrossed with the reading matter that I completely forgot to eat. When I finished reading the book, I noticed a label with an address in the inside back cover.

"'I wrote it down," he said. "Then I made my way to the location. When I found the address, it was this church, but there was no one around, and the doors were closed. Fearing that I might miss out if I didn't get to talk to someone, I decided to just sit in my car and wait.

"Then to my joy the doors opened and people began to walk in. I was excited. Even though I was illegally parked, I left the car and came inside to this sanctuary. I couldn't believe my ears as you talked about the very things I was concerned about.

"Tell me," he asked. "Am I going crazy? I know I talked with that policeman. I shook his hand and saw the car drive off, but the car license plate number does not exist. Am I losing my mind?"

I was awestricken to think that I was hearing about a modern episode of an angel leading a soul to search for God and to find comfort in Him. In taking this man through the Scriptures, I opened to him the reality that angels occasionally appeared in the form of humans to lead the honest in heart or deliver them from trouble. He was greatly relieved and, more than that, he felt humbled to realize that God had sent an angel to comfort him and lead him to salvation.

Another unusual encounter occurred in 1974. I was at a pastors' meeting, when one of the pastors, Bob Edwards,[19] addressed the ministers. The experience had just taken place a couple of weeks prior to this convocation. His countenance still bore the expression of awe. Still reeling from the incident that almost cost his life, Bob began his story.

"Two weeks ago," he began, "I had to go to New York City to attend a meeting."

He told us that he had been informed that it would be better for him to find lodging on the New Jersey side of the Big Apple. Parking in New York would be difficult and expensive, but on the Jersey side it would be no problem. From there he could take a bus over to Manhattan and leave his car in a parking lot. The motel costs would be far less expensive as well, so he drove his old Mercedes Benz to the city.

When he arrived at the motel, he explained to the agent at the counter that this was his first time to New York City and would appreciate directions as to where to park his car to catch the bus going to Manhattan. The man behind the counter was "very understanding, and helpful, and informative," Bob informed us.

The bus stop was not far away, but it would be better if he drove to it, since the bus stop was not in a very safe neighborhood. The parking lot was adjacent to the bus stop, so all he had to do was park his car and take a short walk to catch the bus.

Bob followed the instructions the next morning. He drove directly to the parking lot without any problems. Then he took the short walk to the bus stop and, as suggested, caught the bus and arrived at the 34th Street bus depot. From there he took a taxi and arrived safely at the New York Center on 46th Street between Broadway and 8th Avenue. Everything went exactly as he had been informed.

---

19   This story was relayed by Bob Edwards at a Chesapeake Conference ministerial workers' meeting in 1974.

After the meetings, Bob took another taxi and returned to the Times Square bus depot to catch his bus ride back to New Jersey. Again, everything went like clockwork. He found the right bus and boarded. When the bus started on its way, Bob decided to ask the bus driver for guidance.

"I don't know what bus stop to get off on in order to get to my parked car," he said. After the bus driver was told the name of the parking lot and the street it was on, the bus driver told him it was no problem.

"I will tell you when we get there, so relax and enjoy the ride."

Since the day had been long, and the whole trip to New York that morning had been filled with some apprehension, Bob finally felt he could relax. Then making himself as comfortable as possible on the bus seat, he dozed off.

When he woke up, Bob could see only darkness outside his window. Fear struck him as he noticed that it was midnight, and he was still on the bus. Getting up, he went immediately to the bus driver.

"Sir, did I miss my stop?" Bob asked.

"Oh, I am sorry, mister. I forgot all about you, but we can fix that. I'll tell you what you need to do. I will give you a transfer slip and leave you off at the next bus stop. You should then cross over to the opposite side of the street and catch the next bus going back," the bus driver encouragingly said.

"I became uneasy about the whole thing," Bob informed us.

The bus rolled into the next bus stop and, as promised, Bob was given the transfer slip. "The bus should be here pretty soon," said the bus driver. "Just go and wait right there," he noted, pointing to the place of the bus stop across the street.

Once off the bus, Bob hurried across the street and waited for the next bus. He was relieved to see the bus arrive as soon as it did. He mounted the bus and shared with the bus driver his dilemma. But unfortunately, this bus driver had no knowledge of the parking lot or the street name.

"When we get close to where you think it is, just tell me, and I will let you off," he was told. "Just sit close so that you can point out the area for me."

Bob's eyes were wide open. Though he strained his eyes to see out the window, nothing looked familiar.

"Things looked different at night," he said.

Then the bus driver said, "I think this is about the area that you are looking for."

Bob hesitantly got off the bus, and watched it roll away. Once off the bus he looked around; everything was shut down tight. There was not a soul around. He began to walk, hoping to spot a familiar sight or street but recognized nothing.

Then Bob's ears caught the sound of singing. Down the street there were two men with arms thrown around each other's shoulders weaving side to side as they strolled.

"Two drunken men," Bob thought. "I better hide myself."

He shared with us that he had heard many horrid stories of people being mugged or killed in New York, so he decided to slip into the shadows of one of the receding storefronts. As the singing drew closer, Bob pressed close to the store entrance, hoping not to be spotted.

Then a thought struck him: "Maybe these drunken men will know the whereabouts of the parking lot. I'll chance it. If they try something, they are drunk enough, and I am big enough to get away."

Bob was a strapping 250 pounds plus man, standing at more than six feet. When they arrived near to where he was hiding, he stepped out and greeted the surprised men.

"Good evening gentlemen, I wondered if you could help me."

At first the men were startled. Then one said, "Sure, what do you need."

Bob then shared with them his problem, to which one of them said, "Sure, we will help you."

Grabbing him, each on one arm, they began to shove him into the darkness. He attempted to struggle to get loose, but he discovered that not only were they not as drunk as he supposed, but they were also stronger then he had thought.

His worst nightmare was coming true. His mind raced as he thought he would become another victim of the atrocities in the streets of New York. Then he remembered to send a prayer heaven bound. "God, help me."

Then all of a sudden a car drove up. With headlights lighting up the episode, the driver drove closer.

"Who's that?" questioned one man, loosening his grip in the surprise of the moment.

"It's a friend," Bob exclaimed. With that, he broke loose and ran to the car.

"The driver pointed to the passenger's side and motioned for me to get in. I quickly opened the door and jumped into the car," Bob told us. Once inside, the car drove away.

"I was first relieved, but then I became apprehensive. Did I jump out of the frying pan and into the fire?" he said. "Here I was with a complete stranger not knowing what he was up to or where he was taking me, but as I looked at the stranger, he seemed well-dressed, and his demeanor seemed gentle.

"What are you doing out in such a dangerous place, and at such an hour of the night?" he questioned.

Bob then began to explain his plight. As they conversed, Bob said that he began to feel safe and relax.

"I know where that parking lot is. I will drive to the back of it, and enter in through the opening. When we reach your car, I will point my headlights toward the driver's side. You get out and jump into your car. As soon as you are in, lock your doors. I will wait until your car starts, then you will be okay," the man gently suggested.

"Just as he said," Bob continued, "we arrived at the parking lot. Then he drove to the backside and entered through the opening he had mentioned.

When we reached my car, I did as he told me. I jumped into my car, locked my doors, and then proceeded to pull on the glow plug to start my diesel engine. Once the glow light went out, I turned the key and started my car. I turned on my lights and then looked out to wave to the waiting car. When I looked, there was no car to be seen. He had gone," Bob ended.

Bob then said that he drove through the opening in the back of the car lot and headed for his motel. When he arrived, the motel agent said, "Decided to take in the lights?"

"No!" Bob replied. Then he proceeded to share the horrific events of the night and the miraculous deliverance of the kind man who had showed up just at the nick of time.

In the morning Bob left the motel and headed back to the parking lot to pay the fee for the parking. Upon his arrival he got out of his car, and with his ticket in hand, he walked up to the agent.

"I came to pay for my parking fee. I got here way after you closed last night and drove out through the back opening in your fence. So, I have returned to pay the fee."

"What are you talking about, mister?"

"I parked here yesterday, but when I returned I was driven by a kind man who drove me to the back entrance," Bob replied.

"Mister, are you nuts? Look and see if there is an opening or back entrance in the fence," the man muttered.

As Bob looked toward the back fence, he carefully scanned it. A sense of awe came over him when he realized there was not an opening in any place along the fence.

"Mister, are you alright?" questioned the man.

"Yea, I am okay," responded Bob.

Puzzled and stunned, he walked back to his car. As he drove off he marveled at this strange experience that had happened to him.

"This could only have been an angel," he thought.

Then with a tone of reverence Bob said to us, "I sat by an angel and knew it not."

Pg. 18

HOW DELIVERANCE COMES

In the case of Connie, here is how she got deliverance. First of all, she needed to acknowledge her unwillingness to obey the Lord and His teachings. The Scriptures warn that if we turn our ear from hearing the truth, God will send us a strong delusion. Notice these texts:

He that turneth away his ear from hearing the law, even his prayer shall be abomination. (Proverbs 28:9)

Even him, whose coming is after the working of Satan with all power and signs and lying wonders, And with all deceivableness of unrighteousness in them that perish; because they received not the love of the truth, that they might be saved. And for this cause God shall send them strong delusion, that they should believe a lie: That they all might be damned who believed not the truth, but had pleasure in unrighteousness. (2 Thessalonians 2:9–12).

After this, I shared with her the experience of King Saul. "King Saul," I began, "was the first King of Israel. He had been greatly honored and exalted by God. In fact, look at what the Bible says."

Then turning once more to the Scriptures, I began reading:

Now the Lord had told Samuel in his ear a day before Saul came, saying, To morrow about this time I will send thee a man out of the land of Benjamin, and thou shalt anoint him to be captain over my people Israel, that he may save my people out of the hand of the Philistines: for I have looked upon my people, because their cry is come unto me. And when Samuel saw Saul, the Lord said unto him, Behold the man whom I spake to thee of this same shall reign over my people. (1 Samuel 9:15–17).

Then skipping over to chapter 10, and verse 6, I continued reading the words of Samuel as he spoke to Saul.

The spirit of the Lord will come upon thee, and thou shalt prophesy with them, and shalt be turned into another man. And let it be, when these signs are come unto thee, *that* thou do as occasion serve thee; for God *is* with thee. And thou shalt go down before me to Gilgal; and, behold, I will come down unto thee, to offer burnt offerings, *and* to sacrifice sacrifices of peace offerings: seven days shalt thou tarry, till I come to thee, and show thee what thou shalt do. And it was *so*, that when he had turned his back to go from Samuel, God gave him another heart: and all those signs came to pass that day. And when they came thither to the hill, behold, a company of prophets met him; and the spirit of God came upon him, and he prophesied among them" (1 Samuel 10:6–10).

"Think of it Connie. Here was a man who was greatly exalted by God before the people. That's how he began, but look how he ended," I said. Once more, I turned to the Holy Bible and read:

But the spirit of the Lord departed from Saul, and an evil spirit from the Lord troubled him. And Saul's servants said unto him, Behold now, an evil spirit from God troubleth thee. Let our lord now command thy servants, which are before thee, to seek out a man, who is a cunning player on an harp: and it shall come to pass, when the evil spirit from God is upon thee, that he shall play with his hand, and thou shalt be well. . . . And it came to pass, when the evil spirit from God was upon Saul, that David took an harp, and played with his hand: so Saul was refreshed, and was well, and the evil spirit departed from him" (1 Samuel 16:14–16, 23).

"When a person knows what is right and, from the light received, understands the truth, but turns his or her back to it, he or she in essence is turning away from God, who is the only protection. When God is brushed off, the deserter is left on his own, and Satan takes control. This is what happened to King Saul, and it is what is happening to you."

At this she saw clearly what her role had been, and what she could do to reverse her condition. Falling to her knees, she humbly confessed her sins to God. What repentance! With tears streaming down her cheeks, she begged God for deliverance. When she finished her wrestling with God, she found peace and deliverance.

Another important step is acknowledging one's own transgressions or sins. If we are to be pardoned, we must confess; however, we cannot confess if we do not recognize our failings. The Scriptures say, "If we confess our sins, He is faithful and just to forgive us our sins, and cleanse us from all unrighteousness" (1 John 1:9). The psalmist declared, "I will declare mine iniquity; I will be sorry for my sin" (Psalm 38:18). The wise man wrote, "He that covereth his sins shall not prosper: but whoso confesseth and forsaketh them shall have mercy" (Proverbs 28:13, emphasis added).

Being honest with God and with self is paramount if we are to be forgiven and be at peace with God. God's command to the Israelites was "it shall be, when he shall be guilty in one of these things, that he shall confess that he hath sinned in that thing" (Leviticus 5:5, emphasis added). For most, these are usually the necessary and only steps to experience deliverance from a troubled conscience or possession as in the case of Connie.

I saw Connie about twenty years later; we crossed each other's paths at a church's anniversary. When she saw me, she ran over and gave me a hug. She reminded me about her experience and deliverance, and then she told me that from the moment she surrendered, she never again was possessed by another spirit other than Christ's.

MENTAL ILLNESSES

The level of "mentally ill" people in America is on the increase.[20] Among them are probably some who are possessed but, due to the denial of science concerning this reality, they continue to be slaves of demonic possession. The drugs that keep the poor victims in a mental stupor exacerbate this condition. If possession is the source of their maladies, they can be, and sometimes are, ruined mentally by the destruction resulting from the drugs. Treatments used early in medicine, such as the frontal lobotomy, and electric shock treatments, often left patients irreversibly mentally incapacitated.[21]

> Many sincere Christians, unfamiliar with human physiology, are greatly surprised to discover that certain of the more gross, abnormal, bizarre forms of behavior often superficially associated with 'possession' are also present in certain kinds of mental illnesses in which demon possession does not appear to be a factor. We speak of such unnatural things as; foaming at the mouth; noisy, obscene blasphemous utterances in unnatural, altered (and often guttural) vocal registers, or shrill, spine-chilling screams; falling into trance-like states; being thrown to the floor, or violently against the wall or furniture.[22]

Other ailments include major depression, schizophrenia, bipolar disorder, obsessive-compulsive disorder (OCD), panic disorder, post-traumatic stress disorder (PTSD), and borderline personality disorder. All of these mental aberrations, accompanied by their physical and sometimes erratic demonstrations, are sometimes seen in genuine cases of demon possession; they are also common responses from mental disorders. Thus, the ignorance of an individual concerning mental disorders such as epilepsy, which can bring about convulsions, often leads to explanations of these phenomena by means of the spirit world, ultimately "finding demons" where none exist.

Epilepsy is characterized by recurrent, disorganized, abnor-

20   Bruce E. Levine, "The Astonishing Rise of Mental Illness in America," ConterPunch, April 28, 2010, http://www.counterpunch.org/2010/04/28/the-astonishing-rise-of-mental-illness-in-america/ (accessed September 12, 2011).
21   "Electroshock Therapy," Electroboy: Fighting Depression and Bipolar Disorder, http://www.electroboy.com/electroshocktherapy.htm (accessed September 9, 2012).
22   "'Spiritual Warfare' and 'Deliverance Ministry' and Seventh-day Adventists," a report of the Biblical Research Institute, General Conference of Seventh-day Adventists, 1983, http://www.sdanet.org/atissue/warfare/bri.htm.

mal electrical firing in brain cells, which can disrupt normal functioning of the brain. This disruption can cause recurrent seizures, which is the main symptom of epilepsy. While these seizures are usually caused by abnormal electrical activity in the brain, they can manifest very differently from person to person. For instance, one type of seizure may cause a brief loss of consciousness, whereas another seizure type may cause uncontrollable jerking of the entire body.[23]

"Simple partial seizures can be caused by congenital abnormalities (abnormalities present at birth), tumor growths, head trauma, stroke, and infections in the brain or nearby structures."[24] Those with epilepsy suffer from approximately 40 different types of seizures. Recently, the reported case of Susannah Cahalan by BBC sheds light on this.

In 2009, Susannah Cahalan was a healthy 24-year-old reporter for the *New York Post*, when she began to experience numbness, paranoia, sensitivity to light and erratic behavior.

She began to experience seizures, hallucinations, increasingly psychotic behavior and even catatonia. Her symptoms frightened family members and baffled a series of doctors.

[In one episode her boyfriend] heard guttural sounds coming from me. He thought maybe I was just angry because I hadn't slept for days, and he knew that it was really frustrating. And so he thought, "Maybe she's just venting her frustration." But the grunts were very unnatural sounding, so he turned and looked at me. And he saw that my eyes were wide open but completely unseeing, and at that point he tried to shake me and say, "Are you OK, Sue? What's going on?" And at that point, my arms whipped out, and I had a grand mal seizure, and I was convulsing. And I bit my tongue so that blood and kind of a combination of blood and foam was coming out of my mouth. And he had the presence of mind — and I think this is incredible — to know that this was a seizure because I had never had a seizure before.[25]

She was then taken to the hospital and there she experienced other symptoms. She slurred her words. She drooled, and did not have proper control over her swallowing.

23   Reza Shouri, MD, "Symptoms of Epilepsy,"About.com Epilepsy & Seizures, August 11, 2008, http://epilepsy.about. com/od/symptomsandcauses/a/symptoms.htm (accessed December 10, 2012).
24   Laith Farid Gulli MD, Alfredo Mori MD, *Gale Encyclopedia of Neurological Disorders* (Detroit: The Gale Group Inc., 2005), http://www.minddisorders.com/Py-Z/Seizures.html (accessed September 12, 2012).
25   Julie Stapen/Free Press, "A Young Reporter Chronicles Her 'Brain On Fire,'" npr.org books, November 14, 2012, http://www.npr.org/2012/11/14/165115921/a-young-reporter-chronicles-her-brain-on-fire (accessed December 11, 2012).

I kept my arms out in unnatural poses. At one point, I was like the Bride of Frankenstein — I kept my arms out rigidly. I was slow. I could hardly walk, and when I did, I needed to be supported ... I started [acting] very psychotic. I believed that I could age people with my mind. If I looked at them, wrinkles would form, and if I looked away, they would suddenly, magically get younger. And I believed that my father had murdered my stepmother. I believed all these incredibly paranoid — a huge, extreme example of persecution complex. And then as the days went on, I stopped being as psychotic, and I started entering into a catatonic stage, which was characterized by just complete lack of emotion, inability to relate, or to read, or hardly to be able to speak.

[She explained that her] grunts and these guttural sounds that came from me sounded superhuman to someone who might be inclined to think that way. ... When you see videos of people — in fact, when I see videos of myself — demonic possession is not far from your mind.[26]

Fortunately for her, she was diagnosed and treated by Dr. Souhel Najjar for anti-NMDA receptor encephalitis, a rare autoimmune disease that can attack the brain. After her recovery she interviewed people that had been affected by the same disease.

One woman …asked for a priest because she said, "The devil is inside of me. I need it out." A little girl was grunting — they had a monitor in her room — and she was grunting so unnaturally that her parents looked at each other and said, "Is she, is she possessed?"[27]

The Psychiatric symptoms as described throughout the neurological literature can be roughly divided into the following categories: agitated aggression; anxious avoidance, which encompasses more generalized anxiety states, phobic preoccupations, and obsessive-compulsive behaviors; withdrawn depression; psychosis, including auditory and visual hallucinations, paranoid ideations, and delusions; sleep disruption, either hypersomnia or insomnia; catatonia; and dysregulated mood with lability, disinhibition, and/or hypersexuality.[28]

There's no question that an exorcist ignorant of these diseases could very easily think that a person demonstrating any of the above mentioned symptoms can erroneously arrive at the mistaken notion that the problem is demonic possession.

---

26   Ibid.
27   Ibid
28   http://ajp.psychiatryonline.org/article.aspx?articleid=106753 (assessed December 11, 2012)

Another malady is schizophrenia; personality changes characterize this illness. This is a long-term mental disorder of a type involving a breakdown in the relation between thought, emotion, and behavior, leading to faulty perception, inappropriate actions and feelings, withdrawal from reality and personal relationships into fantasy and delusion, and a sense of mental fragmentation.[29] The most pronounced case is that of Dr. Jekyll and Mr. Hyde; the case of a person alternately displaying opposing good and evil personalities.[30]

Dysthymia, also known as neurotic depression, is mental abnormality that shows itself in a "depressed mood for most of the day, for more days than not, as indicated either by subjective account or observation by others, for at least 2 years." Dysthymic presence, while depressed, includes two (or more) of the following symptoms:

1.   poor appetite or overeating
2.   insomnia or hypersomnia
3.   low energy or fatigue
4.   low self-esteem
5.   poor concentration or difficulty making decisions
6.   feeling of hopelessness

The disturbance does not occur exclusively during the course of a chronic psychotic disorder, such as schizophrenia or delusional disorder.[31]

"Another mental disorder is called bipolar disorder, formerly known as manic depression; it is marked by alternating periods of elation and depression. It causes serious shifts in mood, energy, thinking, and behavior. The swings can sway from the lows of depression on one extreme, to the highs of mania on the other. These mood swings are more than just a momentary good or bad feeling. Unlike ordinary mood swings, the intensity of the mood changes is so extreme that they interfere with the person's ability to think clearly, debilitating their capacity to cope with the ordinary demands of life. These episodes can actually last for days, weeks, or months. During the period of the mood disturbance, three (or more) of the following symptoms have persisted (four if the mood is only irritable) and have been present to a substantial degree:

Inflated self—esteem or grandiosity

Decreased need for sleep (e.g., feels rested after only three hours of sleep)

More talkative than usual or pressure to keep talking

Flight of ideas or subjective experience that thoughts are racing

Distractibility (i.e., attention too easily drawn to unimportant or irrelevant external stimuli)

Increase in goal-directed activity (socially, at work or school, or

---

29   "Schizophrenia," Oxford Dictionaries, http://oxforddictionaries.com/definition/english/schizophrenia (accessed September 9, 2012).
30   "Strange Case of Dr Jekyll and Mr Hyde," Wikipedia: The Free Encyclopedia, http://en.wikipedia.org/wiki/Strange_Case_of_Dr_Jekyll_and_Mr_Hyde (accessed September 8, 2012).
31   "Diagnostic criteria for 300.4 Dysthymic Disorder," BehaveNet, http://behavenet.com/node/21573 (accessed September 5, 2012).

sexually) as psychomotor agitation

•   Excessive involvement in pleasurable activities that have a high potential for pain consequences (e.g., unrestrained buying sprees, sexual indiscretions, or foolish business investments)."[32]

"Persons affected by this disorder will impulsively quit a job during a manic episode, gamble away all they have, or charge up huge amounts on credit cards. Feeling a surge of energy may cause them to 'feel rested after sleeping three hours.' The opposite can take place during a depressive episode. The same person, experiencing a depressive feeling of self-loathing and hopelessness over being unemployed and in debt, might feel constantly devoid of rest and too tired to get out of bed."[33]

Because of these mood swings, sometimes leading to erratic behavior, exorcists can view them demon possessed people. In fact, Dr. Neil Nedley, author of the book, *Depression, the Way Out,* stated: "Oh, yes, this has occurred several times."[34] Dr. Nedley is an expert in this area, and conducts clinics to help sufferers learn to cope, control, or overcome depression. He developed the residential Nedley Depression Recovery Program for patients who are treatment resistant. His website is www.drnedley.com.

One of the most notorious modern-day cases of a mistaken ailment and consequently attempted exorcism is that of Anneliese Michel. She lived from September 21, 1952, to July 1, 1976. She was a Catholic from Germany who believed she was possessed by six or more demons and, subsequently, underwent an exorcism. Two motion pictures, *The Exorcism of Emily Rose* and *Requiem* are based on her story.

From the age of 16 to her death at age 23, Anneliese experienced, as a direct or indirect result of an exorcism ritual, what medical professionals recognize as a severe psychiatric disturbance. Both priests, who performed the exorcism, and Anneliese's parents were convicted of manslaughter. The Catholic Church, which had authorized the exorcism, reversed its position and declared Anneliese Michel a case of mental illness. Many people, however, still believe she was genuinely possessed by demons, and her gravesite is a destination for pilgrims to this day.[35]

Let us now make a shift from the physical to the spiritual. From the examples given in the Scriptures, people clearly can become demented as a result of being possessed. Let's consider a few.

Acts of violence can result from being possessed. King Saul became possessed

32   Neil Nedley, Depression the Way Out, (Ardmore, OK: Nedley Publishing, 2009), p. 240.
33   Ibid.
34   Personal conversation with Dr. Nedley, December 30, 2011.
35   "Anneliese Michel," Wikipedia: The Free Encyclopedia, http://en.wikipedia.org/wiki/Anneliese_Michel, (accessed September 13, 2012).

after his unbending resistance to yield to the Spirit of God. Once the Spirit of God abandoned him, another spirit took possession. This resulted in mood swings: at times he was happy with David; at other times he was determined to murder him. Notice the extreme swings. At first, he adored him: "Saul took him [David] that day, and would let him go no more home to his father's house" (1 Samuel 18:2). Then Saul hated him:

> Saul was very wroth, and the saying displeased him; and he said, They have ascribed unto David ten thousands, and to me they have ascribed but thousands: and what can he have more but the kingdom? And Saul eyed David from that day and forward. And it came to pass on the morrow, that the evil spirit from God came upon Saul, and he prophesied in the midst of the house: and David played with his hand, as at other times: and there was a javelin in Saul's hand. And Saul cast the javelin; for he said, I will smite David even to the wall with it. And David avoided out of his presence twice. (1 Samuel 18:8–11)

The story of the demoniac took place near the eastern shore of the Sea of Galilee in the region of the Decapolis:

> They came over unto the other side of the sea, into the country of the Gadarenes. And when he was come out of the ship, immediately there met him out of the tombs a man with an unclean spirit, Who had his dwelling among the tombs; and no man could bind him, no, not with chains: Because that he had been often bound with fetters and chains, and the chains had been plucked asunder by him, and the fetters broken in pieces: neither could any man tame him. And always, night and day, he was in the mountains, and in the tombs, crying, and cutting himself with stones. But when he saw Jesus afar off, he ran and worshipped him, And cried with a loud voice, and said, What have I to do with thee, Jesus, thou Son of the most high God? I adjure thee by God, that thou torment me not. For he said unto him, Come out of the man, thou unclean spirit. And he asked him, What is thy name? And he answered, saying, My name is Legion: for we are many. And he besought him much that he would not send them away out of the country. Now there was there nigh unto the mountains a great herd of swine feeding. And all the devils besought him, saying, Send us into the swine, that we may enter into them. And forthwith Jesus gave them leave. And the unclean spirits went out, and entered into the swine: and the herd ran violently down a steep place into the sea, (they were about two thousand;) and were choked in the

> sea. And they that fed the swine fled, and told it in the city, and in the country. And they went out to see what it was that was done. (Mark 5:1–14)

Then Mark gives us an added interesting detail.

> They come to Jesus, and see him that was possessed with the devil, and had the legion, sitting, and clothed, and in his right mind: and they were afraid. And they that saw it told them how it befell to him that was possessed with the devil, and also concerning the swine. And they began to pray him to depart out of their coasts. And when he was come into the ship, he that had been possessed with the devil prayed him that he might be with him. Howbeit Jesus suffered him not, but saith unto him, Go home to thy friends, and tell them how great things the Lord hath done for thee, and hath had compassion on thee. (Mark 5:15–19)

Notice that the Scriptures declare that the madman, who had recently been in bondage to satanic forces, was found in his "right mind" and clothed. Obviously, any person found today spending his time in the cemetery and carrying on as this man was, we would call insane.

Another biblical mention of mental illness resulting from possession is found in Matthew, chapter 4.

> His fame went throughout all Syria: and they brought unto him all sick people that were taken with divers diseases and torments, and those which were possessed with devils, and those which were *lunatick*, and those that had the palsy; and he healed them" (Matthew 4:24, emphasis added).

In this chapter the "lunatick" was distinguished from one who is demon-possessed, but a comparison of Matthew 17:14–18 and Mark 9:17 shows that the New Testament writers apparently saw a close relationship between the two. From the symptoms described in these two texts, the sufferer mentioned was probably a victim of epilepsy. At that time there was no remedy for mental illness; anyone considered to be crazy was called "demon-possessed" and deemed hopeless. Concerning Jesus, his enemies with hopes of discrediting him charged, "He hath a devil, and is mad; why hear ye him?" (John 10:20).

Since there was no known cure, those victimized were left to suffer with their condition. Hope sprang up when it was noised abroad that Jesus could deliver. For those considered lunatics, Jesus' power was the remedy looked for by the loved ones of the afflicted. Thus, they took their victims to Christ to be released.

DIVERS MANIFESTATIONS OF BIBLICAL POSSESSION

The Scriptures give us varying examples of possession; they range from bizarre exhibitions, to a normal appearing well-dressed psychic walking down the street. In all, Satan has chosen his decoys well. Some possessions are blatantly visible; others are clothed in the garb of professionalism. The following examples give us descriptions of victims and demons alike. Notice the diverse responses from demons when being expelled. Also note the semblance of those victimized post deliverance.

Demons Are Boisterous

The people with one accord gave heed unto those things which Philip spake, hearing and seeing the miracles which he did. For unclean spirits, *crying with loud voice,* came out of many that were possessed with them: and many taken with palsies, and that were lame, were healed. (Acts 8:6, 7, emphasis added)

Act Religious—Damsel That Commended Paul

It came to pass, as we went to prayer, a certain damsel possessed with a spirit of divination met us, which brought her masters much gain by soothsaying: the same followed Paul and us, and cried, saying, These men are the servants of the most high God, which shew unto us the way of salvation. And this did she many days. But Paul, being grieved, turned and said to the spirit, I command thee in the name of Jesus Christ to come out of her. And he came out the same hour. (Acts 16:16–18)

Do Violence
The Jewish Exorcists

Then certain of the vagabond Jews, exorcists, took upon them to call over them which had evil spirits the name of the Lord Jesus, saying, We adjure you by Jesus whom Paul preacheth.

And there were seven sons of one Sceva, a Jew, and chief of the priests, which did so. And the evil spirit answered and said, Jesus I know, and Paul I know; but who are ye? And the man in whom the evil spirit was leaped on them, and overcame them, and prevailed against them, so that they fled out of that house naked and wounded. (Acts 19:13–16)

King Saul

It came to pass as they came, when David was returned from the slaughter of the Philistine, that the women came out of all cities of Israel, singing and dancing, to meet king Saul, with tabrets, with joy, and with instruments of musick. And the women answered one another as they played, and said, Saul hath slain his thousands, and David his ten thousands. And Saul was very wroth, and the saying displeased him; and he said, They have ascribed unto David ten thousands, and to me they have ascribed but thousands: and what can he have more but the kingdom? And Saul eyed David from that day and forward. And it came to pass on the morrow, that the evil spirit from God came upon Saul, and he prophesied in the midst of the house: and David played with his hand, as at other times: and there was a javelin in Saul's hand. And Saul cast the javelin; for he said, I will smite David even to the wall with it. And David avoided out of his presence twice. (1 Samuel 18:6–11)

Cause Vexation, Erratic Behavior, Foaming, Gnashing of Teeth, Thrashes

When they were come to the multitude, there came to him a certain man, kneeling down to him, and saying, Lord, have mercy on my son: for he is lunatick, and sore vexed: for ofttimes he falleth into the fire, and oft into the water. And I brought him to thy disciples, and they could not cure him. Then Jesus answered and said, O faithless and perverse generation, how long shall I be with you? how long shall I suffer you? bring him hither to me. And Jesus rebuked the devil; and he departed out of him: and the child was cured from that very hour. Then came the disciples to Jesus apart, and said, Why could not we cast him out? And Jesus said unto them, Because of your unbelief: for verily I say unto you, If ye have faith as a grain of mustard seed, ye shall say unto this mountain, Remove hence to yonder place; and it shall remove; and nothing shall be impossible unto you. Howbeit this kind goeth not out but by prayer and fasting. (Matthew 17:14–21)

One of the multitude answered and said, Master, I have brought unto thee my son, which hath a dumb spirit; And wheresoever he taketh him, he teareth him: and he foameth, and gnasheth with his teeth, and pineth away: and I spake to thy disciples that they should cast him out; and they could not. He answereth him, and saith, O faithless generation, how long shall I be with you? how long shall I suffer you? bring him unto me. And they brought him unto him: and when he saw him, straightway the spirit tare him; and he fell on the ground, and wallowed foaming. And he asked his father, How long is it ago since this came unto him? And he said, Of a child. And ofttimes it hath cast him into the fire, and into the waters, to destroy him: but if thou canst do any thing, have compassion on us, and help us. Jesus said unto him, If thou canst believe, all things are possible to him that believeth. And straightway the father of the child cried out, and said with tears, Lord, I believe; help thou mine unbelief. When Jesus saw that the people came running together, he rebuked the foul spirit, saying unto him, Thou dumb and deaf spirit, I charge thee, come out of him, and enter no more into him. And the spirit cried, and rent him sore, and came out of him: and he was as one dead; insomuch that many said, He is dead. But Jesus took him by the hand, and lifted him up; and he arose. (Mark 9:17–27)

It came to pass, that on the next day, when they were come down from the hill, much people met him. And, behold, a man of the company cried out, saying, Master, I beseech thee, look upon my son: for he is mine only child. And, lo, a spirit taketh him, and he suddenly crieth out; and it teareth him that he foameth again, and bruising him hardly departeth from him. And I besought thy disciples to cast him out; and they could not. And Jesus answering said, O faithless and perverse generation, how long shall I be with you, and suffer you? Bring thy son hither. And as he was yet a coming, the devil threw him down, and tare him. And Jesus rebuked the unclean spirit, and healed the child, and delivered him again to his father. (Luke 9:37–42)

Change a Person's Tone of Voice

Thou shalt be brought down, and shalt speak out of the ground, and thy speech shall be low out of the dust, and thy voice shall be, as of one that hath a familiar spirit, out of the ground, and thy speech shall whisper out of the dust. (Isaiah 29:4)

When they shall say unto you, Seek unto them that have familiar spirits, and unto wizards that peep, and that mutter: should not a people seek unto their God? for the living to the dead? (Isaiah 8:19)

Lead to Betrayal and Treason

Supper being ended, the *devil having now put into the heart of Judas Iscariot, Simon's son, to betray him*; Jesus knowing that the Father had given all things into his hands, and that he was come from God, and went to God; He riseth from supper, and laid aside his garments; and took a towel, and girded himself. (John 13:2–4, emphasis added)

Cause Blindness and Speech Impediments

He was casting out a devil, and it was dumb. And it came to pass, when the devil was gone out, the dumb spake; and the people wondered. (Luke 11:14)

As they went out, behold, they brought to him a dumb man possessed with a devil. And when the devil was cast out, the dumb spake: and the multitudes marvelled, saying, It was never so seen in Israel. But the Pharisees said, He casteth out devils through the prince of the devils. (Matthew 9:32–34)

Then was brought unto him one possessed with a devil, blind, and dumb: and he healed him, insomuch that the blind and dumb both spake and saw. (Matthew 12:22)

Cause Physical Infirmity

He was teaching in one of the synagogues on the sabbath. And, behold, there was a woman which had a spirit of infirmity eighteen years, and was bowed together, and could in no wise lift up herself. And when Jesus saw her, he called her to him, and said unto her, Woman, thou art loosed from thine infirmity. And he laid his hands on her: and immediately she was made straight, and glorified God. (Luke 13:10–13)

Can Have Superhuman Power

When he was come to the other side into the country of the Gergesenes, there met him two possessed with devils, coming out of the tombs, exceeding fierce, so that no man might pass by that way. (Matthew 8:28)

Because that he had been often bound with fetters and chains, and the chains had been plucked asunder by him, and the fetters broken in pieces: neither could any man tame him. And always, night and day, he was in the mountains, and in the tombs, crying, and cutting himself with stones. (Mark 5:4, 5)

Cause Blindness and Dumbness

As they went out, behold, they brought to him a dumb man possessed with a devil. (Matthew 9:32)

Then was brought unto him one possessed with a devil, blind, and dumb: and he healed him, insomuch that the blind and dumb both spake and saw. (Matthew 12:22)

At even, when the sun did set, they brought unto him all that were diseased, and them that were possessed with devils. (Mark 1:32)

They also which saw it told them by what means he that was possessed of the devils was healed. (Luke 8:36)

For unclean spirits, crying with loud voice, came out of many that were possessed with them: and many taken with palsies, and that were lame, were healed. (Acts 8:7)

It came to pass, as we went to prayer, a certain damsel possessed with a spirit of divination met us, which brought her masters much gain by soothsaying. (Acts 16:16)

Altered Personality Changes

The Lord said unto Samuel, How long wilt thou mourn for Saul, seeing I have rejected him from reigning over Israel? fill thine horn with oil, and go, I will send thee to Jesse the Bethlehemite: for I have provided me a king among his sons. . . . the spirit of the Lord departed from Saul, and an evil spirit from the Lord troubled him. And Saul's servants said unto him, Behold now, an evil spirit from God troubleth thee. Let our lord now command thy servants, which are before thee, to seek out a man, who is a cunning player on an harp: and it shall come to pass, when the evil spirit from God is upon thee, that he shall play with his hand, and thou shalt be well. (1 Samuel 16:1, 14–16)

Saul said unto his servants, Provide me now a man that can play well, and bring him to me. Then answered one of the servants, and said, Behold, I have seen a son of Jesse the Bethlehemite, that is cunning in playing, and a mighty valiant man, and a man of war, and prudent in matters, and a comely person, and the Lord is with him. . . . it came to pass, when the evil spirit from God was upon Saul, that David took an harp, and played with his hand: so Saul was refreshed, and was well, and the evil spirit departed from him. (1 Samuel 16:17, 18, 23)

It came to pass as they came, when David was returned from the slaughter of the Philistine, that the women came out of all cities of Israel, singing and dancing, to meet king Saul, with tabrets, with joy, and with instruments of musick. And the women answered one another as they played, and said, Saul hath slain his thousands, and David his ten thousands. And Saul was very wroth, and the saying displeased him; and he said, They have ascribed unto David ten thousands, and to me they have ascribed but thousands: and what can he have more but the kingdom? And Saul eyed David from that day and forward. And it came to pass on the morrow, that the evil spirit from God came upon Saul, and he prophesied in the midst of the house: and David played with his hand, as at other times: and there was a javelin in Saul's hand. And Saul cast the javelin; for he said, I will smite David even to the wall with it. And David avoided out of his presence twice. And Saul was afraid of David, because the Lord was with him, and was departed from Saul. Therefore Saul removed him from him, and made him his captain over a thousand; and he went out and came in before the people. (1 Samuel 18:6–13)

Cause Dementia:

When he was come out of the ship, immediately there met him out of the tombs a man with an unclean spirit, Who had his dwelling among the tombs; and no man could bind him, no, not with chains: Because that he had been often bound with fetters and chains, and the chains had been plucked asunder by him, and the fetters broken in pieces: neither could any man tame him. And always, night and day, he was in the mountains, and in the tombs, crying, and cutting himself with stones. But when he saw Jesus afar off, he ran and worshipped him, and cried with a loud voice, and said, What have I to do with thee, Jesus, thou Son of the most high God? I adjure thee by God, that thou torment me not. For he said unto him, Come out of the man, thou unclean spirit. And he asked him, What is thy name? And he answered, saying, My name is Legion: for we are many. And he besought him much that he would not send them away out of the country. Now there was there nigh unto the mountains a great herd of swine feeding. And all the devils besought him, saying, Send us into the swine, that we may enter into them.

And forthwith Jesus gave them leave. And the unclean spirits went out, and entered into the swine: and the herd ran violently down a steep place into the sea, (they were about two thousand;) and were choked in the sea. And they that fed the swine fled, and told it in the city, and in the country. And they went out to see what it was that was done. And they come to Jesus, and see him that was possessed with the devil, and had the legion, sitting, and clothed, and in his right mind: and they were afraid. (Mark 5:2–15)

Spirit of Conniving and Sorcery

When they had gone through the isle unto Paphos, they found a certain sorcerer, a false prophet, a Jew, whose name was Barjesus: Which was with the deputy of the country, Sergius Paulus, a prudent man; who called for Barnabas and Saul, and desired to hear the Word of God. But Elymas the sorcerer (for so is his name by interpretation) withstood them, seeking to turn away the deputy from the faith. Then Saul, (who also is called Paul,) filled with the Holy Ghost, set his eyes on him, and said, O full of all subtlety and all mischief, thou child of the devil, thou enemy of all righteousness, wilt thou not cease to pervert the right ways of the Lord? And now, behold, the hand of the Lord is upon thee, and thou shalt be blind, not seeing the sun for a season. And immediately there fell on him a mist and a darkness; and he went about seeking some to lead him by the hand. (Acts 13:6–11)

Each case presented varied outward conduct. Except for the demoniac, the others were usually difficult to detect because the individuals mentioned gave the appearance that they were in control. Their actions were not constant but spasmodic. King Saul was paranoid and had flashes of anger. The damsel lauded the work of the apostles, but she normally divined or did the work of a fortuneteller. Elymas desired the secret of the power so that he could perform miracles as did the apostles, but his occupation was that of a magician.

hardened (daily)
Resisted
indulged
maintained his own judgement + opinions
hearer not doer.
in bondage to own choosing

THEN SATAN ENTERED

The experience of Judas gives us an insight as to how Satan takes possession of humans. The takeover of this disciple did not begin with an abrupt or instant act. Rather, it was a step-by-step process. We begin with Jesus and his disciples in the upper room. "And supper being ended, the devil having now put into the heart of Judas Iscariot, Simon's son, to betray him." Obviously, he had already begun the downward path prior to this episode, and his greed became transparent when Jesus gave a gentle rebuke concerning Mary Magdalene's deed (see John 12:3–7). With a rankled spirit (see Matthew 26:14, 15), he apparently determined to get even. Jesus had just made a statement in reference to his being betrayed by one of them.

> Simon Peter therefore beckoned to him [John], that he should ask who it should be of whom he spake. He then lying on Jesus' breast saith unto him, Lord, who is it? Jesus answered, He it is, to whom I shall give a sop, when I have dipped it. And when he had dipped the sop, he gave it to Judas Iscariot, the son of Simon. And after the sop Satan entered into him. Then said Jesus unto him, That thou doest, do quickly. (John 13:24–27)

Satan possessed Judas. This shrewd commandeer of the enemy plunged him into the act of betrayal. "For thirty pieces of silver—the price of a slave—he sold the Lord of glory to ignominy and death."[36] In speaking about Judas, John stated on one occasion, "This he said, not that he cared for the poor; but because he was a thief, and had the bag, and bare what was put therein" (John 12:6). Though he had "a strong love for money", "he had not always been corrupt enough to do such a deed as this."[37] The problem lies in the fact that he never came to the point of yielding "his worldly ambition or his love of money."[38] Though he had accepted the position as an apostle of Christ, he did not allow himself to be under the Lord's molding. Feeling that he could maintain his own judgment and opinions, he nurtured an independent temperament to criticize and accuse.[39]

---

36   E. G. White, *The Desire of Ages*, 716.
37   Ibid.
38   Ibid., 717.
39   Ibid., author's paraphrase.

A year before the betrayal, Jesus hinted that he read Judas' heart. "Have I chosen you twelve, and one of you is a devil" (John 6:70). At the last supper, Jesus once more gave evidence that he was divine and able to read Judas' heart. He was not a practitioner of Christ's counsel but, rather, only a hearer.

Two disciples stood in distinct contrast: John and Judas. While John in humility gained precious lessons from the Savior, the other demonstrated arrogance and an unyielding self-will to the subduing, transforming power of Christ. Both had the same opportunity: Judas daily resisted, indulging in his selfish desires; John, in contrast, daily died to self and overcame sin. The latter was sanctified through the words of Christ; the other was taken in bondage to Satan by his own choosing.

Judas could have repented, even after he had given his word twice to betray Christ, but he hardened his heart. Eventually, this state of heart and mind gave entrance to Satan. This is why the Bible states, "Rebellion is as the sin of witchcraft, and stubbornness as iniquity and idolatry" (1 Samuel 15:23). The phrase, "*entered into him*" (John 13:27, emphasis added), simply implies that the devil took complete possession of him. Up to this point, Judas still had the opportunity to repent, but in hardening his heart, he passed the boundary line of no return.

The turning point for Judas came when Jesus preached the sermon in the synagogue at Capernaum about a year earlier (see John 6:22–65). While others separated themselves from Christ, Judas continued to associate with Him and the other disciples, but, in heart, he had deserted Jesus. As the Savior continued to teach, Judas made no open opposition, but the current that he had placed himself in became too strong to resist. Had he yielded up his egocentricity to the subduing influence of Christ, he would not have been led to the point of no return. It was not until the episode at Simon the leper's feast, that Jesus' commendation of Mary's act of devotion and indirect rebuke of his extremely greedy attitude provoked Judas into action. Jesus' rebuke of Judas' cloaked selfish statement of care for the poor rankled him. Resentfulness led to wounded pride, which kindled a revengeful spirit. Judas' determination to get back at Christ became such a strong torrent of ill will toward his Leader that it swept him helplessly into the cruel act of betrayal and treason. Once he got to the point of no return, being led at will by the evil one, Judas went to the "chief priests and captains" (Luke 22:3, 4).

The overmastering of Judas by the enemy of souls should serve as a strong warning to those on the precipice of evil. Not until Judas witnessed the malicious heartless treatment of the Savior by the religious leaders did reality set in, but by then the devil goaded him with the magnitude of his evil, and Judas could find escape from his tortured conscience only by committing suicide. Something similar will be the experience of everyone who persists in resisting the promptings of God's Spirit in defense of self. Unless the depraved elements of the heart are resisted and overcome, Satan will surely latch on to them and use them to drag the soul down into degradation against God's will.

It is a frightful scriptural revelation that a person, as in the case of Judas, with keen intellect can be a puppet in the hands of the archenemy and, yet, appear self-possessed—never a hint of being manipulated and appearing as saintly and in control as was church deacon Dennis Lynn Rader, the BTK (bind, torture, kill) serial killer. Outwardly, people like Mr. Rader may appear professional, tidy, self-composed, brilliant, and harmless; inwardly, their wicked master is pulling the strings of control, harboring unimaginable evil to perpetrate while moving undetected.

The same was true in the modern-day film, *Sleepers*. These terrorists were able to work incognito, living in a neighborhood as well-ordered citizens, drawing no other attention than a "Good morning." They gained the respect of their neighbors until they had complete confidence, but when the moment came (whether the latent period had been as long as ten years or less), they perpetrated the most heinous and gruesome crimes as in the assault on the New York Twin Towers of 9/11.

When the heart is opened to unbelief, hate, envy, or rebellion, the devil supplies all the ingredients for suspicion, doubt, and self-justifiable resistance. In this age, if those who come under the precious influence of biblical truth do not become transformed in character, they will, like Judas, go from light to darkness—and how great will be their darkness. We are warned:

> Let no man say when he is tempted, I am tempted of God: for God cannot be tempted with evil, neither tempteth he any man: But every man is tempted, when he is drawn away of his own lust, and enticed, Then when lust hath conceived, it bringeth forth sin: and sin, when it is finished, bringeth forth death. (James 1:13–15)

Judas' experience is a prime example of the downward trend taken by many who become possessed. It serves not only as a warning, but also as a revelation into how to avoid becoming a victim of Satan.

Humanity is a frightful power for evil without the controlling power of God's Spirit. The vacuum created by unbelief and hatred of reproof will generate devilish influences. In the final events of earth's history, principalities and powers, the rulers of the darkness of this world, and spiritual wickedness in high places will all unite in a desperate companionship. Relatives and friends will be leagued with demons against God in the person of His saints. As Christ was victimized by the confederation of Judas and his controlling demon, so will God's people be subjects of reprisal, calumny, and persecution.

The words of Christ will meet a woeful fulfillment. Jesus foretold: "And ye shall be betrayed both by parents, and brethren, and kinsfolks, and friends; and some of you shall they cause to be put to death. And ye shall be hated of all men for my name's sake. But there shall not an hair of your head perish. In your patience possess ye your souls" (Luke 21:16-19).

DEMONS KNOW WHO THE TRUE STRONGMAN IS

As mentioned before, the controversy between the fallen angels and Christ and his angels started in heaven. Though Christ was now clothed with human flesh, those demons that had been expelled from the realms beyond did not fail to recognize who their opponent was. The animosity was blatant. Note Luke's record of one encounter.

> When he went forth to land, there met him out of the city a certain man, which had devils long time, and ware no clothes, neither abode in any house, but in the tombs. When he saw Jesus, he cried out, and fell down before him, and with a loud voice said, What have I to do with thee, Jesus, thou Son of God most high? I beseech thee, torment me not. (For he had commanded the unclean spirit to come out of the man. For oftentimes it had caught him: and he was kept bound with chains and in fetters; and he brake the bands, and was driven of the devil into the wilderness.) And Jesus asked him, saying, What is thy name? And he said, Legion: because many devils were entered into him. And they besought him that he would not command them to go out into the deep. And there was there an herd of many swine feeding on the mountain: and they besought him that he would suffer them to enter into them. And he suffered them. (Luke 8:27–32).

Jesus did not permit any allusion that there was any inkling of unity between His enemies and Himself; this is evident by His command to hold their peace. "He healed many that were sick of divers diseases, and cast out many devils, and suffered not the devils to speak, because they knew Him" (Mark 1:34). "Devils also came out of many, crying out, and saying, Thou art Christ the Son of God. And he rebuking them suffered them not to speak: for they knew that he was Christ" (Luke 4:41). "Unclean spirits, when they saw him, fell down before him, and cried, saying, Thou art the Son of God. And he straitly charged them that they should not make him known" (Mark 3:11, 12). The demons, appearing as if they recognized their leader bowed down, and by thus doing, they wished to give the impression and implication that He was in league with them. Therefore, Christ's refusal of their testimony invalidated the suggestion.

Today spiritualists profess Christ, and even claim that their abilities are God-given; however, the clear biblical examples already considered shed light on this modern day conundrum. The apostle Paul warns:

> Be ye not unequally yoked together with unbelievers: for what fellowship hath righteousness with unrighteousness? And what communion hath light with darkness? And what concord hath Christ with Belial? Or what part hath he that believeth with an infidel? And what agreement hath the temple of God with idols? Wherefore come out from among them, and be ye separate, saith the Lord, and touch not the unclean thing; and I will receive you. (2 Corinthians 6:14–17)
>
> [Again he stated:] "What say I then? That the idol is anything, or that which is offered in sacrifice to idols is anything? But I say, that the things which the Gentiles sacrifice, they sacrifice to devils, and not to God: and I would not that ye should have fellowship with devils. Ye cannot drink the cup of the Lord, and the cup of devils: ye cannot be partakers of the Lord's table, and of the table of devils" (1 Corinthians 10:19–21).

While in the next chapter I share an experience about my former belly-dancer girlfriend and a psychic that took place in my mother's house in 1967, there is something about that encounter that I want to point out here. After going through an impromptu, bizarre, psychical encounter, the spiritualist made a statement when, out of curiosity, I asked if she believed in Christ. At the time I was not a believer myself, and I am not sure what prompted that question. Nevertheless, she said, "If anybody dares to say anything bad about my Christ, I will put a spell on them."

Strange—while professing to be a follower of Christ, she threatened to do what Christ Himself forbade His disciples to do when "he turned, and rebuked them, and said, Ye know not what manner of spirit ye are of. For the Son of man is not come to destroy men's lives, but to save them. And they went to another village" (Luke 9:55, 56). Another thing that was weird is that "spells" come from satanic sources. Therefore, the fact that a spell was threatened made her connection obvious. A spell "is an ability to control or influence people as though one had magical power over them."[40] Humans do not of themselves have this ability; the source is either from above or from below. In this case, spells are from beneath. The Bible clearly states, "Doth a fountain send forth at the same place sweet water and bitter? Can the fig tree, my brethren, bear olive berries? either a vine, figs? so can no fountain both yield salt water and fresh" (James 3:11, 12).

---

40 *New Oxford American Dictionary*, s.v. "spell."

On another occasion a woman, who was deeply into spiritualism, tried to convince me that, although her friend was demon-possessed, there were times when an angel from heaven spoke to her, giving good advice and forecasting future events. While she was telling me this, her friend, who was sitting in a chair across from me, went into another episode of demonic possession.

This strange one-sided bedfellow (for it is clear that the Lord is not involved) has multiplied far into many branches of modern-day occult and spiritualistic ideologies. But there is no concord between Christ and Satan (2 Corinthians 6:15). Once this fact is accepted, it will place a formidable barrier against any form of this supposed amalgamation of God and Satan. The only safety is to adhere tenaciously to a "Thus saith the Lord!"

ENCOUNTERS WITH THE POSSESSED

In a former chapter we covered the diverse manifestation of devil possession in the Scriptures. In the forgoing, we will look at present-day examples. The names utilized in the incidents are fictitious.

GO-GO DANCER

Place:	**Vampire's apartment, Brooklyn, New York**
Victim:	**Go-go dancer named Lila**
Witness:	**Band members and other go-go dancers present**
Year:	**Circa 1966**

Lila was one of our nine go-go dancers. Among all the girls that were part of our rock 'n' roll act, she was unique. Her friend once placed a record on a record player and began to play it. The record had an African chant. She seemed to go into a trance as she twirled to the music. She then fell to the floor, and began to go into convulsions. I watched with apprehension. After a while, the spell seemed to break, and she was back to normal. Because we looked at what happened as temporary, and apparently not destructive to her, our apprehension turned to a sadistic entertainment. As the Scripture says, "It is as sport to a fool to do mischief" (Proverbs 10:23).

One particular evening we were anxious for some entertainment, so we placed a record on the phonograph. Soon, the go-go dancer began her usual contortions and fell to the floor. This time she began to writhe like a serpent; then she took a deep breath and lay still for a while. We all watched with bated breath and breathed a sigh of relief when she regained consciousness. Though her eyes were opened, and she was fully conscious, she could not speak.

"A dumb spirit has possessed her," somebody whispered.

While she was under this possession, all she could do was motion with her hands. She acted as if there was something urgent she needed to share with us. We gave her the writing pencil and paper she motioned for, and she began writing. She scribbled out a message; when finished, she handed the written note to Manny. Manny quickly read it.

"I have been shown that you should not take the trip you are planning on. If you do, you will be in an accident."

After delivering the warning, Lila went back into her convulsions and then returned to normal. Whatever was supposed to have happened never did. As for Lila, she separated from us after the contracted performance, and I never saw her again.

BELLY DANCER

Place: **My mother's house on Barbey Street, Brooklyn, New York**
Victim: **Helena**
Witness: **My mother, a spiritist landlady, and myself**
Year: **1967**

The time had come, I felt, that my mother should meet my girlfriend Helena. We made our way through the maze of subways, reached the last stop, and then walked for a few city blocks. After we arrived at my mother's house, Helena eased into the relationship quite smoothly. I was glad. We visited for a while. Then my mother asked if we wanted to visit the lady upstairs. Why? I was not sure, but we consented. We climbed the steps, and upon reaching the doorway, we knocked and waited. The door opened. There behind the open door stood the lady of the house. She kindly invited us in. We were then directed to sit on her davenport, where we chatted for a while. Then, without any pre-warning, something strange began.

The woman of the house started to act weirdly. My girlfriend got up and went into a dancing gyration. Doing her usual motions (she was a belly dancer by profession), she began to twirl around in the living room. She seemed to be in a trance. The woman of the house began to speak with a hissing sound. I remember her saying, "Don't anyone pray! Don't anyone pray!"

Looking back, I think that it was a rather strange demand. Neither my girlfriend nor I were praying people and, at that time, my mother was herself involved with the occult. Why she commanded that no one pray was a mystery.

The sight was creepy—my girlfriend dancing in a trance, and the woman hissing like a snake, speaking with a strange voice and encircling her. This episode went on for about an hour. Eventually, my girlfriend came out of the trance, and the woman ceased hissing. It was an awkward experience, unexplainable yet undeniable. We then returned to my mother's apartment. After a few moments, we bid mother farewell and left. There was no question in my mind that something, or someone, possessed both women. Neither was in control: one had her speech controlled while the other had her mind and body manipulated.

Wanting to escape the eeriness of it all, we made a speedy exit. We went down the street and turned the corner for the train station. On the way we passed by a vacant lot. As we were walking, Helena's sandal laces became undone. She bent down and tied them, and then we proceeded. Again, the laces became loose. With a weary yet scary look on her face, she said, "My sandals have come undone again." I knelt down and tied the laces around her leg as tight as possible.

We started on our way again. But the episode repeated itself; the laces loosened and limply dropped to the concrete sidewalk. Bending down, I wrapped her lace around her calf tightly, and determined to hasten her on the way. She took one step only and the sandal straps were undone. At this, she turned to the open lot and said, "Someone was killed in this lot and her spirit is here."

I began to feel the hair stand up on the back of my neck. With greater determination I decided to get away from there as quickly as possible, tied laces or not, I pulled her until we got to the train. When we got home, I dared not raise the subject. She did not ever bring it up either.

This girl at times had embarrassingly strange behavior, and I had wondered why until this episode with my mother and the medium. One day we went shopping. When in the store, she began putting merchandise in her purse. Then she went over to the shoe department, pretended she was trying on some shoes, put her own in the box, and walked out. She was a kleptomaniac. Because she was such a beautiful girl and dressed quite exquisitely, no one suspected her. I asked her why, with the amount of money she made, that she took risks stealing such trinkets. She answered, "I don't know." A few months later, after that hairy encounter at my mother's house, we broke up. Our paths were never to cross again.

HIPPIE YOUNG ASTRAL-TRAVELER WOMAN

Place: Santa Fe, New Mexico
Victim: Jane
Witness: Church members
Year: Circa 1976

It was Sabbath morning in my English congregation. By this time I was eight years removed from show business and five years into ministry. In Santa Fe, New Mexico, I had two parishes. I normally alternated between the congregations every other week. One congregation's worship service was in English. This group met in the rented Women's Club building. The other was a Hispanic congregation, which met in a beautiful Spanish-style, adobe church building.

On this particular day, I noticed two individuals new to the worship activities. By their attire and appearance, I gathered they were hippies, and they were! When the services were finished, they approached me. After I had finished dismissing the congregation, we stepped to one side of the exit and conversed about their need. It was not the usual request. No, it was not money or a handout. The young man was the spokesman.

"She wants to be baptized," he began. "I told her that if she was going to be delivered, she needed to get baptized."

Turning to her, I asked, "Why do you feel you need to get baptized?"

Then the whole saga unveiled itself. Sam was a self-proclaimed prophet. He seemed to have some understanding of Christianity, however convoluted.

Jane was involved with the occult. She was an astral-traveler and a rebirther. She was into macrobiotics and chasing after the Native American spirits. The latter was why she had moved to New Mexico. Besides this, she had had hepatitis, resulting from a dirty hypodermic needle when injecting heroin. Into this dysfunctional lifestyle she dragged her two small children, for whom she expressed great concern. The spirits, which were constantly present in her dwelling, harassed her and her children. Knowing her lifestyle, I wondered if the bizarre description she gave was the result of hallucinations from drug abuse or actual reality. If true, the constant demon aggravation in her home gave reason for her apprehensive misgivings. I thought that she, no doubt, had cause to be.

Sam had her convinced that if she were to be baptized, she would rid herself of this torment. The key was to find someone "qualified" to do it, and so here they were. Jane wasted no time in making her matter known and suggested the ritual be performed immediately. Her anxiety wore well on her expressive Sicilian eyes and olive complexion. Her tone of voice revealed a certain ardor that matched her desire.

Quickly surveying the circumstances, I surmised that Jane was a genuine seeker. Sam, on the other hand, appeared to be an opportunist, utilizing this spiritual cloak to gain more confidence from her in his self-appointed role. It did not take long to validate my initial assessment. Not willing to dash any hope, or to add frustrated disappointments, yet sensing that I needed more time with her, I said that a visit was in line.

"I need to visit with you before the ceremony can be performed," I told her.

Time was needed to help her understand that the ceremony in and of itself was not sufficient; it had no intrinsic power. There was no magic in baptism. She would not yet be able to understand that because she was so wrapped up in mystical ideas.

People caught up in the occult usually believe and attribute power to symbols, artifacts, stars, signs, and other such things. Her house had "dream-catchers," amulets, talisman, fetish, etc. Smart devils! They are too successful in making human beings think that some puny potion, bizarre-looking objects, signs of the cross, or other items can have power over them. Thus, this becomes the very means of alluring people into being charmed, and then their minds are more accessible.

As a boy, I was a movie addict. I remember this notion of the occult was strongly suggested by such movies as *Mark of the Vampire*, *The Wolf Man*, etc.

Usually a crucifix was used to back off Bela Lugosi, the acting vampire. Strange powers were attributed to some chair, sending the victim back in time or some sign turning the witch into ashes. Mysticism played a great part in the oddity of some trinket leading the unwary to depend on a magical saying or brilliant stone for deliverance.

Crafty demons! They succeed in leading frail humans to believe that by flipping a light switch, these mighty beings can be forced to flee or be banished. Others are driven to blast their music, which is essentially demonic itself. Yet somehow there is the comfort (in their thinking, anyway) that the noise keeps the spirits away. These are just ancient superstitions practiced with modern noisemakers, like space-age people replacing the fire with the electric bulb with the hopes of accomplishing the same task.

Of course today with modern technology, Hollywood produces scenes that are surreal. Magical powers are vested in young Harry Potter, Spider Man, and the likes, craftily performing amazing stunts that defy the imagination. All of these leave the certain impression that some lucky moment may come when in jubilance an unearthed gadget will make the discoverer able to perform superhuman acts. Altogether, this contributes to solidify the error that leads people into dependence on things that have no power to deliver but, on the contrary, plunges credulous souls deeper into the clutches of the enemy.

A biblical story may erroneously be wrested to support this delusion. The power of God accompanied the apostle Paul's efforts, and many were healed of physical infirmities. "God wrought special miracles by the hands of Paul: so that from his body were brought unto the sick handkerchiefs or aprons, and the diseases departed from them, and the evil spirits went out of them" (Acts 19:11, 12). In Ephesus, "these manifestations of supernatural power were far more potent than had ever before been witnessed." They "were of such a character that they could not be imitated by the skill of the [magicians] or the enchantments of the sorcerer. As these miracles were performed in the name of Jesus of Nazareth, the [onlookers] had opportunity to see that the God of heaven was more powerful than the magicians who were worshipers of the goddess Diana." This resulted in the Lord exalting His servant far "above the most powerful and favored of the magicians."[41]

"Sorcery had been prohibited in the Mosaic law." Death was the punishment threatened to anyone caught practicing it. Yet, from time to time apostates, like the witch of Endor, had been secretly practicing this prohibited activity. During "Paul's visit to Ephesus, there were in the city 'certain of the vagabond Jews, exorcists,' who, seeing the [miracles performed] by him, 'took upon them to call over them which had evil spirits the name of the Lord Jesus' [Acts 7:13]. . . . 'Seven sons of one Sceva, a Jew, and chief of the priests'" (verse 14) made

---

41   E. G. White, *The Acts of the Apostles*, 286.

an attempt. "Finding a man possessed with a demon, they [approached] him [and demanded], 'We adjure you by Jesus whom Paul preacheth' [verse 14]. But 'the evil spirit answered and said, Jesus I know, and Paul I know; but who are ye? And the man in whom the evil spirit was leaped on them, and overcame them, and prevailed against them, so that they fled out of that house naked and wounded'"[42] (Acts 19:15–17).

Unmistakable proof was given that it was not the name, or some trinket that had inherent power. Rather, it was genuine faith and a living connection with the Savior that made of His servants true conduits of His power. This episode also spoke eloquently of the sacredness of Christ's name as well as the peril incurred when invoking it as a mere magic wand and without genuine faith in the divinity of the Savior. "Fear fell on them all, and the name of the Lord Jesus was magnified" (Acts 19:17).

This display of power through the ordained channels shone the light of truth onto the Ephesians. The teachings shared by the apostles displaced the darkness that enshrouded them. Though they had accepted Christianity, some of them "had not fully renounced their superstitions." Magic continued to be practiced to some extent, but when they were "convinced of their error, 'many that believed came, and confessed, and shewed their deeds'" (Acts 19:18). Even some of the sorcerers were convicted to abandon their practices, and "many of them also which used curious arts brought their books together, and burned them before all men: and they counted the price of them, and found it fifty thousand pieces of silver. So mightily grew the word of God and prevailed" (Acts 19:19, 20).[43]

The Ephesian converts demonstrated that they abhorred the things they had once delighted in by burning their books. They became aware that by practicing magic, they had "offended God and imperiled their souls." Hence, their righteous anger was aroused against this evil called magic, and by their actions, they "gave evidence of true conversion."[44]

"These treatises on divination contained rules and forms of communication with evil spirits. They were the regulations of the worship of Satan—directions for soliciting his help and obtaining information from him. By retaining these books the disciples would have exposed themselves to temptation; by selling them they would have placed temptation in the way of others. They had renounced the kingdom of darkness, and to destroy its power they did not hesitate at any sacrifice. Thus truth triumphed over men's prejudices and their love of money."[45] Christianity gained a signal victory in the very stronghold of superstition by the manifestation of Christ's power.

Knowing that Jane's view was not unlike those of the people in Paul's day, I gathered that I had my work cut out for me. I made an appointment to visit

42   Ibid., 287, 288.
43   Ibid., 288, with author's paraphrase.
44   Ibid.
45   Ibid., 288, 289.

at her place and evaluate the situation. She was content with that and left the church. The following week, I passed by the place to inform her that, after a pre-engagement with the Navajo tribe, I would return and spend time with her. I could tell by the look of her disappointed stare that she was not happy. Nevertheless, I could not bring myself to baptize her without first helping her understand the condition for God's blessing that results from baptism.

The next Sabbath both she and Sam returned. Jane, more frustrated than ever, couldn't wait for the service to end so that she could talk with me.

"I decided not to wait for you, so I went ahead and had Sam baptized me," she announced. "However, the spirits are still harassing us. You must do it!"

"If I am to do it, I will need to spend time with you and help you understand what conditions you must meet to be delivered. Are you willing to do anything?" I asked.

"Yes!" she responded.

"All right," I said, "I will meet you at your home this week and begin studying with you."

Jane had a voracious hunger for the knowledge of God. Though steeped into so many different types of ideologies, isms, etc., she was merely seeking for meaning in her life. As we studied, changes began to take place, and for the better. No sooner did she learn than she applied what she had learned.

One night Jane came to our mid-week Bible studies at the home of one of the members. We had barely started when there was a rap at the door. The lady of the house opened it. There stood Sam and another self-proclaimed prophet friend of his. They walked in and proceeded to accost me verbally.

"You Pharisee," came the denunciation. Sam was charging me with teaching falsehood. Then he turned to Jane and demanded, "It is either him or me."

Looking at him, I said, "You have it all wrong Sam. It is either God or you. That is the decision she has to make."

"Are you coming?" he demanded, looking at Jane.

There was a pause of silence. All of the onlookers waited for her answer.

"No!" responded Jane.

At this Sam went into a tirade and, with his buddy, stomped out of the house and into the darkness. I had sensed the charged air when they stepped in. It felt like a host of demons had walked in with them. However, the opposite was true when they departed. The atmosphere changed. The tension was gone. Jane looked relieved.

"What do you want to do Jane?" I asked.

"I don't feel like I can go home tonight. He is angry!" she frighteningly whispered.

My wife assured her that she could stay over at our place and then go home in the morning. She gave a sigh of relief and gladly accepted the gesture.

In the morning I took her to her place. When we arrived, she was troubled. The house appeared ransacked. She went to see if her stashed money was still there; it wasn't. Her fears were substantiated. It was Sam. He had gone before her and taken all that was worth anything and left her penniless.

"Now what do I do?" she questioned while crying. "He has taken my food and rent money."

It was obvious to me. She and her children would have to stay with us until she could get her on her feet.

Jane never had to be exorcised. Though steeped in witchcraft, she simply was searching. When she found what her heart yearned for, she was delivered from all that she had experienced and seen. It was a progressive climb in spirituality and a leaving spiritualism behind. For Jane, it was like the snake shedding its old skin as it developed the new.

FEARFUL TO SLEEP

Place:	**Norway European Bible School**
Victim:	**Young married student**
Witness:	**Husband, private interview**
Year:	**2002**

In the month of May 2002, I was teaching in Norway, the land of trolls. One morning I happened to broach the subject of possession. After class a female student requested a private audience.

"I am scared to death. I cannot sleep at night unless I have the lights on," she confided.

Mary (not her real name) was a young married woman in her late twenties. As a Christian, she was somehow entrapped in the fear that her life was at risk. The only thing that protected her at night was the light, she thought. Terrified and afraid to close her eyes, she had suffered this bondage for years. Night and darkness served to bring her dread. The thing that she thought delivered her was the very thing that kept reminding her of the evil lurking in the darkness—the light.

This reminds me of a made-up story. A witch doctor, anxious to make some quick money by deception, came up with a magical potion. He claimed that, through this potion he could make gold. To prove it, he made a demonstration. Calling the onlookers to pay close attention, he began his trick. Pouring water into the pot, he proceeded to cast in different objects—crocodile teeth, earthworms, etc.—that were supposed to add to the magic. To finish, he lifted his hand into the air, waved his spoon, and chanted some words. While the onlookers gazed on his uplifted hand, he slipped golden nuggets into the pot with the other hand. Then, stirring the concoction with his wooden spoon, he scooped up the nuggets. Amazed, the crowd applauded. Then he offered to sell the secret to anyone who was interested in making golden nuggets.

There were not a few takers. Pulling each individual aside, he first received the fee, and then unveiled the secret. After taking the 'takers' through the process, he warned:

"There is one thing you must never do! You must never remember the red-faced monkey. If you do, the potion will not work."

"Well, that was fair enough," thought the buyers.

Upon reaching home, the process began. Then, reaching the final step, the would-be rich thought on the last point—the red-faced monkey!

With Mary, I instructed her that she need not fear death, for Christ had conquered it for her. I shared with her a verse in Hebrews 2:14, 15:

Forasmuch then as the children are partakers of flesh and blood, he also himself likewise took part of the same; that through death he might destroy him that had the power of death, that is, the devil; and deliver them who through fear of death were all their lifetime subject to bondage.

"You see, the enemy is trying to keep your attention focused on what he does and, therefore, keeps your mind filled with him. The answer is to think about what Christ can do and fill your mind with Him." Then I shared Bible promises and had prayer with her.

The next morning, she and her husband were ecstatic. She slept the entire night—and with the lights out.

APPARITIONS IN NEW YORK CITY

Place: Lower Eastside Manhattan
Victim: Couple attending a series of meeting
Witness: Those present in the class
Year: June 1998

One of my most recent experiences concerning apparitions was in the Lower Eastside of Manhattan in New York City. I was holding a series of talks in that area from May 13 to June 8. The residents from the adjacent neighborhood buildings in the Lower Eastside projects were invited. One night I presented the subject on the great spiritual battle presently ensuing. Then, allowing for a question-and-answer period available to those interested, I began answering their inquiries.

Once I broached the subject of apparitions, there seemed to be an air of fright that took hold of those present. When I asked, "How many of you are experiencing what I am talking about?" At least twenty-one out of the twenty-four gave their testimonies concerning their recent experiences. A few had seen a black figure stand at the foot of their beds. Though conscience of its presence, and desirous to evade it's influence, they could neither move nor talk. They seemed to be paralyzed, unable to appeal for any help. This, they said, occurred several times before they attended the meetings.

Others talked about things moving by themselves or hearing strange sounds and footsteps. Still others talked of apparitions, and some of eerie feelings having their surroundings charged with a dense atmosphere.

PASTOR CABRAL AND THE EXORCIST FRIEND

Place: **Queens Spanish Church, Queens, New York City**
Victim: **Young Hispanic man**
Witness: **Pastor Cabral, Pastor Merino, exorcist**
Year: **Circa 1990**

"Glad to see you. I didn't know who was at the door, but I am thankful it is you," whispered Pastor Cabral.

He had cautiously pried the church door slightly open to discover who was knocking. (He was a fellow colleague whom I had gone to visit.) He then opened the church door and beckoned me to quickly enter. Once in, he hastily barred the entrance. It was obvious he did not want any intruders.

"We are exorcising someone," he said in a low voice. "Follow me."

We went up the staircase and made our way into his office and passed to an adjacent room. On the floor was a young man writhing, while another pastor demanded a spirit to leave him. The scenario appalled me. The poor young man had the look of terror in his eyes. His body was being slammed against the wall; the preacher kept on repeating, "*Te reprendo*" ("I rebuke you"). With him was another young pastor, an observer.

I was moved with compassion. Standing there and just witnessing without doing something was difficult. I could hardly bare the sight as the terrified victim screamed in torment. The impression came over me that the pastor performing the exorcism was just as frightened as the boy. He kept at a safe distance. While he was in this precautious self-protection mode, the boy kept being battered. Not being able to continue withholding the pitiful sight any longer, I knelt by the young man, grabbed him, and pressed him to my chest while I prayed.

It was not long before the restless storm broke, and the body I held relaxed into a quiet calm. The boy was now in full consciousness and relieved. The young pastor had a look of bewilderment. He stared at me and mentioned that he was amazed I would approach such a dangerous encounter so closely. The exorcist pastor said nothing while the other pastor just praised the Lord that the boy was delivered.

DR. JOYCE BAUERS

Place: Mission College, Black Hills Health and Education Center
Victim: Dr. Joyce Bauers (fictitious name)
Witness: Staff and students
Year: October 1998

She was a model student. Joyce had enrolled into the fall semester taking the evangelism course offered at our school. She passed with flying colors. Upon the conclusion of the term, my wife realized that in Joyce she had a qualified person to teach physiology. We were anxious to begin the new course in allied health, but we couldn't because there was a need of having someone with the right credentials. Here she was! A perfect match or so we thought.

Class began. The number of students was a mere twelve, but it was a good enthusiastic group. This lady fit the position like hand and glove. The students loved her.

"Great teacher!" they exclaimed.

She appeared to be a lady with integrity and high moral standards, but there were times when her demeanor belied this. We thought it was just a matter of the students' inexperience that led to the misinterpretation.

Then it happened. While I was away on a speaking engagement, my wife called me.

"Something strange is going on," she said.

"What do you mean?" I asked.

"Luisa was in my office, and she seemed greatly concerned and somewhat scared," my wife responded.

"About what?" I asked.

"She came with a letter that the professor had given her. It was addressed personally to her from 'an angel of the Lord,'" my wife continued. She then queried, "What should I do?"

"Wait until I get back, and I will deal with it," I assured her.

When I returned to the campus, I encountered students on a warpath against the "witch." The other teachers were upset; an atmosphere thick with suspicion and anarchy was prevalent. As I began to investigate, my discovery found not one letter but several that had been addressed and delivered to the particular people who were suffering from ailments. All the letters were sent by the same messenger, with the same apparent concern for the students' wellbeing.

I must confess that the spirit of the students leading out in the "hang the witch" revolt made me suspect demonic play. I felt that the same spirit was also controlling the professor. The unreasonable fanatic mob frenzy was like that of the biblical story of the swine driven by the demons in their wild descent to their demise in the sea (see Matthew 8:28–32). Other teachers resigned in protest of my not handling the problem immediately; students found all sorts of "biblical" reasons for immediate extrication of the person in question

Though greatly troubled, I wanted to give the lady the benefit of doubt. However, being a health educator myself, I knew that the recommended prescription was contrary to common laws of health because those laws also violated the biblical counsel. Hence, I knew that the remedy was not from above but from beneath. Had the persons signaled out followed the written suggested advice, the results would have been detrimental, further impairing their health.

I decided to visit the teacher. Upon my arrival, I could sense a defensive air about her.

"Can you tell me about these letters that you have been passing around?" I asked.

In her confident professional manner she began her defense. "I have a friend," she started, "who receives messages from an angel. I have seen her go into trances while we were walking. Unable to move from the spot, she would tell me that there would be someone who would be coming down the street that she was supposed to help. She told me that she could not move from her fixed position. In fact, she acted like she was nailed to the spot." Joyce continued, "As we waited there, inadvertently, a person would come who was in need. I have seen her help so many people resulting from the visions she has received."

"From whom does she get the messages that you have delivered to the guests and students on campus?" I inquired.

"There is an angel that speaks to her, and she begins to talk in an angelic language," she responded.

"Does she understand what she is saying?" I queried.

"No!" she answered.

"How do you know that what she is writing is what she is getting from this supposed celestial visitor?" I questioned again.

"Well," she said, "the Bible speaks of an angelic language that no one understands."

"No," I remonstrated, for I knew what she was referring to from the Bible. "There is no such thing! What the apostle Paul said was, 'If I could speak with the tongue of angels,' not that he could speak with the language of angels. Paul, in the book of Corinthians, was not establishing a new way of communication for human beings. On the contrary, he was using an exaggeration to give strength to his argument that love was above all. There is no recorded biblical account of any human speaking in any other language than the common dialects known to man," I insisted.

"I know this is of God! Someone else brought up that point to me. So I asked her to try to interpret what she was hearing and how she does it," she retorted.

"The Bible does not allow for the same person speaking in tongues to interpret, but rather for someone else to translate. That way, 'in the mouth of two witnesses shall the thing be established.' Besides," I continued, "how could this be of God when the counsel given is contrary to the health counsels found in Holy Writ? I think you need to seriously reevaluate this."

As we continued our discussion, she confessed that there were occasions when an evil spirit would take control of her friend. This concerned her. Therefore, she had taken the lady to a pastor and attempted to get her delivered. Because the deliverance did not occur, she assumed that the pastor and the elders were not connected enough to render the remedy desired. These alternating, occasional manifestations convinced her that they were of the devil. However, she was as equally persuaded that the experiences of the angel were from God. Again, I made another effort to help her understand, and again she refused to acknowledge my conclusion. At this, I felt I had no other alternative but to ask her to leave the campus.

During our discussion Joyce had shared with me her frustration with the pastors who were unable to help her friend get rid of the spirits that possessed her. The next day I decided to call the pastor.

"It was a weird experience," the pastor said. He went on to say that they attempted to exorcise the friend, but she seemed to revert back.

"There seemed to be an unusual relationship between Joyce and her friend. Why she is mixed up with this woman is an enigma," the pastor explained. "She is such a bright and highly educated woman. It is just a shame."

I discovered that the pastor was not the only one from whom Joyce tried to get help. She had taken her friend to a health institute, where her troubled friend had an episode. The efforts there had also been unsuccessful. Angry that the people in the health institute could not extricate the evil part of Bonnie, Joyce decided to take her to another location for help. But there, too, the pastor's effort had proven fruitless.

Why she then decided to come to our school is still a mystery to me. Obviously, she must have known from the course study at our institution that we would not countenance her dabbling with spiritism on the campus. She intentionally kept her friend's satanic connections secret until she could disseminate enough apparent goodwill to win an acceptance of her deluded practice. Whatever her intentions, she now had to be asked to leave.

Though livid, she reluctantly conceded to my recommendation. Feeling relieved that she appeared amiable, I thought the problem gone. But the devil does not give up easily. Bonnie then showed up on campus. I decided to encourage a visiting pastor/professor to go with me. I knew it to be ill-advised to tackle something of this nature by myself. When we reached her apartment, the woman was apparently not present.

As we began to talk to Joyce, the woman slipped from the bedroom into our presence like one anxious to catch us at our word. It was hard not to conclude that the woman was a witch. Her long black hair hung over the right side of her face. Wearing a long black dress with a dark shawl draped over her shoulder, she had dark mysterious eyes that peered at us with a look of steel. It seemed as if she was attempting to intimidate us with her stare.

She sat across from us in the recliner. Joyce sat on the other living room couch to her right. I began the discussion.

"Tell me about yourself," I suggested.

The strange visitor began to reveal her experience. No longer uncertain to my visiting professor or to me, these women were directly connected to evil forces. They attempted to connect their peculiar experiences to God and His Bible, citing some biblical references that in no way could be crafted to support their error. My visiting friend began to appeal to these women to abandon their ideas and practices; however, they continued to hold to their position. I finally looked Joyce straight in the eye and said, "As long as you stubbornly cling to your errors, I cannot help you."

Then it happened. Bonnie began to speak, but it was not her voice.

"It's a demon," Joyce warned.

The voice was heinous. She oscillated between the voice of a human and the sound of an animal, groaning like a lion. The whole atmosphere became oppressively heavy. I could feel the hairs on the nap of my neck rise. We knew what to do—throw ourselves on our knees and begin to pray. We assaulted the throne of heaven, claiming God's power for deliverance. Her body began to contort. Then, almost instantly, she took a deep breath and remained motionless.

We stopped praying, in hopes that it was over, but it wasn't. The woman's mouth began to move—her eyes still closed. Allegations poured out of her mouth concerning some supposed sin we were committing, but we knew better. Paying no mind to the demon's distraction tactic, we proceeded praying. Then there was a repeat of body action—stopped breathing, silence, and stillness. While there was an apparent lifelessness on the part of the woman, Joyce began to talk.

"This has happened several times before," she noted, but she was interrupted when the woman began to claw her own throat with her long nails.

We jumped forward and grabbed her arms to keep the demon from doing the physical damage. Once more, we began to earnestly pray. The same thing happened. I went quickly next door to the adjoining apartment and invited another employee to join us in the battle. However, I noticed the fear on his face when he came into the room. We had no time to search for others. The scene began to repeat itself. This time we decided to continue our petitioning until the deliverance was final. It took three hours of wrestling and praying. Then it finally broke.

Bonnie became fully conscious. There was no effort on her part now to argue her former position. On the contrary, an expression of gratitude took the place of argument and denial. She stated that her captivity had been of long duration, and that she was relieved to finally have deliverance. We had a final prayer, and then we strongly urged Joyce to immediately leave the campus.

I requested the staff member who had witnessed the event to arrange to have a truck rented that day and move her off the campus. This he did, but when I went to find Joyce, she had disappeared. She was off the campus, and so was her friend, but the truck and belongings were still on campus.

Toward the evening, I noticed her Blazer speeding toward the main road off the campus. I gave chase, continuing to flash my headlights and beep my horn, but she kept going. Finally, we came to the main road where she had to stop before turning. I caught up with her. When she rolled down the window, there was such an evil look that if looks could kill, my life would have been snuffed out instantly. It was eerie! Not cowering, which I suppose was the intent of the angry stare, I challenged, "Why have you not moved out? What are you waiting for?"

"I can't move until twenty-four hours are completed," she responded.

"An observer of times," I thought, "another link to her involvement with the occult."

My mind immediately went to a passage of Scripture, "There shall not be found among you any one that maketh his son or his daughter to pass through the fire, or that useth divination, *or an observer of times*, or an enchanter, or a witch. Or a charmer, or a consulter with familiar spirits, or a wizard, or a necromancer" (Deuteronomy 18:10, 11, emphasis added). The tone of voice gave evidence that someone else was in control. She tried to threaten me; I responded by quoting the Scripture noted above. To this she turned and sped away into the night. The next day she showed up and moved.

Several days later, my wife brought me a letter. It was from Bonnie. She was still in the area. In it she expressed gratitude for the encounter, though now feeling at a loss for direction. She wanted to see me, to ask for advice. I was leery, but determined to accommodate her. My wife and I decided to visit. When we searched for her whereabouts, we found that she was working for a low-rated motel. When asked for her quarters, we were directed to a basement dwelling. My wife waited in the car while I made the visit. I knocked on her door. She opened and invited me inside.

"I am so thankful that you came. I did not think that you would even consider coming after what we put you through," she began. "Joyce and I have parted ways. I am trying to witness to these people of the power of God to deliver, and His goodness and mercies toward us. However, I am having a hard time. It is so discouraging to witness to people and not even get any indication that anything is happening."

"How can I help you?" I asked.

"Just pray for me that I will remain close to the Lord, and that I will be able to find another job that will afford me to live the Christian life," she requested.

I prayed with her and left, sensing that the woman had truly been delivered and was now on the right path.

APPARITION IN PALAU

Place: **Palau Mission Academy**
Victim: **Students in the dorm**
Witness: **Staff and students**
Year: **Fall 1986**

When I went to Palau as a missionary, an island country in the Pacific, I was asked to present a week of prayer and to preach at our high school. On the first night everything went well. It seemed like the students were attentive and eager to hear what the Bible had to say. This was a bit unusual in as much as most of the students came from non-Christian homes. Normally, when the Word of God is presented to a group of people whose background includes magic, spiritualism, and witchcraft, etc., one can anticipate something to occur.

One night after the meeting and the young people were back in their respective dorms, blood-curdling screams from the young ladies dorm interrupted the quiet of the night. They reported in the morning that they had seen an old woman with white hair clad in a garment of white walking through their dormitory. The boys upstairs, hearing the girls' screams, were amused by the silliness of their foolish terror. The woman disappeared.

My wife, upon hearing of the occurrence, knew what we were dealing with, and she chose to sleep with the girls the following night. The next evening, the apparition appeared in the boys' dormitory. One of the boys was Korean, and his Buddhist beliefs apparently gave no credence to any such occurrence. He thought it was all "stupid and silly." Being amused by the supposed superstition, he laughed at the other young men who had been greatly frightened. In the morning, as he was musing about the happening, he looked up. There in front of him was the woman of the same description. Seeing the apparition himself caused him great terror. It was no laughing matter now. His hair stood up, and running through the hallway, the other boys could hear his hoarse voice screaming. While the strange occurrence first took place in the girl's dorm at night, the apparition now appeared in broad daylight on the boy's floor.

When I returned to the school that evening, the staff and students relayed the incident. This time, while my wife slept downstairs, and led the girls in singing hymns and praying, I slept with the boys on their floor and did the same. That night I told all of the students that someone in the dorm was inviting this evil presence into our midst. I explained that though the invitation might not be verbal, it might be by things held in store by the students. It might be a false god, like rock n' roll music, jewelry, or anything else attached to witchcraft or spiritualism.

"If you want to get rid of the evil presence," I told them, "you will have to be willing to get rid of all that the devil could claim as his own."

Having placed a 50-gallon drum outside the dorm, I gave the students an opportunity to rid themselves of the accursed things. We waited. Then, one by one, the students left our presence and returned with trinkets, CDs, magic balls that were purported to give answers to the tests, Ouija boards, and other such things. They threw them into the barrel, and we set them afire. This we did to follow the biblical example of the people in Paul's day, who burned all their sorcery paraphernalia, books, and artifacts.

This act on their part cleansed the dormitory of all and anything that the devil could claim as a channel of invitation. After that, we were free from any apparitions and demonic presence. In addition, many students decided in favor of Christ and gave public testimony, through the Christian ordinance of baptism, of their newfound faith.

POSSESSED YOUNG MAN

Place: **Dorm Room, BHHEC**
Victim: **Married student**
Witness: **Wife, staff, and students**
Year: **Fall 1997**

Ben had arrived on campus with his wife. Because he was recommended and brought by a staff member, he did not go through the normal process of having his references checked. His demeanor seemed congenial; nothing seemed out of the ordinary.

One early afternoon, I was urgently requested to go to the student's room. I decided to take with me the staff member who knew him. There was obviously some problem; we made our way as quickly as possible. When we arrived at the dorm, we headed toward the couple's room. Even though I knocked, I did not hesitate to go in. Upon entering, I noticed the wife cowering and curled up on her bed against the corner wall.

As soon as we entered, Ben began to act strangely. Moving away from us, he began acting as if he all at once became frightened. Not being acquainted with his history or problems, I began to try to converse with him, to put him at ease. His eyes gave bizarre, heinous stares. Then it happened. Language came out of his mouth that was beyond vulgar. Speaking as if he were Satan, he was gloating about what he had done to Christ on the cross. Then the door to the room opened. Students in the adjacent room wondered what was taking place. The filthy loud words drew their attention, so I encouraged them to quickly close the door and gather to pray, which they did.

The possessed young man then launched forward at the staff member and took a swing at him. The staff member dodged. I then threw myself on my knees, grabbed the young man, and prayed over him while I held him. It was quite tense. I continued to pray while he continued to swear and curse. The spiritual tug of war lasted about half an hour. Then I felt the resistance subside. The man grew quiet and then completely relaxed. The victory had been gained. Back in his own mind, Ben asked, "What happened?"

I told him about the struggle and the victory the Lord had given. He gathered back with his relieved and grateful wife, now no longer fearful.

The praying young men returned to find out what was taking place, sensing that a change had come. It had! We then all knelt down and praised the Lord for the deliverance and victory.

YOUNG POSSESSED SON

Place: **In a home in Waitara, Australia**
Victim: **Young African/Australian man**
Witness: **Pastor Bruce Price and family**
Year: **Circa 1993**

I was giving a series of evangelistic talks in the Waitara Church in Australia. One night I made an appeal, and several people came to the altar. After the services were finished, a mother with a heavy heart requested a private interview. She said that her son acted strangely; his behavior was erratic and unpredictable, and she—though reluctant to think so--feared that it might be demonic possession. His actions were reminiscent of past episodes that she had witnessed of devil possession in her Caribbean homeland.

We were not sure what the case really was, so Pastor Price and I had a season of prayer before going to the residence. When the Pastor and I arrived, we met a waiting, anxious mother who escorted us into the living room. There we had prayer with her and her husband. After this the young man was invited to meet us. He was not aware of the purpose of our visit. Initially, he acted and talked normally until we opened the Bible. Then, almost immediately, his voice and body movements changed.

Pete (not his real name) began to go through the typical contortions of a possessed person. Pastor Price and I hastened to our knees to pray. We prayed while we held the man. After a short while, his body lost its tension and laid still. We thought it was over, but then it started again. This tussle continued, and we wrestled for about two hours, after which Pete took a deep breath and began singing hymns. At once the atmosphere changed. Pete was delivered. A few weeks later, he was one of the baptismal candidates who gave his testimony of the wonderful way the Lord had delivered him.

OUR BATTLE

For we wrestle not against flesh and blood, but against principalities, against powers, against the rulers of the darkness of this
world, against spiritual wickedness in high places. Wherefore
take unto you the whole armour of God, that ye may be able to
withstand in the evil day, and having done all, to stand. Stand
therefore, having your loins girt about with truth, and having
on the breastplate of righteousness; And your feet shod with the
preparation of the gospel of peace; Above all, taking the shield
of faith, wherewith ye shall be able to quench all the fiery darts
of the wicked. And take the helmet of salvation, and the sword
of the Spirit, which is the word of God: Praying always with all
prayer and supplication in the Spirit, and watching thereunto
with all perseverance and supplication for all saints. (Ephesians
6:12–18)

Once we realize that our battle is with superior beings, we place ourselves
on the road to victory. Because the battleground is in the mind and with
the thought processes, this is where the conquering must take place. Hence,
we must gain the ability to become aware of the enemy. Early detection is
imperative. However, in order to recognize another voice making suggestions,
we cannot depend upon our own conscience or feelings because the mind has
been sensitized to sin, and trained by being constantly bombarded with satanic
suggestions. Therefore, it must be educated to become sensitive to differentiate
between right and wrong—between the holy and profane. Only the Word of
God, when accepted as the source of all truth and righteousness, and when
taken into the mind, can accomplish the task. In this spiritual arena, only the
Bible is the source of spiritual truth. "Without the Bible we should be bewildered
by false theories. The mind would be subjected to the tyranny of superstition
and falsehood."[46]

The Holy Scriptures "are able to make thee wise unto salvation through
faith which is in Christ Jesus. All scripture is given by inspiration of God,
and is profitable for doctrine, for reproof, for correction, for instruction in

46   E. G. White, "The Power of the Word of God," *The Review and Herald*, November 10, 1904.

righteousness: That the man of God may be perfect, thoroughly furnished unto all good works" (2 Timothy 3:15–17). With all of these qualities, the role of the Word is paramount when contesting with demonic powers.

The mind, when left to its own hereditary and cultivated propensities is not capable of discerning Satan's infiltration. The only true detector of evil is the Law of God, as revealed in His Word. Paul wrote, "I had *not* known sin, but by the law: for I had *not* known *lust*, except the law had said, *Thou shalt not* covet" (Romans 7:7, emphasis added). The prophet Isaiah declares, "To the law and to the testimony, if they speak not according to this word, it is because there is no light in them" (Isaiah 8:20). Knowing and acknowledging what sin is (The transgression of the law of God [1 John 3:4] enables the victim to compare his thoughts with God's principles.)

The Bible reveals what is righteous and what is evil. The Lord unequivocally describes the opposite of righteousness.

> Now the works of the flesh are manifest, which are these; adultery, fornication, uncleanness, lasciviousness, Idolatry, witchcraft, hatred, variance, emulations, wrath, strife, seditions, heresies, Envyings, murders, drunkenness, revellings, and such like: of the which I tell you before, as I have also told you in time past, that they which do such things shall not inherit the kingdom of God. (Galatians 5:19)

Any thought that may be moving in these channels is obviously from Satan. This is why Jesus said:

> For from within, out of the heart of men, proceed evil thoughts, adulteries, fornications, murders, thefts, covetousness, wickedness, deceit, lasciviousness, an evil eye, blasphemy, pride, foolishness: all these evil things come from within, and defile the man. (Mark 7:21–23).

If there is no desire or tendency to have evil thoughts, and yet they appear, then the source is obvious. At this point, once the thoughts are detected, the Scriptures become a mighty antidote to vanquish the suggestions. This is what Christ did. In the wilderness temptation, Jesus cited the Bible and its principles to repulse the temptation. "It is written" was His defense. Paul stated that thoughts can be altered.

> For the weapons of our warfare are not carnal, but mighty through God to the pulling down of strong holds; Casting down imaginations, and every high thing that exalteth itself against the knowledge of God, and bringing into captivity every thought to the obedience of Christ. (2 Corinthians 10:4, 5).

It is here that the Word of God plays a crucial role. "For the word of God is quick, and powerful, and *sharper than* any *twoedged* sword, piercing even to the dividing asunder of soul and spirit, and of the joints and marrow, and is a discerner of the thoughts and intents of the heart" (Hebrews 4:12, emphasis added). Remember, the only way that Satan can take control of the mind or intellect is for us to yield it to him.

In order to avoid a mental mutiny, the will must be reinforced by divine thoughts. The apostle Peter wrote, "Whereby are given unto us exceeding great and precious promises; that by these ye might become partakers of the divine nature, having escaped the corruption that is in the world through lust" (2 Peter 1:4). Notice that through the many wonderful promises found in the Word we can become partakers of the "divine nature." The psalmist puts it this way: "Wherewithal shall a young man cleanse his way? by taking heed thereto according to thy word. Thy word have I hid in my heart, that I might not sin against thee" (Psalm 119:9, 11). Paul wrote, "Let this mind be in you, which was also in Christ Jesus" (Philippians 2:5).

The will of God is revealed in the sacred pages of the Scriptures. That divine will must be understood and internalized in order for us to endure the trials that come. Moreover, in order to honor Him, there must be a correct conception of his character, government, and purposes, and then we must live in harmony with them. The words "a new heart will I give you" in Ezekiel 36:26 mean that He will give us a new mind. A clear conception of Christian duty and an understanding of the truth always attend this change of mind.

In proportion to our understanding, the Word of God will be the clearness of our view of truth. By giving the Scriptures close, prayerful attention, the comprehension will become clear and the judgment sound. By turning to God, the seeker will reach a higher grade of intelligence. The perusal of the Word of God will strengthen the understanding, and give light and knowledge. When the Bible is studied and obeyed as it should be, the mind will be expanded and the taste will be refined. The psalmist prayed, "Order my steps in thy word: and let not any iniquity have dominion over me" (Psalm 119:133).

We gain an understanding from the Bible of the correct relationship between our efforts and God's undertaking for our deliverance. "When the heart yields to the influence of the Spirit of God, the conscience will be quickened, and the sinner will discern something of the depth and sacredness of God's law, the foundation of His government in heaven and on earth. The 'Light, which lighteth every man that cometh into the world,' illumines the secret chambers of the soul, and the hidden things of darkness are made manifest. John 1:9."[47]

When the teachings of the Bible are made the controlling influence in our lives, and when the mind and heart are brought under its restraining power, the evils that now exist in our thinking will find no place. The teachings of the Word of God should, therefore, control mind and heart so that the life may

---

47   E. G. White, *Steps to Christ*, 24.

demonstrate the enabling power of God's grace. Through His Word we become connected to Him.

A caution is in order here. Only genuine faith that the Bible in truth is the Word of God triggers and unleashes its power. A Bible seated on a lintel or placed on a coffee table, though revered, will do nothing for the household or individual. Though the Bible's thoughts are inspired, the particular words in and of themselves have no intrinsic power. The words must be believed and assimilated into the heart and mind in order to receive any benefit. "For the word of God is quick, and powerful, and sharper than any twoedged sword, piercing even to the dividing asunder of soul and spirit, and of the joints and marrow, and is a discerner of the thoughts and intents of the heart" (Hebrews 4:12).

Attempting to use the words of the Bible without having a living faith in them is futile. This fact is evident in the temptation of Christ by the devil, when Satan quoted the Scriptures. While his quoting a scriptural text revealed that he was well acquainted with the Bible's contents, his knowledge did not transform him into a loving, Christ-like being. The seven sons of Sceva used the name of Jesus as if the name alone had power, but they discovered that quoting the sacred name carried with it no results. As faith takes hold of the truths conveyed by the words, they produce power in the life.

The lack of faith in the Word renders it impotent to the unbeliever. "Without faith it is impossible to please him: for he that cometh to God must believe that he is, and that he is a rewarder of them that diligently seek him" (Hebrews 11:6). Combining truth with error, or supplanting Biblical teachings with religious rituals or traditions can also accomplish this neutralizing effect. Jesus warned the people of His day that they were guilty of this evil. He said, "Making the word of God of none effect through your tradition, which ye have delivered: and many such like things do ye" (Mark 7:13).

By faith in the Word of God great things have been done. Believers "through faith subdued kingdoms, wrought righteousness, obtained promises, stopped the mouths of lions. Quenched the violence of fire, escaped the edge of the sword, out of weakness were made strong, waxed valiant in fight, turned to flight the armies of the aliens. Women received their dead raised to life again" (Hebrews 11:33–35).

The promise is "if any of you lack wisdom, [James wrote] let him ask of God, that giveth to all men liberally, and upbraideth not; and it shall be given him. But let him ask in faith, nothing wavering. For he that wavereth is like a wave of the sea driven with the wind and tossed" (James 1:5, 6). Yes, "every word of God is pure: he is a shield unto them that put their trust in him" (Proverbs 30:5).

> [Jesus said,] I am the vine, ye are the branches: He that abideth
> in me, and I in him, the same bringeth forth much fruit: for
> without me ye can do nothing. If a man abide not in me, he is

cast forth as a branch, and is withered; and men gather them, and cast them into the fire, and they are burned. If ye abide in me, and my words abide in you, ye shall ask what ye will, and it shall be done unto you. Herein is my Father glorified, that ye bear much fruit; so shall ye be my disciples. As the Father hath loved me, so have I loved you: continue ye in my love. If ye keep my commandments, ye shall abide in my love; even as I have kept my Father's commandments, and abide in his love. (John 15:5–10)

The freedom of man is only possible when the condition of becoming one with Christ is realized. Christ said, "The truth shall make you free" (John 8:35), and He is the truth. Consequently, the restoration to one's self comes by a willing subjection to God.

The only way in which we can gain a more perfect comprehension of truth is by keeping the heart tender and subdued by the Spirit of Christ; sin can triumph only by enfeebling the mind and destroying the liberty of the person. The soul must, therefore, be cleansed from vanity and pride and vacated of all that has held it in custody. Christ must be enthroned within! This is the greatest challenge for mankind—giving up self. Crucifying the flesh is torturous, but how sweet when the victory comes.

Man cannot overcome his own astuteness, prowess, perspicacity, or intelligence. "Can the Ethiopian change his skin [asked the Lord], or the leopard his spots? Then may ye also do good, that are accustomed to do evil" (Jeremiah 13:23). The intellect, education, and natural ability all have a part to play, but when it comes to victory over self and the devil, they are powerless. By them, an external show of right behavior can be produced, but they are useless at transforming the heart. It is impossible for us, of ourselves, to escape from the ditch of sin in which we are sunken. Our hearts are evil, and we cannot change them. "Who can bring a clean thing out of an unclean? not one" (Job 14:4). "The carnal mind is enmity against God: for it is not subject to the law of God, neither indeed can be" (Romans 8:7).

The power to change is not inherent or self-generated. That power, which must work within, must come from above. For "every good gift and every perfect gift is from above, and cometh down from the Father of lights, with whom is no variableness, neither shadow of turning. Of his own will begat he us with the word of truth, that we should be a kind of firstfruits of his creatures" (James 1:17, 18). David acknowledged the source of his deliverance when he wrote, "He sent from above, he took me, he drew me out of many waters. He delivered me from my strong enemy, and from them which hated me: for they were too strong for me" (Psalm 18:16, 17). "There must be a power working from within, a new life from above, before men can be changed from sin to holiness. That power is Christ. His grace alone can quicken the lifeless faculties of the soul, and attract it to God, to holiness."[48] Simply stated, only the gospel of the grace of God can uplift the soul, and nothing can stir the heart and awaken the power of the soul other than the contemplation of the love of God made palpable by His Son.

Through the omnipotent power of the Holy Spirit the grace of Christ is made available to sinners, and becomes the defense of every contrite soul. Therefore, Christ will not permit one who in penitence and faith claims His protection to pass under the enemy's power. He has committed Himself through heaven's Comforter to be by the side of His tempted and tried ones. Hence, there cannot be any such thing as failure, loss, impossibility, or defeat. As did Paul, they can say, "I can do all things through Christ who strengthens me" (Philippians 4:13 NKJV). Then the tempted and tried should not wait to adjust all the difficulties, but rather look to Jesus, their Helper.

> When, under the temptations of Satan, men fall into error, and their words and deportment are not Christ-like, they may not realize their condition, because sin is deceptive, and tends to deaden the moral perceptions. But through self-examination, searching of the Scriptures, and humble prayer, they will, by the aid of the Holy Spirit, be enabled to see their mistake. If they then confess their sins and turn from them, the tempter will not appear to them as an angel of light, but as a deceiver, an accuser of those whom God desires to use to his glory. Those who acknowledge reproof and correction as from God, and are thus enabled to see and correct their errors are learning precious lessons, even from their mistakes. Their apparent defeat is turned into victory. They stand trusting not to their own strength, but to the strength of God. They have earnestness, zeal, and affection, united with humility, and regulated by the precepts of God's word. Thus they bring forth the peaceable fruits of righteousness. The Lord can teach them his will, and they shall know the doctrine, whether it be of God. They walk not stumblingly, but safely, in a path where the light of heaven shines.[49]

---

48   Ibid., 18.
49   E. G. White, "The Duty of Confession," *The Review and Herald*, December 16, 1890.

GAINING THE MASTERY

The body should not be the master of the life; the mind should. In the battle for the mastery, the desires of the flesh must be kept in check. In his warfare over temptation, the apostle Paul wrote testimony to the Corinthian believers: "I keep under my body, and bring it into subjection: lest that by any means, when I have preached to others, I myself should be a castaway" (1 Corinthians 9:27). To the Galatians he wrote:

This I say then, Walk in the Spirit, and ye shall not fulfill the lust of the flesh. For the flesh lusteth against the Spirit, and the Spirit against the flesh: and these are contrary the one to the other: so that ye cannot do the things that ye would. And they that are Christ's have crucified the flesh with the affections and lusts. (Galatians 5:16, 17, 24)

Among whom also we all had our conversation in times past in the lusts of our flesh, fulfilling the desires of the flesh and of the mind; and were by nature the children of wrath, even as others. (Ephesians 2:3)

Peter knew this mastering was possible. He wrote, "Dearly beloved, I beseech you as strangers and pilgrims, abstain from fleshly lusts, which war against the soul" (1 Peter 2:11). "That he [man] no longer should live the rest of his time in the flesh to the lusts of men, but to the will of God" (1 Peter 4:2). Victory is certain. The One who demonstrated the unyielding quest to overthrow the foe undergirds its certainty. To vanquish the lower passions was a test He bore, and because He conquered, He is able to urge the weak and fainting with enticements of rewards to achieve what is within their reach—triumph over sin. Jesus encouraged:

He that hath an ear, let him hear what the Spirit saith unto the churches; To him that overcometh will I give to eat of the tree of life, which is in the midst of the paradise of God. . . . He that hath an ear, let him hear what the Spirit saith unto the churches; He that overcometh shall not be hurt of the second death. . . . He that hath an ear, let him hear what the Spirit saith unto the churches; to him that overcometh will I give to eat of the hidden manna, and will give him a white stone, and in the stone a new name written, which no man knoweth saving he that receiveth it. . . . He that overcometh, and keepeth my works unto the end, to him will I give power over the nations. (Revelation 2:7, 11, 17, 26)

Him that overcometh will I make a pillar in the temple of my God, and he shall go no more out: and I will write upon him the name of my God, and the name of the city of my God, which is new Jerusalem, which cometh down out of heaven from my God: and I will write upon him my new name. . . . . To him that overcometh will I grant to sit with me in my throne, even as I also overcame, and am set down with my Father in his throne. (Revelation 3:12, 21)

He that overcometh shall inherit all things; and I will be his God, and he shall be my son. (Revelation 21:7)

If victory were not possible, then all the promised enticements would be like displaying delightful food just beyond the reach of a chained, starving man while the onlooker watches with glee at the frantic, desperate, yet futile efforts. God does not play thus with his children.

When the mind is not under the direct influence of the Spirit of God, Satan can mold it as he chooses. All the rational powers which he can control he will carnalize. He is directly opposed to God in his tastes, views, preferences, likes and dislikes, choice of things and pursuits; there is no relish for what God loves or approves, but a delight in those things which He despises.[50] The devil will use your mind if you give it to him.[51]

[In contrast,] "when the mind is stored with Bible truth, its principles take deep root in the soul, and the preferences and tastes become wedded to truth, and there is no desire for debasing, exciting literature that enfeebles the moral powers and wrecks the faculties God has bestowed for usefulness. Bible knowledge will prove an antidote for the poisonous insinuations received through unguarded reading.[52]

He "who desires to be a partaker of the divine nature" needs to realize "that he must escape the corruption that is in the world through lust." The battle is relentless, because the enemy does not give up easily, but the victory is sure. The struggling of the soul must be constant and earnest against the evil imaginings. The resistance has to be persistently maintained against the temptation to sin in thought or act. Since He has promised to "keep us from falling" (Jude 24), it is

---

50   E. G. White, *In Heavenly Places*, 163.
51   "Ellen G. White Comments" *Seventh-day Adventist Bible Commentary*, vol. 6, ed. Francis Nichol (Washington, DC: Review and Herald Publishing Association), p. 1105.
52   E. G. White, *The Review and Herald*, November 9, 1886.

our privilege; therefore, we must by faith, keep the soul from every stain.[53]

By meditating on the Scriptures, we are to think soberly and candidly upon the things that pertain to our eternal salvation. "We should dwell upon the character of our dear Redeemer and Intercessor." Review in your contemplation the infinite mercy and love of Jesus. The sacrifice made for you will call for most serious and solemn reflection. Let your curiosity delve deeper into the wonders of the glorious plan of salvation. Force your mind to seek to grasp and absorb the rich mystery of godliness; the incarnation, and living trajectory and purpose of the One who came to save us. Our faith and love will grow stronger; our prayers will become more fervent and intelligent. This is the reward for those who constantly contemplate heavenly themes.[54]

It is incumbent upon us to understand how to cooperate with heaven for our victory and salvation. Because "we have a vigilant foe, who is ever upon our track to take advantage of every weakness,"[55] we likewise must be vigilant. "Put ye on the Lord Jesus Christ, and make not provision for the *flesh*, to fulfil the *lusts* thereof" (Romans 13:14, emphasis added). In other words, if you have a weakness toward alcohol, then stay away from it. If you have a bent toward stealing, move away from situations or occasions where the temptation to steal is the strongest. If for some reason it is not possible to avoid the temptation, then resist.

If there is a desire to be free from the bondage of smoking, do not keep the cigarettes at a hand's reach. Throw them away. Also, in the battle for the mastery, we should not allow our minds to be overstrained or the body to be enfeebled. When this happens, Satan "can take advantage, and press the soul with his fiercest temptations," causing a downfall. In order to prevent this, the will must be exercised. "Submit yourselves therefore to God. Resist the devil, and he will flee from you. Draw nigh to God, and he will draw nigh to you. Cleanse your hands, ye sinners; and purify your hearts, ye double minded" (James 4:7, 8). We are admonished to "Be *sober*, be *vigilant*; because your adversary the devil, as a roaring lion, walketh about, seeking whom he may devour " (1 Peter 5:8, emphasis added).

In order to avoid becoming victimized by Satan's devices, we must vigilantly guard the avenues of the soul. Stay away from that which will suggest impure thoughts through reading, seeing, or hearing. The mind must not be permitted to contemplate or ingest every thought or subject that the devil may suggest.[56] We are not to allow our minds to be wastebaskets for the depositing of Satan's scraps. In the battle against evil suggestions, Paul wrote:

---

53   E. G. White, *The Review and Herald*, June 12, 1888, with author's paraphrase.
54   Ibid., with author's paraphrase.
55   E. G. White, "Come Ye Yourselves Apart . . . and Rest Awhile," *The Review and Herald*, November 14, 1893.
56   E. G. White, *The Acts of the Apostles*, 518, author's paraphrase.

Whatsoever things are true, whatsoever things are honest, whatsoever things are just, whatsoever things are pure, whatsoever
things are lovely, whatsoever things are of good report; if there
be any virtue, and if there be any praise, think on these things.
(Philippians 4:8)

Adding Peter's insightful counsel, he wrote:

Therefore, prepare your minds for action, keep sober in spirit,
fix your hope completely on the grace to be brought to you at
the revelation of Jesus Christ. As obedient children, do not be
conformed to the former lusts which were yours in your ignorance, but like the Holy One who called you, be holy yourselves
also in all your behavior. (1 Peter 1:13–15 NASB).

The Holy Spirit is the only one who can "attract the mind upward, and
habituate it to dwell on the pure and the holy."[57] We must, therefore, realize and
crave His abiding divine support and continuous presence in our lives. In order
to gain that help, we must earnestly pray and maintain constant vigilance. In short,
with the help of God we are to be the guardians of our own thoughts. Otherwise, we
will be mere puppets being unconscious of our manipulated thoughts.

How does this work? When a suggestion comes, it is usually in the guise
of your own thoughts. As Satan and his cohorts study humanity, they are able
to detect, by observation and reactions or responses to his suggestions, what
our weaknesses are. When he takes note of the body language, he is able to
determine just how to fashion his specious approach. His strategy is to subtly
implant temptations, so clothed in disguise, that they appear to be the host's
own thoughts. His aim is to have his temptation lodge in the mind.

The duller the conscience, the less the person is cognizant of the devil's
efforts, and the easier it is to yield. The unwary assumes the thoughts to have
their origin in himself and of his own volition, and because of this assumption,
the thoughts are then acted on. Thus, "when lust hath conceived, it bringeth
forth sin, and sin, when it is finished, bringeth forth death" (James 1:15).

However, when a person begins to study and believe the Word of God, and
appropriate its principles, his sensitivity to the enemy becomes heightened and
keener. Through the enlightenment of the Scriptures, the mind becomes more
sharpened and capable of perceiving the influence. "The entrance of thy words
giveth light; it giveth understanding unto the simple" (Psalm 119:130).

The Word of God becomes like an alarm system or security surveillance
camera to the thinking process. The more of the Word a person stores in the
mind, the tighter does the mesh become. It, therefore, affords the mind sharper
discrimination to decipher and to more readily reject undesirable thoughts. The
Word then has a sanctifying effect on the mind and character. The promise is,

---

57   *Patriarchs and Prophets*, 460.

"Sanctify them through thy truth: thy word is truth" (John 17:17). This is why the psalmist pleaded, "Order my steps in thy word: and let not any iniquity have dominion over me" (Psalm 119:133).

When a thought is introduced, it may be immediately detected. However, generally speaking, it may not be recognized until it has lingered for a while. Whenever the thought is recognized, regardless of whether it is instantly, or you realize that you have been harboring the thought for a while, you have to deal with it. As soon as you are cognizant of it, ask first for forgiveness, and then instantly attack the thought with the Word. Select the memorized or chosen promises that address the sinful thought. Bring the verses or verse to the forefront. Then, after you repeat the texts or text over and over again, let the divine thoughts of the Scriptures push out the evil suggestion. Only the divine power of the Omnipotent can controvert the onslaught of the enemy.

At first, it may take perseverance. Do not become discouraged because you did not realize you had been harboring the insinuated thought. It may take a while until it becomes habitual to turn the current of your mind in the right direction. Nevertheless, if you are vigilant, eventually it will happen. Once the victory is gained, it will become easier the next time. The more of the Scriptures put to memory, the more the mind expands and creates a greater capacity and sensitivity to the stealthy approach of the intruder. Thus, the enemy's suggestions are easier to detect.

By the aid of the Holy Spirit, God's words stored up in the memory become like radar. The mind becomes more fitted up with God's standard of truth and purity. This enables the conscience to become more cognizant of the difference between good and evil, between the holy and the profane. The thinking process is thus enlightened and, armed with holy thoughts, capable of not only detecting but also of expulsing the evil thoughts and developing the faith to "quench all the fiery darts of the wicked" (Ephesians 6:16).

The "medium through which truth or error finds a lodging place in the mind" is either through sight or hearing. It is through the same thought-process of the "mind that truth or error is received, but it makes a decided difference whether we believe the Word of God or the sayings of men."[58] By faith in the power of the Word the mind is fortified with the "divine nature, having escaped the corruption that is in the world through lust" (2 Peter 1:4). Through this means, man, by meditating on God's promises, becomes free of external manipulation. He is then able to cast "down imaginations, and every high thing that exalteth itself against the knowledge of God, and bringing into captivity every thought to the obedience of Christ" (2 Corinthians 10:5).

Our confidence is therefore placed, not on self, but upon the Lord for the victory. "The salvation of the righteous is of the Lord: he is their strength in the

---

58   E. G. White, *Selected Messages*, Book 1, 346.

time of trouble. And the Lord shall help them, and deliver them: he shall deliver them from the wicked, and save them, because they trust in him" (Psalm 37:39, 40). Though we are no match for so powerful a foe, we have our "Big Brother" who will aid us in the warfare—the Lord Jesus Christ. The expulsion of corrupt or sinful thoughts is the act of the soul itself. God will not remove them.

A person's thoughts manipulate the hand to steal or the feet to walk in evil paths. The limbs by themselves have no ability to act independently of the mind, which is the control tower of the person. Nevertheless, though we have the ability to control our limbs, we have no inherent power to free ourselves from Satan's control. But "when we desire to be set free from sin, and in our great need cry out for a power out of and above ourselves, the powers of the soul are imbued with the divine energy of the Holy Spirit, and they obey the dictates of the will in fulfilling the will of God."[59]

We are to look upon Satan as a conquered foe. Jesus gained the victory for us on the cross, and it is His desire that we accept that victory as our own. When I was a young boy, I heard and, therefore, knew more about the devil than God. There are professed Christians who "think and speak altogether too much about the power of Satan." They seem mesmerized by the tales of his prowess. "They think of their adversary, they pray about him, [and] they talk about him. [Consequently,] he looms up greater and greater in their imagination."[60] The same is true today, but even if it is true that Satan is a powerful being, we need to remember that we have a more powerful Savior. He cast the evil one from heaven (see Revelation 12:7–9), and He can cast him from our minds. Satan is well pleased when we magnify his power. "Why not disappoint him? Why not talk of Jesus? Why not magnify His power and His love?"[61]

Time has revealed that man, in his own strength, could not overcome Satan, which is why Christ came from the royal courts of heaven to help man. There was no doubt that Adam in Eden, with his superior advantages, might have conquered Satan by withstanding his temptations. The test of the tree of knowledge of good and evil attests to that. However, it was not possible for man after his fall, and when he became separated from God (see Isaiah 59:2), to resist the temptation of Satan in his own strength. In order to restore man to strength and victory over the enemy, Christ humbled Himself, taking man's nature and combining it with his divine power; all this so that He could reach man where he is.

The prophet Micah wrote:
Who is a God like unto thee, that pardoneth iniquity, and passeth by the transgression of the remnant of his heritage? He retaineth not his anger for ever, because he delighteth in mercy.

---

59   E.G. White, *The Desire of Ages*, 466.
60   Ibid., 493.
61   Ibid.

He will turn again, he will have compassion upon us; he will subdue our iniquities; and thou wilt cast all their sins into the depths of the sea" (Micah 7:18, 19).

Here we are told that God will subdue or bring under control our iniquities. Yet, He invites us to cooperate with Him. Therefore, "Let the wicked forsake his way, and the unrighteous man his thoughts: and let him return unto the Lord, and he will have mercy upon him; and to our God, for he will abundantly pardon" (Isaiah 55:7).

Remember, "it is faith that connects us with heaven, and brings us strength for coping with the powers of darkness. In Christ, God has provided all the means for subduing every sinful trait, and resisting every temptation, however strong. [Sadly though,] many feel that they lack faith, and therefore they remain away from Christ." They erroneously think that since they do not have faith, there is no hope for them. Many consider faith a supernatural element bestowed only upon the spiritually elite. This again is a ploy of the archenemy. "Let these souls, in their helpless [sense of] unworthiness, cast themselves upon the mercy of their compassionate Savior." In this matter it is useless to look to self. Look to Christ! "He who healed the sick and cast out demons when He walked among men is the same mighty Redeemer today." Divine faith is not something that you somehow look into the inner recesses of the mind, grab and exercise. It actually comes from God through His Word.[62] "So then faith comes by hearing, and hearing by the word of God" (Romans 10:17).

It is simple! He promised, and you believe the outcome to be true. You act upon the promise looking, not at your inabilities, but rather upon His abilities as described in the promise. The apostle Paul describes faith this way: "What is faith? It is the confident assurance that something we want is going to happen. It is the certainty that what we hope for is waiting for us, even though we cannot see it up ahead" (Hebrews 11:1 TLB). Don't look into the empty caverns of the mind; look to the fullness of His promises that, when taken a hold of, strengthen and fortify the mind. Grasp His promise: "Him that cometh to me I will in no wise cast out" (John 6:37). Like the demon-possessed boy's father, cast yourself at His feet with the cry, "Lord, I believe; help Thou mine unbelief" (Mark 9:24). If you do this, you can never perish—never!

Faith can be strengthened only by humiliation of heart and through fervent prayer with fasting. Self must be emptied and replaced with the Spirit and power of God. Faith, with earnest, persevering entreaties "that leads to entire dependence upon on God, and unreserved consecration to [Him]—can alone [succeed] to bring men the Holy Spirit's aid in the battle against principalities and powers,

the rulers of the darkness of this world, and wicked spirits in high places."[63]

---

62   Ibid., 429, with author's paraphrase.
63   Ibid., 431, with author's paraphrase.

EXORCISING A SPIRIT

The task of delivering a person from demonic possession may be undertaken once there is conclusive evidence that the person is, indeed, possessed. If time permits, persons with a sound Christian walk with Christ, whose lives give evidence of the fact, should be summoned to participate. Each one must make sure that, upon approaching the victim, he or she has confessed all known sins to God. He or she must feel devoid of any guilt that would impede or short-circuit God's power to deliver.

> In such cases of affliction, where Satan has control of the mind, before engaging in prayer there should be the closest self-examination to discover if there are not sins which need to be repented of, confessed, and forsaken. Deep humility of soul before God is necessary, and firm, humble reliance upon the merits of the blood of Christ alone. Fasting and prayer will accomplish nothing while the heart is estranged from God by a wrong course of action. Read Isaiah 58:6, 7, 9–11.[64]

Each person needs to search his or her heart and soul and be assured that he or she is at peace with God. Once this assurance is secured, they then can approach the situation with freedom to appeal to God without a troubled conscience.

The specific venue or place of meeting is not the primary concern. Most of the encounters Christ had with demonically possessed people were in the vicinity of the temple, synagogues, homes, or out in the open. (See Matthew 8:15, 16, 31; 9:33; Mark 1:39; John 18:20.) There were no prearranged or prescheduled meetings. The encounters were all spontaneous and usually abrupt. Except for the case of the father and demon-possessed son encounter with the disciples, the confrontations erupted in reaction to Christ's holy life and ministry. So if the encounter with a possessed person occurs in the same abrupt, unanticipated circumstances, then the spiritual preparation mentioned above demands an instant self-evaluation. Like Christ's prayer practice, the habitual daily communion with God affords the divine connection needed and will suffice to deal with the powers of darkness.

---

64   E. G. White, *Counsels on Health*, 377.

On the other hand, if the intervention permits time for preparation, then an appropriate location should be selected. Those officiating need to evaluate the case to make sure that possession is indeed suspected. When it is determined that spiritual deliverance is needed, then the team performing the deliverance should (if possible) surround the victim in question. Then on bended knee, with the open Bible in hand, all—one by one, doing "all things . . . decently and in order" (1 Corinthians 14:40)—must offer their pleas and petitions to God in behalf of the victim. In these cases the "the earnest prayers of His faithful followers"[65] are necessary. "The effectual fervent prayer of a righteous man availeth much" (James 5:16).

It is crucial here to remember that it is not the *prayer* that has power, but the *One* receiving the prayer Who has the power. It is also imperative that those praying not presume to enter into a discussion or debate with the demons. (See the next chapter.) Remember, you are seeking by earnest prayer to bring the forces of heaven to war with the evil forces of earth. Therefore, the intercession and communication should be with heaven. Bring to your aid the sure promises of God found in the Holy Scriptures.

If the encounter is abrupt, then the person handling the problem, need not kneel down. Rather, they should engage with the same assurance of victory while standing and fixing the attention on the afflicted one. Some resort to making the statement, "I rebuke you." However, the example of the angel when "contending with the devil he disputed about the body of Moses, durst not bring against him a railing accusation, but said, The Lord rebuke thee" (Jude verse 9). Remember, the power is in the Lord, not in the person performing the attempted exorcism.

With the authority vested in the Word of God, the men of God may have to declare, "In the name of the Lord, depart from him/her." Or as Paul stated, "I command thee in the name of Jesus Christ to come out of her" (Acts 16:18). Stick to affirming the directive irrespective of the response that may come from the possessed person. Continue to rely upon that holy name for deliverance. Cite or quote the commands and words of the Scriptures for the needed authority in the struggle. Sing with living faith hymns of victory and praises to the Lord. Be persistent until the victory is secured.

Hymns such as "There's Power In The Blood," "What A Friend We Have In Jesus," Abide With Me," "The Old Rugged Cross," and "Rock of Ages," may be sung interspersed throughout the contest. Most of these hymns are found in most Christian hymn books.

Following, are Bible promises that need to be read our loud. Psalm 91 is my preferred choice. In this psalm the powers at play and the victor are revealed.

---

65   E. G. White, *Testimonies for the Church*, vol. 1, 299.

He that dwelleth in the secret place of the most High shall abide under the shadow of the Almighty. I will say of the Lord, He is my refuge and my fortress: my God; in him will I trust. Surely he shall deliver thee from the snare of the fowler, and from the noisome pestilence. He shall cover thee with his feathers, and under his wings shalt thou trust: his truth shall be thy shield and buckler. Thou shalt not be afraid for the terror by night; nor for the arrow that flieth by day; Nor for the pestilence that walketh in darkness; nor for the destruction that wasteth at noonday. A thousand shall fall at thy side, and ten thousand at thy right hand; but it shall not come nigh thee. Only with thine eyes shalt thou behold and see the reward of the wicked. Because thou hast made the Lord, which is my refuge, even the most High, thy habitation; There shall no evil befall thee, neither shall any plague come nigh thy dwelling. For he shall give his angels charge over thee, to keep thee in all thy ways. They shall bear thee up in their hands, lest thou dash thy foot against a stone. Thou shalt tread upon the lion and adder: the young lion and the dragon shalt thou trample under feet. Because he hath set his love upon me, therefore will I deliver him: I will set him on high, because he hath known my name. He shall call upon me, and I will answer him: I will be with him in trouble; I will deliver him, and honour him. With long life will I satisfy him, and shew him my salvation. (Psalm 91:1–16)

The angel of the Lord encampeth round about them that fear him, and delivereth them. (Psalm 34:7)

He answered, Fear not: for they that be with us are more than they that be with them. (2 King 6:16)

Fear thou not; for I am with thee: be not dismayed; for I am thy God: I will strengthen thee; yea, I will help thee; yea, I will uphold thee with the right hand of my righteousness. (Isaiah 41:10)

My help cometh from the Lord, which made heaven and earth. He will not suffer thy foot to be moved: he that keepeth thee will not slumber. Behold, he that keepeth Israel shall neither slumber nor sleep. The Lord is thy keeper: the Lord is thy shade upon thy right hand. The sun shall not smite thee by day, nor the moon by night. The Lord shall preserve thee from all evil: he shall preserve thy soul. (Psalm 121:2–7)

Ye are of God, little children, and have overcome them: because greater is he that is in you, than he that is in the world. (1 John 4:4)

The Lord is good, a strong hold in the day of trouble; and he knoweth them that trust in him. (Nahum 1:7)

Turn you to the strong hold, ye prisoners of hope. (Zachariah 9:12)

For though we walk in the flesh, we do not war after the flesh: (For the weapons of our warfare are not carnal, but mighty through God to the pulling down of strong holds;) Casting down imaginations, and every high thing that exalteth itself against the knowledge of God, and bringing into captivity every thought to the obedience of Christ. (2 Corinthians 10:3–5)

Return, O Lord, deliver my soul: oh save me for thy mercies' sake. For in death there is no remembrance of thee: in the grave who shall give thee thanks. (Psalm 6:4)

Mine eyes are ever toward the Lord; for he shall pluck my feet out of the net. Turn thee unto me, and have mercy upon me; for I am desolate and afflicted. The troubles of my heart are enlarged: O bring thou me out of my distresses. Look upon mine affliction and my pain; and forgive all my sins. Consider mine enemies; for they are many; and they hate me with cruel hatred. O keep my soul, and deliver me: let me not be ashamed; for I put my trust in thee. Let integrity and uprightness preserve me; for I wait on thee. (Psalm 25:16–21)

In thee, O Lord, do I put my trust; let me never be ashamed: deliver me in thy righteousness. Bow down thine ear to me; deliver me speedily: be thou my strong rock, for an house of defence to save me. For thou art my rock and my fortress; therefore for thy name's sake lead me, and guide me. Pull me out of the net that they have laid privily for me: for thou art my strength. Into thine hand I commit my spirit: thou hast redeemed me, O Lord God of truth. (Psalm 31:1–4)

The Lord shall help them, and deliver them: he shall deliver them from the wicked, and save them, because they trust in him. (Psalm 37:40)

Withhold not thou thy tender mercies from me, O Lord: let thy loving kindness and thy truth continually preserve me. For innumerable evils have compassed me about: mine iniquities have taken hold upon me, so that I am not able to look up; they are more than the hairs of mine head: therefore my heart faileth me. Be pleased, O Lord, to deliver me: O Lord, make haste to help me. Let them be ashamed and confounded together that seek after my soul to destroy it; let them be driven backward and put to shame that wish me evil. (Psalm 40:11–14)

Offer unto God thanksgiving; and pay thy vows unto the most High: and call upon me in the day of trouble: I will deliver thee, and thou shalt glorify me. (Psalm 50:14, 15)

Make haste, O God, to deliver me; make haste to help me, O Lord. Let them be ashamed and confounded that seek after my soul: let them be turned backward, and put to confusion, that desire my hurt. (Psalm 70:1, 2)

In thee, O Lord, do I put my trust: let me never be put to confusion. Deliver me in thy righteousness, and cause me to escape: incline thine ear unto me, and save me. Be thou my strong habitation, whereunto I may continually resort: thou hast given commandment to save me; for thou art my rock and my fortress.

Deliver me, O my God, out of the hand of the wicked, out of the hand of the unrighteous and cruel man. For thou art my hope. (Psalm 71:1–5)

For he shall deliver the needy when he crieth; the poor also, and him that hath no helper. He shall spare the poor and needy, and shall save the souls of the needy. He shall redeem their soul from deceit and violence: and precious shall their blood be in his sight. (Psalm 72:12–14)

Deliver me, O Lord, from mine enemies: I flee unto thee to hide me. Teach me to do thy will; for thou art my God: thy spirit is good; lead me into the land of uprightness. Quicken me, O Lord, for thy name's sake: for thy righteousness' sake bring my soul out of trouble. (Psalm 143:9–11)

They shall fight against thee; but they shall not prevail against thee; for I am with thee, saith the Lord, to deliver thee. (Jeremiah 1:19)

I will make thee unto this people a fenced brasen wall: and they shall fight against thee, but they shall not prevail against thee: for I am with thee to save thee and to deliver thee, saith the Lord. And I will deliver thee out of the hand of the wicked, and I will redeem thee out of the hand of the terrible. (Jeremiah 15:20, 21)

The famous "Lord's Prayer," in Matthew 6:9–13, is another promise of deliverance, a prayer that can be recited in the battle. Romans 7:24, 25 is another. It reads: "O wretched man that I am! who shall deliver me from the body of this death? I thank God through Jesus Christ our Lord." For those who are fearful of death, here are two precious promises:

Forasmuch then as the children are partakers of flesh and blood, he also himself likewise took part of the same; that through death he might destroy him that had the power of death, that is, the devil; And deliver them who through fear of death were all their lifetime subject to bondage. (Hebrews 2:14, 15)

Wherefore he is able also to save them to the uttermost that come unto God by him, seeing he ever liveth to make intercession for them. (Hebrews 7:25)

Remember, again, that it is living faith in the Author of the Word, Jesus Christ, that provides the victory. The demons can detect whether or not those involved have a living connection with the Savior. I have known of cases of those attempting to perform exorcisms, and the demons have been able to point to their secret faults. They do so with the hope of discouraging the efforts, defeating by intimidation, and impugning those trying to help the victim.

Christ is the answer. If those participating have committed mistakes, and in themselves feel unworthy, even then, a humble recognition of their errors to the Lord can remove the barrier and empower and make efficacious the simple and humble, who place their trust in Christ. Lift up Christ as the all-powerful deliverer! Call upon His name as the only name under heaven in which there is salvation. Make your strong pleas at the Throne of Grace. Call upon the help of the Omnipotent. Persevere.

Once the battle is engaged, there is no stopping until the victory is gained. (At times, we needed to pray for hours. At other times, the conquest came without much resistance.) There are circumstances when the enemy has such a stronghold on the victim that the struggle is intense. The atmosphere becomes dense, oppressive. The hair on the flesh may well stand up. There may be writhing. The body of the possessed may move in a sinuous, snakelike movement. Screaming or yelling out filthy profanities or sacrilegious vulgarity may spout from the victim. Nevertheless, the praying team must stick to its objective and not allow these manifestations to distract it. Again, do not dialogue with the demons but with God. If persistent, the objective will be gained, and the soul will be delivered.

The intercession must continue until there is clear evidence that the person is delivered. Usually, the person's convulsions cease, the tremors stop, the screaming or yelling subsides, and the person becomes conscious and coherent. Once this takes place, then it is clear that the victory has been gained.

The Lord provided this promise: "These signs shall follow them that believe; in my name shall they cast out devils" (Mark 16:17).

SELF-PROCLAIMED EXORCIST!

On September 11, 2000, newspapers around the world carried the story about how Satan had invaded the Vatican in Rome and screamed insults at Pope John Paul II (1920–[2005]) through the agency of a teenage girl [Anneliese Michel], reported to have been a "splendid girl in terms of purity and goodness" before being possessed by the devil at the age of 12. The 19-year-old began shouting in a "cavernous voice" during a general papal audience in St. Peter's Square. Despite the efforts of the pope to quiet the attack, the Prince of Darkness laughed at the Holy Father's efforts to drive him away. When Vatican guards attempted to constrain the girl, she violently pushed them back in a display of superhuman strength.

Vatican exorcist Father Gabriele Amorth said that he and another exorcist, Father Giancarlo Gramolazzo, had previously worked with the girl and that the pope had spent half an hour with her the day before the incident and had also exorcised the teenager. However, it soon became apparent when the girl began insulting the pope and speaking in unknown tongues during the papal audience that neither of the exorcisms had managed to banish Satan."[66]

In the Bible there is only one reference to the word "exorcist." Luke wrote, "Then certain of the vagabond Jews, exorcists, took upon them to call over them which had evil spirits the name of the Lord Jesus, saying, We adjure you by Jesus whom Paul preacheth" (Acts 19:13). The Greek word is *exorkistes*, which means, "one who employs a formula of conjuration for expelling demons."[67] It is the practice of expelling demons or other evil spirits from a person they have possessed. These vagabond Jews were "itinerant Jewish exorcists" (Acts 9:13 RSV). These impostors were going about seeking to benefit themselves by employing

66   "Exorcism," *Encyclopedia of the Unusual and Unexplained: Religious Phenomena,* http://www.unexplainedstuff. com/Religious-Phenomena/Exorcism.html (accessed March 4, 2012).

67   *Strong's Analytical Concordance, s.v. exorkistes.*

the names of Paul and Jesus. These Jews professed to cure diseases by charms and spells. Though an ancient practice, it is still a part of many current religions.

Today, an exorcist is an individual supposedly endowed with extraordinary spiritual powers or abilities. In their practice, exorcists make use of prayers, set formulas and gestures, and religious material such as icons, symbols, amulets, etc. They assume these items have inherent powers in themselves.

In antiquity, "the Babylonians, for example, saw every illness as traceable to the work of demons. . . . The typical non-Hebrew dweller in Mesopotamia lived his life constantly in fear and danger of evil spirits. Amulets were widely favored to ward off such encounters, but the chief recourse for protection was found in the form of ceremonies of incantation, administered by a professional priest/exorcist. In the ceremony [not unlike the practice of some in "deliverance ministry" today] the officiating priest sought to discover which demon or demons were troubling the afflicted, the better to conduct successfully the appropriate required ceremony. The ritual not only utilized certain incantation rites but also employed specific verbal formulae blurred magic, religion, and disease."[68]

Whether the person is a practitioner or novice, the potential for error is great, because most do their incantations solely from impressions. The reality is that few understand or know the danger commensurate either to victim or practitioner. The sad story of Anneliese and the pope, and her resulting death, underscores the tragic outcome of would-be exorcists attempting the exercise. Several dangers need mentioning.

1. It is dangerous for mortals to presume that they have power over the enemy. Adam in the prime of his creation, endowed with keen intellect, was no contest for the wily foe. "Adam reasoned with the enemy, thus giving him an advantage. Satan exercised his power of hypnotism over Adam and Eve, and this power he strove to exercise over Christ."[69] Those who assume they can hold some demon to an appointment, and then at that appointed time coerce it to cooperate, are deluded. Rather than leading people away from Satan, they actually make it possible through their daring to make contact with the powers of the darkness. Why did our first parents fall? They entered into conversation with Satan.

Christ the supreme Ruler of the universe did not enter into controversy with the devil. "It is unsafe to enter into controversy, or parley with Satan."[70] "Bear in mind that it is none but God that can hold an argument with Satan."[71] (See Job 1:6–12.) Remember: "None but Christ could engage in battle with him [Satan], enduring successfully the temptations which he had beset the human family."[72]

68   "'Spiritual Warfare' and 'Deliverance Ministry' and Seventh-day Adventists"
69   *Seventh-day Adventist Bible Commentary*, vol. 5, 1081.
70   *Testimonies for the Church*, vol. 3, 483.
71   *Seventh-day Adventist Bible Commentary*, vol. 5, 1083.
72   E. G. White, "Christ's Victory Gained through Pain and Death," *Signs of the Times*, March 26, 1894.

The Saviour of the world had no controversy with Satan, who was expelled from heaven because he was no longer worthy of a place there. He who could influence the angels of God against their Supreme Ruler, and against His Son, their loved Commander, and enlist their sympathy for himself, was capable of any deception. Four thousand years he had been warring against the government of God and had lost none of his skill or power to tempt and deceive.[73]

Satan will go to the extent of his power to harass, tempt, and mislead God's people. He who dared to face, and tempt, and taunt our Lord, and who had power to take Him in his arms and carry Him to a pinnacle of the temple, and up into an exceedingly high mountain, will exercise his power to a wonderful degree upon the present generation, who are far inferior in wisdom to their Lord, and who are almost wholly ignorant of Satan's subtlety and strength. In a marvelous manner will he affect the bodies of those who are naturally inclined to do his bidding. Satan exults that he is regarded as a fiction. When he is made light of, and represented by some childish illustration, or as some animal, it suits him well. He is thought so inferior that the minds of men are wholly unprepared for his wisely laid plans, and he almost always succeeds well. If his power and subtlety were understood, many would be prepared to successfully resist him.[74]

2.   "For they are the spirits of devils, working miracles, which go forth unto the kings of the earth and of the whole world, to gather them to the battle of that great day of God Almighty" (Revelation 16:14). Facing these superior beings in man's puny strength is futile. Yet exorcists insist on "looking" to confront them. They forget that it was a being of keen intellect, one that occupied a high position among the angelic throng, who finally became a rebel. There is no human being with enough intellectual and sufficient astuteness to match him. Adam, who was created in purity of thought and mind, was not able to withstand Satan's subtlety. How then can sinful erring men, after 6,000 years of degeneracy and dwarfing, presume to tackle such a powerful foe?

Men who hold damnable heresies will dare those who teach the word of God to enter into controversy with them, and some who teach the truth have not had the courage to withstand a challenge from this class, who are marked characters in the word of God. Some of our ministers have not had the moral courage to say to these men: God has warned us in His word in regard to you. He has given us a faithful description of your character and

73   E. G. White, *Confrontation*, 45.
74   *Testimonies for the Church*, vol. 1, 341.

of the heresies which you hold. Some of our ministers, rather than give this class any occasion to triumph or to charge them with cowardice, have met them in open discussion. But in discussing with spiritualists they do not meet man merely, but Satan and his angels. They place themselves in communication with the powers of darkness and encourage evil angels about them.[75]

3. Some people profess to have power to cast out devils. They set a date, confront the devil at their own appointed time, and seek to have a conversation with that demon. They attempt to force the devils to identify themselves; then after accomplishing this feat, they "cast them out." For a person, (irrespective of his mental acuity) to attempt to hold a discussion with the prince of the power of the air and match his wits is ludicrous. It is tantamount to a two-year-old boy making an attempt at debating the "Theory of Relativity" with Einstein. So it is with those who venture upon grounds where angels fear to tread.

> Probably the chief characteristic running as a common thread through almost all variations of contemporary "deliverance ministry" is the predilection of entering into dialogue with the spirits in which the demons are asked to identify themselves, indicate the days, months, or years of their "possession," and answer other questions of a similar nature, before being dispossessed of their prey in the name of Jesus Christ.[76]
>
> If the children of men would follow the example of Christ, and hold no converse with the enemy, they would be spared many a defeat at his hands.[77]

This is the warning! "You have even supposed that power is given you to cast out devils. Through your influence over the human mind men and women are led to believe that they are possessed of devils, and that the Lord has appointed you as His agents for casting out these evil spirits."[78] "The work of declaring persons possessed of the devil, and then praying with them, and pretending to cast out evil spirits, is fanaticism, which will bring into disrepute any church which sanctions such work."[79] "Shall self-confident, fanatical men come to these humble souls assuring them that they are possessed of evil spirits, and after praying with them, affirm that the devil is cast out? Such are not the manifestations of the Spirit of God."[80] "When one offers to exhibit these peculiar manifestations, this is decided evidence that it is not the work of God."[81]

We should keep in mind that we have a wily foe to contend with, one that is constantly seeking to draw us away from God. The awareness of this reality will cause us to flee to our refuge and cling to the Lord.

---

75   *Testimonies for the Church*, vol. 3, 485.
76   "'Spiritual Warfare' and 'Deliverance Ministry' and Seventh-day Adventists."
77   E. G. White, "Tempted in All Points Like as We Are," *The Bible Echo*, November 15, 1892.
78   *Selected Messages*, Book 2, 45.
79   Ibid., 46.
80   Ibid., 47.
81   Ibid., 100.

There are many who fail to distinguish between the rashness of presumption and the intelligent confidence of faith. Satan thought that by his temptations he could delude the world's Redeemer to make one bold move in manifesting His divine power, to create a sensation, and to surprise all by the wonderful display of the power of His Father in preserving Him from injury. He suggested that Christ should appear in His real character, and by this masterpiece of power, establish His right to the confidence and faith of the people, that He was indeed the Saviour of the world. If Christ had been deceived by Satan's temptations, and had exercised His miraculous power to relieve Himself from difficulty, He would have broken the contract made with His Father, to be a probationer in behalf of the race."[82]

When He was in the wilderness of temptation, Christ had no controversy with Satan. For 4,000 years Satan had been warring against God's government, and during those millenniums, he had not diminished in the least in his abilities and power to tempt and deceive. He, who could so influence the angels of heaven that he could gain their sympathy against their Supreme Ruler, was capable of any deception.

4. Exorcism can lead the self-proclaimed exorcist into self-exultation and pride, and thus make themselves an easy conveyance and channel for the evil one. Unlike the seventy who were sent out by Christ on their first mission, exorcists of today boast and exult over their power with demons. While the Seventy had supernatural endowments given them by Christ, today's boastful, self-proclaimed exorcists rely on their own prowess. "When the Seventy returned from their journey, they said to Jesus, Lord, even the devils are subject unto us through Thy name (Luke 10:17). Jesus answered, "I beheld Satan as lightning fall from heaven" (verse 18). In other words, it was pride that caused *him* to fall.

5. There is no example in the Scriptures, other than the seven sons of Sceva, of individuals dedicated solely or exclusively to the work of casting out devils. Therefore, there is no biblical model for such an exclusive ministry within the Christian faith. All of Christ's followers were commissioned to the work of saving souls. In the package, lending them efficacy in ministry, they were given different gifts. Yet not once in the lists of spiritual gifts (Romans 12; 1 Corinthians 12; Ephesians 4) is there any mention of exorcism. In other words, because it is not an exclusive gift, then any genuine believer is offered the authority to cast out devils.

Jesus added, "Notwithstanding in this rejoice not, that the spirits are subject unto you; but rather rejoice, because your names are written in heaven" (verse

---

82   *Confrontation*, 84.

20). Do not rejoice in the possession of power, as Christ's disciples did, lest you lose sight of your dependence upon God. Be cautious; otherwise, self-sufficiency will crop up, and you will wind up working in your own strength, rather than in the spirit and power of your Lord. Self is ever ready to take the credit if any measure of success attends the work. Self is flattered and exalted, and the impression is not made upon other minds that God is all and in all. The apostle Paul said, "When I am weak, then am I strong" (2 Corinthians 12:10).

> When we have a realization of our weakness, we learn to depend upon a power not inherent. Nothing can take so strong a hold on the heart as the abiding sense of our responsibility to God. Nothing reaches so fully down to the deepest motives of conduct as a sense of the pardoning love of Christ. We are to come in touch with God, then we shall be imbued with His Holy Spirit, that enables us to come in touch with our fellow men. Then rejoice that through Christ you have become connected with God, members of the heavenly family. While you look higher than yourself, you will have a continual sense of the weakness of humanity. The less you cherish self, the more distinct and full will be your comprehension of the excellence of your Saviour. The more closely you connect yourself with the source of light and power, the greater light will be shed upon you, and the greater power will be yours to work for God. Rejoice that you are one with God, one with Christ, and with the whole family of heaven."[83]

"Ye which are spiritual [encouraged the apostle Paul], restore such an one in the spirit of meekness" (Galatians 6:1). By intercessory prayer, bolstered up by faith, you can force back the power of the evil one. Be as a healing balsam to the bruised and wounded one by speaking words of faith and courage.

6. Leading a person to submit to the exercise of being exorcised (when it is not concretely certain that there is devil possession) can and usually results in the person being emotionally and mentally compromised. Rather than a devil being cast out, the reality is that the person is made subject to demonic presence in his or her life. This can result in depression or other mental abnormalities.

This was the case of a young lady in England who was encouraged to see a Pentecostal preacher claiming the power of deliverance. The girl was subjected to the woman's influence, and the girl ended up having erratic behavior afterward. According to the pastor, she appeared to be irrevocably mentally handicapped.

Perhaps the challenge comes when a person who claims the power of an exorcist actually appears to be successful in his or her practice. Whether there is success or not, the real test of a true agent of the Lord is not in demonstrative displays of power. Rather, the acid test is in his or her fruits of character. Jesus declared:

---

83   *The Desire of Ages*, 493.

Beware of false prophets, which come to you in sheep's clothing, but inwardly they are ravening wolves. Ye shall know them by their fruits. Do men gather grapes of thorns, or figs of thistles? Even so every good tree bringeth forth good fruit; but a corrupt tree bringeth forth evil fruit. A good tree cannot bring forth evil fruit, neither can a corrupt tree bring forth good fruit. Every tree that bringeth not forth good fruit is hewn down, and cast into the fire. Wherefore by their fruits ye shall know them. (Matthew 7:15–20)

The words of Christ were intended to unmask the imposter. Anyone with enough smarts can learn to imitate or perform an act. However, a consistent sterling character is difficult to counterfeit. Like the Egyptian magicians who were able to reproduce the same miracle that God wrought through Moses, there are modern "Egyptian magicians" today whose uncanny abilities astonish the onlooker.

There is no question that the same prowess and power present in Moses' day is active today. Notice what Jesus said in reference to counterfeit practitioners:

Not every one that saith unto me, Lord, Lord, shall enter into the kingdom of heaven; but he that doeth the will of my Father which is in heaven. Many will say to me in that day, Lord, Lord, have we not prophesied in thy name? and in thy name have cast out devils? and in thy name done many wonderful works? And then will I profess unto them, I never knew you: depart from me, ye that work iniquity. (Matthew 7:21–23)

A safe guide for deciphering between the genuine and the false is to observe the "fruit." The true servant of Christ is "firm in principle, fearless in duty, zealous in the cause of God, yet humble and lowly, gentle and tender, patient toward all, ready to forgive, manifesting love for souls for whom Christ died. [When this is evident,] we do not need to inquire: Are they Christians?" The evidence given is unmistakable "that they have been with Jesus and learned of Him." On the contrary, when the opposite traits of pride, vanity, frivolousness, worldly-mindedness; when they are "avaricious, unkind, censorious," there is no need to "be told with whom they are associating, who is their most intimate friend. They may not believe in witchcraft; but, notwithstanding this, they are holding communion with an evil spirit."[84]

Another biblical guide is found in the book of Isaiah. "When they shall say unto you, Seek unto them that have familiar spirits, and unto wizards that peep, and that mutter: should not a people seek unto their God? for the living to the dead? To the law and to the testimony: if they speak not according to this word, it is because there is no light in them" (Isaiah 8:19, 20). Notice that the litmus test here has to do with a measurement by which the genuine will be

---

84   *Testimonies for the Church*, vol. 5, 224.

determined from the fake. The ruler to measure with is the Ten Commandment Law of God. John, the apostle, wrote, "Hereby we do know that we know him, if we keep his commandments. He that saith, I know him, and keepeth not his commandments, is a liar, and the truth is not in him. But whoso keepeth his word, in him verily is the love of God perfected" (1 John 2:3–5).\

Suppose a person declares to be a follower of Christ, but he is embezzling funds. He is stealing; he is not in harmony with God's law. If he makes the claim to follow God, and yet knowingly disregards God's explicit commandments, he cannot be representing the Lord of heaven. If the person uses his ministry to exalt self, or has moral problems, you can write off that person as a true representative of Christ.

Another way to scrutinize the validity of a true or false spirit is to test their relationship with Christ. The Apostle John wrote:

> Beloved, believe not every spirit, but try the spirits whether they are of God: because many false prophets are gone out into the world. Hereby know ye the Spirit of God: Every spirit that confesseth that Jesus Christ is come in the flesh is of God: And every spirit that confesseth not that Jesus Christ is come in the flesh is not of God: and this is that spirit of antichrist, whereof ye have heard that it should come; and even now already is it in the world. (1 John 4:1–5)

The Bible says, "Without controversy great is the mystery of godliness: God was manifested in the flesh, justified in the Spirit, seen of angels, preached unto the Gentiles, believed on in the world, received up into glory" (1 Timothy 3:16). There are no two ways about it. Either Christ is fully God who partook of human flesh and returned to his heavenly abode (see John 1:1–3, 14), or the professor is a liar. Notice it does not say, "god," but rather "God." To doubting Thomas, Christ was not "a god" but "My Lord and my God" (John 20:28). The use of Christ's name, therefore, is not sufficient. Anyone can claim, "Lord, Lord."

THE ROLE OF TEMPTATION

It is clear from the biblical story of Job that Satan cannot touch the mind or intellect, unless we yield it to him. (See Job, chapters 1 and 2.) However, the devil will use the mind if we surrender it to him. Like an invader, he stalks at the door of the mind. He is anxious to see an opening to cast in his thoughts. This is what the Bible terms "temptation." It is no secret that we are all subject to it. Because people are tempted, it becomes one of the most effective ways for the devil to make a person feel shackled to a particular sin or weakness of the flesh. Once the temptation is lurking in the mind, Satan insinuates that this is sin. People who do not know the difference are led to believe that since they are already sinning in the mind due to the temptation suggested, they might as well give in to the thought and carry out the action.

Temptation is not sin. Christ was tempted and yet without sin. It is written of Him (see Matthew 4:1–10): "For we have not an high priest which cannot be touched with the feeling of our infirmities; but was in all points tempted like as we are, yet without sin" (Hebrews 4:15). Temptation becomes sin only when the thought is dwelt or acted upon. For once a person dwells on that thought, it becomes part of the thinking process. Let's see what the Bible tells us about temptation.

1. James 1:2, 12: "My brethren, count it all joy when ye fall into divers temptations. . . . Blessed is the man that endureth temptation: for when he is tried, he shall receive the crown of life, which the Lord hath promised to them that love him. " We should be happy about temptation. Why?

2. We find the answer in James 1:3, 4: "Knowing this, that the trying of your faith worketh patience. But let patience have her perfect work, that ye may be perfect and entire, wanting nothing." Temptation is an endurance test. As we are faced with temptation, and resist and overcome the suggestion, it works patience. This developed patience contributes to increased spiritual strength. As the apostle Peter wrote:

> Beside this, giving all diligence, add to your faith virtue; and to virtue knowledge; and to knowledge temperance; and to temperance patience; and to patience godliness; and to godliness brotherly kindness; and to brotherly kindness charity. For if

these things be in you, and abound, they make you that ye shall neither be barren nor unfruitful in the knowledge of our Lord Jesus Christ. (2 Peter 1:5–8)

What is the source of temptation? In writing to the Thessalonians, Paul wrote, "Lest by some means the tempter have tempted you" (1 Thessalonians 3:5). While it is true that the devil is the tempter, the reality is that there must be a responding chord to tempt. To this issue James wrote:

Let no man say when he is tempted, I am tempted of God: for God cannot be tempted with evil, neither tempteth he any man: But every man is tempted, when he is drawn away of his own lust, and enticed. Then when lust hath conceived, it bringeth forth sin: and sin, when it is finished, bringeth forth death. (James 1:13–15)

The devil may use lust as a means of leading into sin. The question may be asked, "How does the enemy know my weakness?" Because he has tested the victim, he knows there exists a propensity in that direction. He has been using some form of sensory ability to detect which suggestions we are more prone to respond to. All he has to do is make the suggestions and then read the actions and body responses. Once he throws out the temptation, he watches for the sinner to take the bait. If the tactic is successful, he continues to prod until the victim falls prey and becomes habitual in the thought or action. By this means he hopes the sinner continues down the path to destruction until he is locked in the current that leads to death.

Because this is the process taken by the devil, the Lord must work to counter not only the consequence, but also the cause. The good news is that Jesus not only can save us from death, He is also able to deliver us from the temptation that leads to death. The question is "How?" Jesus was also tempted by the devil, and His temptations were very much more severe than are ours. He came off victorious; thus He can impart to us the same power of resistance that He exercised. Because He faced the devil's temptations, and He unflinchingly did not yield to them, He showed us how to overcome.

In Matthew, chapter 4, He responded to the devil three times with the following words: "It is written." We can do the same.

Here is how He can help us.

1. Let us look at Hebrews: "For in that he himself hath suffered being tempted, he is able to succour them that are tempted" (2:18).

For we have not an high priest which cannot be touched with the feeling of our infirmities; but was in all points tempted like as we are, yet without sin. Let us therefore come boldly unto the throne of grace, that we may obtain mercy, and find grace to help in time of need" (Hebrews 4:15, 16).

2. The question is "What should we do when we're tempted?" Verse 16 says: "Let us, then, feel very sure that we can come before God's throne where there is grace. There we can receive mercy and grace to help us when we need it" (NCV). In other words, run to the One who can help.

3. Peter supports this. "The Lord knoweth how to deliver the godly out of temptations, and to reserve the unjust unto the day of judgment to be punished" (2 Peter 2:9).

4. We are not to worry about, or be fearful of temptation. It does not matter where you try to hide, be it a cave, convent, monastery, or if you become a recluse, temptation will find you there.

> Beloved, think it not strange concerning the fiery trial which is
> to try you, as though some strange thing happened unto you:
> but rejoice, inasmuch as ye are partakers of Christ's sufferings;
> that, when his glory shall be revealed, ye may be glad also with
> exceeding joy. (1 Peter 4:12, 13)

5. Our Lord, who permits us to be tempted, uses temptation to prove our faith. Wherein ye greatly rejoice, though now for a season, if need be, ye are in heaviness through manifold temptations: That the trial of your faith, being much more precious than of gold that perisheth, though it be tried with fire, might be found unto praise and honour and glory at the appearing of Jesus Christ" (1 Peter 1:6, 7).

6. God, in allowing us to be tempted, knows that every temptation met, resisted, and overcome will contribute to the growth and sanctification of our characters. That way we can be prepared for the second coming of Jesus.

If the devil succeeds in luring us to fall into the trap of temptation, then he seeks by that very fall to usher in discouragement. Sometimes it seems as if discouragement has a gleam of humility. In reality discouragement is more destructive than a temptation itself. Discouragement is a consequence of wounded self-love. It was this that defeated Israel.

> They journeyed from mount Hor by the way of the Red sea, to
> compass the land of Edom: and the soul of the people was much
> discouraged because of the way. And the people spake against
> God, and against Moses, Wherefore have ye brought us up out of
> Egypt to die in the wilderness? for there is no bread, neither is there
> any water; and our soul loatheth this light bread" (Numbers 21:4, 5).

Elijah was overwhelmed with discouragement and wished he could die (see 1 Kings 19:4). In spite of all that our Lord went through, He refused to become discouraged. "He shall not fail nor be discouraged, till he have set judgment in the earth: and the isles shall wait for his law" (Isaiah 42:4).

Every temptation starts in our thoughts. So is God unfair to permit them to be placed into our frontal lobes? If so, does that give us an excuse for sinning? No! The Bible says explicitly, no! The apostle Paul in 1 Corinthians 10:13 spoke very clearly on this. "There hath no temptation taken you but such as is common to man: but God is faithful, who will not suffer you to be tempted above that ye are able; but will with the temptation also make a way to escape, that ye may be able to bear it."

Don't worry about temptation. It is a sign that the Holy Spirit is working on your heart. By means of temptation the devil tries to make the person fall from his spiritually committed experience, or seeks to discourage the person who desires to become a follower of God. While it is true that unbelievers are controlled by the enemy, they do not understand what temptation is as Christians understand it. So when there is an unclean thought in your mind, you have to decide in that moment to cry to Jesus. Or else, consider your thought very carefully. If the temptation becomes sin, it is your decision, and you are responsible. God has done everything to preserve you from sin.

We have no need to be discouraged when we fail. "For sin shall not have dominion over you" (Romans 6:14). In case we yield to temptation, we have been promised, "My little children, these things I write unto you that you sin not. And if any man sin, we have an advocate with the Father, Jesus Christ the righteous" (1 John 2:1). The biblical preference is not to sin. However, God has promised us: "If we confess our sins, he is faithful and just to forgive us our sins, and to cleanse us from all unrighteousness" (1 John 1:9).

> Therefore I will look unto the Lord; I will wait for the God of my salvation: my God will hear me. Rejoice not against me, O mine enemy: when I fall, I shall arise; when I sit in darkness, the Lord shall be a light unto me. I will bear the indignation of the Lord, because I have sinned against him, until he plead my cause, and execute judgment for me: he will bring me forth to the light, and I shall behold his righteousness. (Micah 7:7–9)
>
> Who is a God like unto thee, that pardoneth iniquity, and passeth by the transgression of the remnant of his heritage? he retaineth not his anger for ever, because he delighteth in mercy. He will turn again, he will have compassion upon us; he will subdue our iniquities; and thou wilt cast all their sins into the depths of the sea. (Micah 7:18, 19)
>
> The Lord thy God in the midst of thee is mighty; he will save, he will rejoice over thee with joy; he will rest in his love, he will joy over thee with singing. (Zephaniah 3:17)

Here is one statement that has been a great encouragement to myself and to many others. "If you have made mistakes, you certainly gain a victory if you see these mistakes and regard them as beacons of warning. Thus you turn defeat into victory, disappointing the enemy and honoring your Redeemer."[85]

---

85   E. G. White, *Christ's Object Lessons*, 332.

Erring humans are prone to mistakes. Even honest hearted people are not exempt. But the problem is not in that we can make a mistake but, rather, what do you do after? Don't to throw in the towel. Consider what has been done, and if possible determine what led to the fall. Then resolve to guard it as a beacon of warning. This way, you can turn your defeat into victory, overcome the enemy and glorify God. The lessons that God sends will always, if learned, bring help in due time. The Bible says, "The steps of a good man are ordered by the Lord: and he delighteth in his way. Though he fall, he shall not be utterly cast down: for the Lord upholdeth him with his hand" (Psalm 37:23, 24). By "trusting, hoping, believing, holding fast the hand of infinite power, you will be more than conquerors."[86] The weak link in this whole matter is self and the inability to recognize that fact.

> When the mind dwells upon self, it is turned away from Christ, the source of strength and life. Hence it is Satan's constant effort to keep the attention diverted from the Saviour and thus prevent the union and communion of the soul with Christ. The pleasures of the world, life's cares and perplexities and sorrows, the faults of others, or your own faults and imperfections—to any or all of these he will seek to divert the mind. Do not be misled by his devices. Many who are really conscientious, and who desire to live for God, he too often leads to dwell upon their own faults and weaknesses, and thus by separating them from Christ he hopes to gain the victory. We should not make self the center and indulge anxiety and fear as to whether we shall be saved. All this turns the soul away from the Source of our strength. Commit the keeping of your soul to God, and trust in Him. Talk and think of Jesus. Let self be lost in Him. Put away all doubt; dismiss your fears. Say with the apostle Paul, "I live; yet not I, but Christ liveth in me: and the life which I now live in the flesh I live by the faith of the Son of God, who loved me, and gave Himself for me." Galatians 2:20. Rest in God. He is able to keep that which you have committed to Him. If you will leave yourself in His hands, He will bring you off more than conqueror through Him that has loved you."[87]

---

86   E. G. White, "A Word of Cheer," *The Southern Work*, December 4, 1902.
87   *Steps to Christ*, 71, 72.

THE THOUGHTS—THE BATTLEGROUND

The work of the archenemy begins in the thoughts. If the thought processes can be captured, then the actions will follow. Hence, the devil seeks through veiled suggestions to charm the mind. Once the temptation is accepted and allowed to take over the reasoning powers, actions follow the thoughts. This is as natural as leaven saturating the meal or salt permeating the food.

Satan first gained access to the celestial beings. He began by complaining "of the supposed defects in the management of heavenly things, and sought to fill the minds of the angels with his disaffection. Because he was not supreme, he sowed seeds of doubt and unbelief. Because he was not as God, he strove to instill into the minds of the angels his own envy and dissatisfaction. Thus the seeds of alienation were planted, afterward to be drawn out and presented before the heavenly courts as originating, not with Satan, but with the angels. So the deceiver would show that the angels thought as he did."[88]

That which Satan had instilled in the minds of the angels—a word here and a word there—opened the way for a long list of suppositions. In his artful way he drew expressions of doubt from them. Then, when interviewed, he accused those whom he had educated.

> The records of some are similar to that of the exalted angel who was given a position next to Jesus Christ in the heavenly courts. Lucifer was enshrouded with glory as the covering cherub. Yet this angel whom God had created, and entrusted with power, became desirous of being as God. He gained the sympathy of some of his associates by suggesting thoughts of criticism regarding the government of God. This evil seed was scattered in a most seducing manner; and after it had sprung up and taken root in the minds of many, he gathered the ideas that he himself had first implanted in the minds of others, and brought them before the highest order of angels as the thoughts of other minds against the government of God. Thus, by ingenious methods of his own devising, Lucifer introduced rebellion in heaven.[89]

88   E .G. White, *The Truth about Angels*, 37.
89   *Seventh-day Adventist Bible Commentary*, vol. 4, 1143.

Satan's beguiling delusions were so concocted that to catch him in his wiles was almost impossible. So subtle was his canny charm that the heavenly host, though of sharp intellect, did not catch on to the scheme in its heinous reality. This condition had existed a long period of time before Satan was unmasked. The outcome of bringing into the open the devil's true motives was war in heaven. Satan was expelled, along with all who would not stand on the side of loyalty to God's government.

Imperceptively, Lucifer "gained the sympathy of some of his associates by suggesting thoughts of criticism regarding the government of God. This evil seed was scattered in a most seducing manner; and after it had sprung up and taken root in the minds of many, he gathered the ideas that he himself had first implanted in the minds of others, and brought them before the highest order of angels as the thoughts of other minds against the government of God."[90]

The clever fiend succeeded in seducing the unsuspecting heavenly intelligences.

> The angels whom he could not bring fully to his side, he accused of indifference to the interests of heavenly beings. The very work, which he himself was doing, he charged upon the loyal angels. It was his policy to perplex with subtle arguments concerning the purposes of God. Everything that was simple he shrouded in mystery, and by artful perversion cast doubt upon the plainest statements of Jehovah. And his high position, so closely connected with the divine government, gave greater force to his representations.[91]

Having accomplished his artful wiles, he was successful in leading the heavenly intelligences into rebellion. Once meeting his objective, he goaded them with the thought that they had gone too far. The dreadful outcome of this rebellion is revealed in the book of Revelation. "There was war in heaven: Michael and his angels fought against the dragon; and the dragon fought and his angels, and prevailed not; neither was their place found any more in heaven" (Revelation 12:7, 8).

The arch apostate possessed keen, shrewd, and cunning ability to implant mental suggestions among beings whose intellect far exceeds that of all humans. His success with the angelic host emboldened him and increased his ability to deceive. If he could implant thoughts in beings that excel in strength, if he could imbue them with his spirit, then what match would man be against such a foe apart from his dependence on God?

---

90   *The Truth about Angels*, 35, 36.
91   Ibid., 36.

SATAN'S CONTROL OVER MEN

Satan has no power to coerce the limbs or motion apart from the consent of the mind. He works through what the Bible calls "temptation." All free moral agents can be tempted by virtue of the fact that they were created with reasoning powers. This is why perfect beings in heaven, while not created with the propensity to sin, could still be tempted. Both human beings as well as angels were endowed with a free will. Hence, they can reason, judge, and thus be capacitated. Concerning the angels free volition, the Bible says, "The angels which kept not their first estate, but left their own habitation, he hath reserved in everlasting chains under darkness unto the judgment of the great day" (Jude 6). Here in this text the fallen angels are indicted for the choice that they made in leaving their first estate.

God alerted man of the dangers of approaching the tree of knowledge of good and evil. This warning gives weight to the reality that Adam was invested with this God-given attribute. Adam had the prerogative of choosing to believe or not to believe God. The ancient record says: "The Lord God commanded the man, saying, Of every tree of the garden thou mayest freely eat: but of the tree of the knowledge of good and evil, thou shalt not eat of it: for in the day that thou eatest thereof thou shalt surely die" (Genesis 2:16, 17). Just as God held Adam accountable, He has made mankind answerable for his own choices and actions.

Precisely because of this responsibility, God enjoins upon us the importance of exercising our wills. Eventually, every individual is to render to God in the judgment an account of his or her words, thoughts, and actions. "God shall bring every work into judgment, with every secret thing, whether it be good, or whether it be evil" (Ecclesiastes 12:14). Jesus said, "I say unto you, that every idle word that men shall speak, they shall give account thereof in the day of judgment. For by thy words thou shalt be justified, and by thy words thou shalt be condemned" (Matthew 12:36, 37).

Because God has endowed man with "thought process," Satan has studied the channels through which Divinity communicates with humanity. Satan's work fills men's hearts with doubt. He leads them to look upon God as a stern judge. He tempts them to sin, and then to regard themselves as too vile to approach their heavenly Father or to excite His pity. The Lord understands all this. Jesus assured His disciples of God's sympathy for them in their needs and weaknesses. Not a sigh is breathed, not a pain felt, not a grief pierces the soul, but the throb vibrates to the Father's heart.

So how is it that the enemy implants thoughts in our minds? For centuries Satan has studied the human anatomy. The devil has been making keen observations. By the familiar channels in which he observes how an individual thinks, he thus implants the thoughts accordingly. Either they come as verbal suggestions, as he did to Christ, or picture suggestions. See Matthew 4:1–11.

Scientists have also been keenly interested in the thinking processes of the mind. "A new study by University of Pennsylvania and Thomas Jefferson University scientists brings this work one step closer to actual mind reading by using brain recordings to infer the way people organize associations between words in their memories."[92]

My wife had an unusual experience in a mall in Portland, Oregon. Coming across a sweater in one of the stores, she found thoughts in her mind. They were suggesting that she should not steal it. Strangely, the sweater was a purple color and one that she said, "I would not be caught dead in it." Second of all, she would not take it even if offered for free because she disliked it so much.

That evening we sat to watch the news, and one report addressed her weird incident. In that particular mall they were experimenting with subliminal messages in the canned music. The issue became a big news item. Because of shoplifting, the mall was using this method to cut down on the theft. The news station played the music so it could be heard normally, and they were able to extract the messages laced within the music. The words were, "I am honest," "I should not steal." A lawsuit ensued, and the mall was forced to abandon its mind-manipulation tactics.

"For as he thinketh in his heart, so is he" (Proverbs 23:7). The body motions respond to the activity of the reasoning powers. Hence, physical motions are activated by what a person thinks. In order for a person to kill, steal, commit an immoral act, or any other activity, whether good or bad, his thought processes must dictate the desire. The thoughts become action and the evil is committed. In this sense the adage, "The devil made me do it," is true. He implants the suggestion, the unwary victim dwells on the thought, the thought engages the motion, and the act is carried out. So what then is the remedy? If Satan seeks to divert the mind to low and sensual things, bring it back again and place it on eternal things; and when the Lord sees the determined effort made to retain only pure thoughts, He will attract the mind, like the magnet, purify the thoughts, and enable them to cleanse themselves from every secret

92   "Mind Reading from Brain Recordings? 'Neural Fingerprints' of Memory Associations Decoded" ScienceDaily (June 26, 2012) Accessed: November 18, 2012. http://www.sciencedaily.com/releases/2012/06/120626172721.htm

sin. "Casting down imaginations, and every high thing that exalteth itself against the knowledge of God, and bringing into captivity every thought to the obedience of Christ" (2 Corinthians 10:5).

> The first work of those who would reform is to purify the imagination. If the mind is led out in a vicious direction, it must be restrained to dwell only upon pure and elevated subjects. When tempted to yield to a corrupt imagination, then flee to the throne of grace and pray for strength from Heaven. In the strength of God the imagination can be disciplined to dwell upon things which are pure and heavenly.[93]

Some, upon sensing their helpless condition, recognize their dependence on God. Although cognizant of their condition, they still want to hold on to some cherished sin or habit. They rationalize that the transgression is not really that offensive to God. By thinking to make a compromise between them and God, they hope that a halfway commitment will at least demonstrate a willingness to receive the help needed.

> [But] a partial surrender to truth gives Satan free opportunity to work. Until the soul-temple is fully surrendered to God, it is the stronghold of the enemy. . . . When the mind becomes confused, when right is considered unessential, and error is called truth, it is almost impossible to make these deceived souls see that it is the adversary who has confused their senses and polluted the soul-temple. A tissue of lies is placed where truth, and truth alone, should be. The word of God is a dead letter to them, and the Saviour's love is unknown.[94]

Some seek to gratify their curiosity and thus tamper with the devil. The Ouija Board has been just a game, but too many have discovered it more than that. Some have seen the answering stick move across the board by itself. Through this, others have entered into the mesmerizing realm of the occult. They have no real faith in spiritualism, and they would start back with horror at the idea of being a medium. Yet they place themselves in a position where Satan can exercise his bewitching power upon them. They do not mean to enter deep into this arena, but their unresisting yielding to the charm of the mysterious leads them on; these people are venturing upon the devil's ground, and they unknowingly allow him to control them. This powerful destroyer considers such his lawful prey, and he will exercise his power upon them against their will. When they wish to control themselves, they cannot. They yielded their mind to Satan, so he holds them captive. No power can deliver the ensnared soul but the power of God in answer to the earnest prayers of His faithful followers.

---

93   E. G. White, *Mind, Character, and Personality*, vol. 2, 595.
94   E. G. White, "Come Out from among Them, and Be Ye Separate," *The Review and Herald*, November 28, 1899.

RESIST THE DEVIL, AND HE WILL FLEE

"Resist the devil, and he will flee from you. Draw nigh to God, and he will draw nigh to you" (James 4:7, 8). First, you must become aware that there is such a being before you can resist; second, there must be recognition of the utter inability of human strength when dealing with such a foe. So how can someone so weak and dependent have the strength or will-power to resist such a powerful and wily being?

Close vigilance and intense prayer are two of our urgent needs. Through watchfulness we can keep at bay those almost undetectable stealthy approaches of the enemy. Self-analysis, when juxtaposed with the scrutiny of holy Biblical principles, can aid us in this close personal surveillance. In our prayers we can pray the prayer of David: "I will set no wicked thing before mine eyes." "Search me, O God, and know my heart: try me, and know my thoughts: and see if there be any wicked way in me, and lead me in the way everlasting" (Psalm 101:3; 139:23, 24, respectively).

We must be distrustful of ourselves and our motives. "The heart is deceitful above all things, and desperately wicked: who can know it?" (Jeremiah 17:9). We must be willing to make efforts commensurate with our true condition (if we realize it) and with the craved deliverance. Paul scolded the Hebrew readers and said, "Ye have not yet resisted unto blood, striving against sin" (Hebrews 12:4). Jesus said, "Strive to enter in at the strait gate: for many, I say unto you, will seek to enter in, and shall not be able" (Luke 13:24).

The sentiments of envy, jealousy, suspicion of others, evil surmising, evil speaking, impatience, selfishness, greed, vanity, and prejudice the devil stealthily implants in our hearts must be uprooted. Having these evils persisting in the heart will neutralize the will for good, strengthen the propensities for evil, and produce traits that will contaminate the soul.

Self is the main source of our problem. We have cultivated our inherited tendencies, and there are times when we justify these tendencies. We see corruption and evils in the churches. We experience personal affronts. Then we notice that the same evils lodge in our own hearts, so we despair and wonder if there is hope for anyone. In feeling that we are not worthy, we may yield to the temptation because we feel that God will not hear us or help us. So, at the point when we most need help, the enemy persuades us not to pray and seek the Lord. We think we must first correct our attitudes before we seek help. Here, in the garb of wanting to be gallant and fix our own problems, we place ourselves just where Satan wants us. Remember what was said in the quote in the chapter entitled "The Role of Temptation": "*By separating them from Christ he hopes to gain the victory.*"[95] Remember, Jesus said, "Without me, ye can do nothing" (John 15:5).

Paul well understood by personal experience the struggle before each believer. For this reason he delineated counsel apropos for the battle. To the Hebrews he wrote:

> Let us lay aside every weight, and the sin which doth so easily beset us, and let us run with patience the race that is set before us, [2]Looking unto Jesus the author and finisher of our faith; who for the joy that was set before him endured the cross, despising the shame, and is set down at the right hand of the throne of God. (Hebrew 12:1, 2)

The focus for victory is not on self but on Him who not only won the battle over sin and its originator; but who also has the power to inspire us to begin and finish the fight. Christ begins by "justifying" us, which qualifies us for the race. However, the work of justification is only the beginning of the Christian experience. We are not only to begin "the race that is set before us" (Hebrew 12:1), but are to continue to "go on unto perfection" (Hebrews 6:1). That requires that we "grow in grace, and in the knowledge of our Lord and Saviour Jesus Christ" (2 Peter 3:18). This is the work of sanctification. Our quest is to be reached as we go from one victory to another through Him who "giveth us the victory" (1 Corinthians 15:57), and who willingly "liveth in me" (Galatians 2:20). The old self must be "transformed by the renewing of" our minds (Romans 12:2) and let "this mind be in you, which was also in Christ Jesus" (Philippians 2:5).

The idea that "I cannot go to Christ when I am in trouble since I don't seek him when I am okay" is dangerous. It sounds pious and full of good and noble purposes. Suppose a child has been warned not to go out into the street to play because he will get hurt. Irrespective of the warning, the child disobeys and gets hurt. The mother, hearing the screams says, "I do not want him to come to me until he takes care of himself, then he can come to me." Can you imagine any loving mother doing that to her child? First of all, most children are incapable of taking care of their own injuries. Second, even if they were capable, no loving parent would not want to be involved in aiding, whether the child can help himself or not. In this matter, the sinner has no strength to heal himself. Satan knows that which is precisely why he tempts to keep the sufferer away from the Deliverer.

---

95   *Steps to Christ*, 71, 72, emphasis added.

[So] we should not make self the center and indulge anxiety and fear as to whether we shall be saved. All this turns the soul away from the Source of our strength. Commit the keeping of your soul to God, and trust in Him. Talk and think of Jesus. Let self be lost in Him. Put away all doubt; dismiss your fears. Say with the apostle Paul, "I live; yet not I, but Christ liveth in me: and the life which I now live in the flesh I live by the faith of the Son of God, who loved me, and gave Himself for me" Galatians 2:20. Rest in God. He is able to keep that which you have committed to Him. If you will leave yourself in His hands, He will bring you off more than conqueror through Him that has loved you.[96]

Be sober, be vigilant; because your adversary the devil, as a roaring lion, walketh about, seeking whom he may devour: Whom resist stedfast in the faith, knowing that the same afflictions are accomplished in your brethren that are in the world. (1 Peter 5:8, 9) Like a roaring lion, Satan is seeking for his prey. He tries his wiles upon every unsuspecting youth; there is safety only in Christ. It is through His grace alone that Satan can be successfully repulsed. Satan tells the young that there is time enough yet, that they may indulge in sin and vice this once and never again; but that one indulgence will poison their whole life. Do not once venture on forbidden ground. In this perilous day of evil, when allurements to vice and corruption are on every hand, let the earnest, heartfelt cry be raised to heaven. "Wherewithal shall a young man cleanse his way?" [Psalm 119:9]. And may his ears be open, and his heart inclined to obey the instruction given in the answer: "By taking heed thereto according to thy word" [Psalm 119:9].[97]

The only safety is to make God our trust. Without divine help, we will be unable to control passions and appetites. In Christ is the very help needed. You can say with the apostle: "Nay, in all these things we are more than conquerors through him that loved us" (Romans 8:37). Again: "But I keep under my body, and bring it into subjection" (1 Corinthian 9:27). God has promised us: "Let the wicked forsake his way, and the unrighteous man his thoughts: and let him return unto the Lord, and he will have mercy upon him; and to our God, for he will abundantly pardon" (Isaiah 55:7).

---

96   Ibid.
97   *Testimonies for the Church*, vol. 2, 409.

DELIVERANCE MINISTRIES

One feature in "deliverance ministry" is the tendency to see a demon or a good angel involved in every human decision and activity. There are two equally serious but opposite extremes to avoid as one is confronted by this baffling phenomena that appears to be supernatural.

a. A virtual denial of the existence of Satan's supernatural workings. This we already covered in a preceding chapter.

b. Satan-made-me-do-it mentality in which the devil is identified as the immediate cause of every misfortune and sinful deed.

Ultimately, all evil is traceable to Satan, the originator of sin. However, Satan and his evil angels are not always directly accountable for every human evil. A mother's dabbling with narcotics, smoking, or alcohol has been linked to children being born with varying mental and physical handicaps. Genetic inheritance also plays a part in passed-on human disabilities. In addition, the environment may contribute to complications in one's mental and physical condition. People may suffer from asbestos, radon gas, allergies from pesticides in food, lead in their teeth fillings, mold spores in the air, lactose resistance, radiation poisoning, etc.

Nevertheless, this does not rule out the possibility of demonic interaction with people who are thus in violation of divine law for human wellness. Nor does it rule out the interplay of demonic influence with people who are doing the best they can with their lives. In other words, one cannot summarily assume that all weaknesses or calamities are of the devil or just nature. Each case must be decided on its own basis and dealt with by taking all of these factors into consideration.

The fact is that fallen man is Satan's lawful captive. As already stated, this was of man's own volition. The good news is that God did not permit this deceitful takeover without a contest. That challenge came in the person of Christ who, on behalf of heaven, made it his mission to rescue man from the power of His great adversary. Man is naturally inclined to follow Satan's suggestions. He cannot successfully resist so terrible a foe unless Christ, the mighty Conqueror, dwells in him, guiding his desires and giving him strength. God alone can limit the power of Satan. Remember, Christ cast out Satan from heaven, and Christ can still dethrone him. Satan declares that he is "going to and fro in the earth, and walking up and down in it" (Job 1:7). He is not off his watch for a single moment, through fear of losing an opportunity to destroy souls. It is important to understand this so as to escape his snares.

While some deceived souls are advocating that he does not exist, he is taking them captive and is working through them to a great extent. Millions are allied to him either through an acknowledged alliance, or through complete ignorance of his existence. Through these agents he exerts his deceptions. On the other hand, Satan knows too well the power that a humble believer can have over him when his or her strength is in Christ. When they humbly entreat the mighty Conqueror for help, the weakest believers, who rely firmly upon Christ, can successfully repulse Satan and his entire host. He is too cunning to come openly, boldly, with his temptations; for then the drowsy energies of the Christian would arouse, knowing he or she can depend upon the strong and mighty Deliverer. Consequently, he steals in unperceived, and works in disguise through the children of disobedience who profess godliness.

Satan will go to the extent of his power to harass, tempt, and mislead. The same being who dared to face, and tempt, and taunt our Lord will exercise his power to a terrible degree upon humanity today. This he will easily accomplish because of the professed believer's inferior wisdom in Christ and his or her almost total ignorance of Satan's subtlety and strength.

He will be able to manipulate the bodies of those who are inclined to do his bidding. He will also, in an awe-inspiring manner, create a euphoric atmosphere in order to cause a feeling of ecstasy that the deluded worshipers will assume to be generated by God. When the devil is thought to be but a mere fiction, he exults. It also suits him well when he is made light of and represented as some half animal, half human creature relegated to some fairy tale. The labels on spice bottles picturing him in his domain makes him an all too familiar personage, neither to be feared nor be concerned about. By all of these false representations created and propagandized by him, he has succeeded in painting himself as inferior. This causes minds to be opened for his delusions. If his power and cunning were understood, many would be prepared to resist him.

Satan was once an exalted angel. Though he was cast out of heaven, his powers have not been abated. On the contrary, subsequent to his fall he has turned his mighty prowess and power against heaven's government. The longer he has observed man, the more he has gained in his knowledge of the weaknesses and vulnerability of his prey.

His only match is Christ, who, when attacked by the most fierce enticements, did not sin. Not even by a thought did He concede in the hellish encounter. The same may be true of us. Christ was fitted for the conflict by the indwelling of the Holy Spirit that fused his humanity with divinity. Because of His victory, He was able to make possible the link of our frail human nature to His powerful divine nature. Having this union with Him, as long as it is tenaciously maintained by faith, will free us from the tentacles of sin.[98]

How this is accomplished, Christ has shown us. By what means did He overcome in the conflict with Satan? By the Word of God. Only by the word could He resist temptation. "It is written," He said. . . . [By His word we are furnished with] "exceeding great and precious promises: that by these ye might be partakers of the divine nature, having escaped the corruption that is in the world through lust." 2 Peter 1:4. Every promise in God's Word is ours. "By every word that proceedeth out of the mouth of God" are we to live [Matthew 4:4]. When assailed by temptation, look not to circumstances or to the weakness of self, but to the power of the word. All its strength is yours. "Thy word," says the psalmist, "have I hid in mine heart, that I might not sin against Thee." "By the word of Thy lips I have kept me from the paths of the destroyer." Psalm 119:11; 17:4.[99]

Satan well knows the power of the Scriptures. That is why he quoted the verses to Christ during his endeavor to tempt Him (see Matthew 4:5, 6). It is from this perspective that he works to undermine faith in the Bible. If he succeeds, he then directs the unwary to other sources of light and power. By this means he gains entrance into minds; therefore, it is dangerous to turn from the plain teachings of the Scriptures. Those who do are inviting the control of demons. The apostle Paul said, "The time will come when they will not endure sound doctrine; but after their own lusts shall they heap to themselves teachers, having itching ears" (2 Timothy 4:3).

> Even him, whose coming is after the working of Satan with all power and signs and lying wonders, and with all deceivableness of unrighteousness in them that perish; because they received not the love of the truth, that they might be saved. And for this cause God shall send them strong delusion, that they should believe a lie" (2 Thessalonians 2:9–11).

This veering away from the holy counsel of God by criticism and speculation has created a vacuum, resulting in the acceptance of spiritualism and theosophy (a philosophy maintaining that knowledge of God may be achieved through spiritual ecstasy, direct intuition, or special individual relations). These modern forms of ancient heathenism have inserted themselves into the thinking not only of the world but also of professed believers.

The conduits that God utilizes to shine divine illumination into the soul are by the direct agency of His Spirit, His Word, or His servants (be it human or angelic). When one ray of light is ignored or discounted, there is a partial

98　*The Desire of Ages*, 123, author's paraphrase.
99　Ibid.

benumbing of the spiritual perceptions. The senses become less keen in discerning a second revealing of light, resulting in increased darkness until it is night in the soul.

Thus, the only way to avoid being dominated by the wicked one is to yield the heart and soul to Christ. A new power takes possession of the heart when a person willingly surrenders to the Lord. An internal change of the desires and will is produced. This is something that man can never accomplish by his own volition. This divine act places a supernatural element into human nature. When this occurs, the soul becomes impregnable to the assaults of the devil. That soul that is yielded to Christ becomes His own stronghold. By His divine power Christ purposes that no other authority will be permitted to inhabit the surrendered disciple. The assurance that "greater is He that is in you, than he that is in the world" becomes a reality.[100]

Therefore, there is no question that we must be under the control of the one or the other of the two great powers that are contending for the supremacy of each soul. Jesus stated, "No man can serve two masters: for either he will hate the one, and love the other; or else he will hold to the one, and despise the other. Ye cannot serve God and mammon" (Matthew 6:24). On another occasion He said, "Enter ye in at the strait gate: for wide is the gate, and broad is the way, that leadeth to destruction, and many there be which go in thereat: because strait is the gate, and narrow is the way, which leadeth unto life, and few there be that find it" (Matthew 7:13, 14). Paul wrote, "Know ye not, that to whom ye yield yourselves servants to obey, his servants ye are to whom ye obey; whether of sin unto death, or obedience unto righteousness?" (Romans 6:16).

The admonition to exercise choice is abounding throughout the Bible. Joshua adjured the Israelites and demanded a decision from them. He proclaimed:

> If it seem evil unto you to serve the Lord, choose you this day whom ye will serve; whether the gods which your fathers served that were on the other side of the flood, or the gods of the Amorites, in whose land ye dwell: but as for me and my house, we will serve the Lord. (Joshua 24:15)

Elijah made a similar appeal to Israel. His challenge was, "How long halt ye between two opinions? If the Lord be God, follow him: but if Baal, then follow him" (1 Kings 18:21).

"It is not necessary to deliberately choose the service of the kingdom of darkness in order to come under its dominion." All that needs to happen is to neglect the union of the heart with Christ. It is incumbent upon each one of us to co-operate with the heavenly agencies; if not, "Satan will take possession of the heart, and will make it his abiding place."[101]

---

100   Ibid., 324, author's paraphrase.
101   Ibid., with author's paraphrase.

In order to resist temptation to sin and the unholy effects of self-love and self-indulgence, we must have a vital connection with God. This can happen only when we have an indwelling Christ, and complete faith in His righteousness, in the heart. This is our only defense. Some are strong willed enough to leave their bad habits. Dread or fear of consequences may even cause some to part ways with Satan, but without a living connection with God, they shall eventually be overcome. "Without a personal intimate relationship with Christ, and a continual communion, we are at the mercy of the enemy."[102] Sooner or later Satan will have his way.

Jesus said, "Learn of me, for I am meek and lowly in heart: and ye shall find rest" (Matthew 11:29). If we are to be victors, we must "enter the school of Christ." There we can daily receive training with continual increments of knowledge and growth in Christ. Through this schooling, "the soul must be delivered from all that is opposed to loyalty to God." As we daily sit at the feet of Jesus, we can learn how to be meek and lowly. By emulating His character, striving to be more like Him, we are delivered from our ideas, habits, and practices that have been entwined into the fabric of our nature by the prince of the air.[103]

Christ accepted the position for the plan that God devised for Him. Since every son and daughter of Adam must meet the devil singlehanded, Christ consented to do the same. If man walks in the way and will of his Maker, the same heavenly powers provided for the aid of Christ to fight successfully the great conflict, are made available to him. As Christ was upheld by heaven's keeping power, so will he who relies on God as Christ relied on Him.[104]

"The Lord is faithful," wrote Paul, "who shall stablish you, and keep you from evil" (2 Thessalonians 3:3). Yes, the power available to Christ to overcome is made available to all who place their trust in Him. The same heavenly intelligences that ministered unto him are also commissioned to minister to those who shall be heirs of salvation. These provisions have been made so that they may overcome every temptation, great or small, as Christ overcame. However, this proviso is not available but to those who earnestly conform to the revealed will of God. Those who parlay with sin and then flee to God when in danger deceive themselves. Remember, without God's aid, failure is certain. There is not a soul secure who thinks he can choose between God and the devil at will.

---

102   Ibid., with author's paraphrase.
103   *Ibid., 330, with author's paraphrase.*
104   E. G. White, *Manuscript Releases*, vol. 6, 383, author's paraphrase.

BEING REPOSSESSED

Another phenomenon to be considered relative to this subject is that of repossession. Though, by the powerful freeing power of Christ, a person may be completely delivered from the iron clutches of the archenemy, he is not henceforth carefree. What ensnared him to begin with can trap him again. With this concern in mind, I believe, Jesus said to the forgiven adulterous woman: "Go and sin no more" (John 8:11).

While speaking to an incredulous gathering, Jesus unveiled to them the consequence of indifference and spiritual carelessness. There was the danger that individuals would trust their supposed safety and not watch. There was concern that a person who found forgiveness and pardon would, presuming upon the goodness of God, think himself to be eternally saved and beyond the reach of being lost. To those Jesus warned:

> The men of Nineveh shall rise in judgment with this generation, and shall condemn it: because they repented at the preaching of Jonas; and, behold, a greater than Jonas is here. The queen of the south shall rise up in the judgment with this generation, and shall condemn it: for she came from the uttermost parts of the earth to hear the wisdom of Solomon; and, behold, a greater than Solomon is here. When the unclean spirit is gone out of a man, he walketh through dry places, seeking rest, and findeth none. Then he saith, I will return into my house from whence I came out; and when he is come, he findeth it empty, swept, and garnished. Then goeth he, and taketh with himself seven other spirits more wicked than himself, and they enter in and dwell there: and the last state of that man is worse than the first. Even so shall it be also unto this wicked generation. (Matthew 12:41–45)

Paul challenged the Roman believers over this point. Just like some Christians in Paul's day who assumed that once they were saved, they were home free, there are sincere Christians today who likewise hold to the same belief. This idea is termed by some "once saved, always saved." Knowing this all-to-well pitfall of the Jews, he uses their election and downfall to underscore the danger. Writing to the Gentile believers he cautioned:

> Thou wilt say then, The branches were broken off, that I might be grafted in. Well; because of unbelief they were broken off, and thou standest by faith. Be not highminded, but fear: For if God spared not the natural branches, take heed lest he also spare not thee. Behold therefore the goodness and severity of God: on them which fell, severity; but toward thee, goodness, *if thou continue in his goodness*: otherwise thou also shalt be cut off. (Romans 11:19–22, emphasis added)

To the Hebrews he wrote, "But Christ as a son over his own house; whose house are we, *if we hold fast the confidence and the rejoicing of the hope firm unto the end*" (Hebrews 3:6, emphasis added).

He warned that that stick-to-it-iveness is essential in the Christian walk. "See that ye refuse not him that speaketh, [he urged]. For if they escaped not who refused him that spake on earth, much more shall not we escape, if we turn away from him that speaketh from heaven" (Hebrews 12:25). The Old Testament followers assumed they had eternal safety on the fact of their proven lineage. Once they were in, it was impossible to be lost. Their contradictory lifestyle, hidden wickedness, and practice of sin they believed had no effect on their salvation.

In a certain city, a lady requested an appointment with me. Upon meeting, she told me her concerns. Her husband was constantly getting drunk and running around with other woman. When I heard that I said, "As a Christian you are probably very concerned about his salvation."

"Oh no, he is saved!" she said. "I am not worried about that. I just wish that he would quit running around with other women."

This idea is opposed to the clear Biblical teaching. The apostle Peter urged,

> For if after they have escaped the pollutions of the world through the knowledge of the Lord and Saviour Jesus Christ, they are again entangled therein, and overcome, the latter end is worse with them than the beginning. For it had been better for them not to have known the way of righteousness, than, after they have known it, to turn from the holy commandment delivered unto them. But it is happened unto them according to the true proverb, The dog is turned to his own vomit again; and the sow that was washed to her wallowing in the mire. (2 Peter 2:20–22)
>
> Ye therefore, beloved, seeing ye know these things before, beware lest ye also, being led away with the error of the wicked, fall from your own steadfastness. (2 Peter 3:17)

Even the angels of heaven are not exempted from this conclusion. Jude wrote, "The angels which kept not their first estate, but left their own habitation, he hath reserved in everlasting chains under darkness unto the judgment of the great day" (Jude 6). The fallen angels at one time enjoyed being in a "saved" relationship with God—saved in the sense that ultimately salvation is nothing more or less than to dwell with God. From the eternal bliss, they chose a different route. Hence, as mentioned before, they were expelled from heaven never more to return.

> It is not only by resistance, but by neglect that the soul is destroyed. . . . There were many in Christ's day, as there are today, over whom the control of Satan for the time seemed broken; through the grace of God they were set free from the evil spirits that had held dominion over the soul. They rejoiced in the love of God; but, like the stony-ground hearers of the parable, they did not abide in His love. They did not surrender themselves to God daily, that Christ might dwell in the heart; and when the evil spirit returned, with "seven other spirits more wicked than himself," they were wholly dominated by the power of evil.[105]

"The last state of that man is worse than the first. Even so shall it be also unto this wicked generation," Jesus said (Matthew 12:45). There is not a person so hardened as one who has been privileged with great light, and yet snubs the Spirit of grace. The apostle Paul wrote:

> It is impossible for those who were once enlightened, and have tasted of the heavenly gift, and were made partakers of the Holy Ghost, and have tasted the good word of God, and the powers of the world to come, if they shall fall away, to renew them again unto repentance; seeing they crucify to themselves the Son of God afresh, and put him to an open shame. (Hebrews 6:4–6)

The usual demonstration in which a person inches on the path to sinning against the Holy Spirit is in their persistent unyielding to His promptings to repent. It is like pushing the snooze button on the alarm clock until the habit leads to a deaf ear to the ringing. Hence, every step in the refusal to yield to surrender to Christ is a step toward the rejection of forgiveness, without which salvation is not attainable. This ultimately leads toward the sin against the Holy Spirit.

Once that threshold is crossed, there is no turning back, no redress, nor is there any more vacuum to fill. The space is commandeered and saturated by the enemy, who at this point latches on to the victim with a sedation, which anesthetizes the conscience. Thus, the result is that the person no longer feels his need of God, and if he intellectually recognizes a lack, there is no ability to be reconnected to the source of power. The choice is eternal in nature.

However, even if the person is possessed, the conscience is still capable of sensing guilt and conviction; as in the case of the demoniac, there is still

105   *The Desire of Ages*, 323.

probation available. Through Christ, deliverance is still possible. The victim can be yanked out of the enemy's clutches and be restored to a sane relationship with his Maker.

The man in the parable from whom the evil spirit had been cast out, but who did not fill the soul with Christ, forcibly exemplifies the need of not only emptying the heart of evil, but of filling the vacuum with the Divine occupant. When the demon returned and discovered that the heart from which he was expelled was "swept and garnished," he was delighted to find it still empty. This time he brought seven companion spirits more wicked than himself and made the condition of the man worse than the first (Luke 11:24–26).

Though the man in this allegory refused to do the work of the devil, the trouble with him was that after the heart was cleaned up and decorated, he failed to invite the presence of the heavenly companion. It is, therefore, not enough to clear and empty the heart. The vacuum must be filled with the spirit of Christ. The graces of the Lord must saturate the heart and mind. We may be sufficiently strong-willed to leave behind many bad habits, and yet the victories are the result of an indwelling Christ, who alone can give lasting victory. We must realize our great deficiency and, then, conversely, the great reservoir of power that is placed at our command. By inviting Christ into our hearts, and maintaining a daily, abiding relationship with him, we may shut the door to any reoccurrence of demonic presence.

In a certain city I studied the Bible with a lady. She was very desirous to know and to put into practice whatever she learned, and she continued the studies for several months. After the completion of the series of studies, she requested baptism. After the baptism, she became very faithful in church attendance and avid in her continued reading of the Scriptures.

After about a year, her attendance and participation in church activities began to dwindle. At first she would miss a service now and then. Then her absence began to be noticeable; she would not attend for weeks. Because her husband was a Jew, but not religious, I wondered if that was a factor in her lack of church attendance. I decided to pay her a home visit.

After arriving and going through the normal greetings and casual "How do you do," I got to the purpose of my visit. She admitted her lukewarmness and delinquent church attendance. Then she changed the subject by asking a question.

"May I share something strange with you?" she asked.

"Of course," I said.

"I don't know if I am losing my mind," she began.

"I have been having some strange experiences."

"Like what?" I asked.

"Well, several months ago, I was lying on my bed. All of a sudden the atmosphere in my room became very heavy and oppressive. Then at the end of my bed, a dark form appeared. I became terrified. I wanted to scream for help, but a paralysis came over me. I just could not move.

"The black form just stood there glaring at me. It was evil. I then remembered that my only hope was to call on the name of Jesus, but I could not even move my mouth. It was a terrible ordeal. Then somehow, I managed to call on the name of the Lord, and the thing disappeared. The experience was so surreal that at first I thought it was a frightful nightmare that I had just awakened from. But no, I had been awake. And unlike the relief that comes when you awake and realize that it was a mere dream, I was left stunned with fear. I shuttered with the thought that there might be a repeat of the same. I hoped that was the end of it, but it has happened several times after.

"What was that?" she anxiously asked.

"It was a demonic presence," I said.

"Why would it come to me? I do not play with Ouija Boards or have any interest in the occult. Why would the devil visit me?"

"Well," I asked, "have you changed anything in your spiritual life since you committed yourself to Christ?"

"No," she said, "not that I know. Well, there is one thing. One day, months after I was baptized, I was cleaning around my bedroom. Then, when I was cleaning my nightstand, I pulled the drawer, and there were the earrings and necklace that I had taken off and had forgotten that I had placed them there.

"As I looked at the jewelry, I was struck with their beauty. I seemed charmed by them. Then picking them up, I went to the mirror to see how they would look on me. As I placed them on my ears and around my neck, they looked so attractive on me. So little by little they once more became a part of my attire. When I went to church, I made sure I did not wear them. Then, since I could not wear my jewels to church, I began to feel uncomfortable in going. It became more natural to stay away. It was after that when I had the experience with the visitant," she concluded.

Yes, many unwary sincere persons do not understand the connections that satanic agencies use as channels for their purposes. I have mentioned the girl, who upon hearing a certain African chant, would become demon-possessed. The practitioners of Voodoo use items belonging to others as channels by which to cast spells or curses on the owner of those items. The Canaanite cult (and most cults in the ancient Near East) included fertility rites involving sympathetic magic based on the assumption that people are supernaturally affected through an object that represents them. Israel was warned to resist this practice because it was completely corrupt and demonic.

The use of rhythmical drumbeats to encourage possession is a normal occurrence in Haiti. Statues or icons of satanic images are also conduits. Anything whose origin is from the occult Satan can use as a come-on for a visit.

It was he who was made with jewels and precious stones as his natural covering. (See Ezekiel 28:13–18.) Therefore, for a person who has come to the knowledge of what the wearing of ornaments can symbolize, the wearing of jewelry acts as an invitation giving permission for demons to respond to that invitation.

When people ask what to do to get rid of evil presences in their homes, I counsel them to get rid of anything that has spiritual significance hanging on the walls, etc. It may be something as innocent as a "lucky charm." Luck or gamble has its origin with Satan. He tried to tempt Christ with a gamble that if presumptuous, angels would catch him before he hit the ground (see Matthew 4:3–10). Certain music, like rock 'n' roll, will serve as an allurement to demonic presence. Sacred music will do the opposite as in the case of King Saul (see 1 Samuel 14:16–23). Amulets[106] are likewise strong channels for demonic interaction. Since they of themselves have no living sense, then the activity generated comes from living beings, utilizing them as mere channels for their work of darkness.

When the lady in the story gave up the wearing of her jewels, the visitations ceased. She was delivered. By breaking the link that demons had to her, and reestablishing her connection with Christ, she found peace.

---

106   An amulet is an ornament or small jewel supposed to have power to protect against evil, danger, or disease.

DEMONS ON ASSIGNMENTS

From a comprehensive look into the Scriptures, there appears to be specific assignments by the prince of darkness for his cohorts. While it is true that these traits did not originate when they were created, it is obvious that these imps have artfully developed skills through the centuries to successfully overcome men. Summarily, the skills are deviant and only tend to morally corrupt, embolden rebellion and defiance, steep into an addiction, and strengthen lustful tendencies or greed.

The Bible mentions a "lying spirit" (1 Kings 22:23, 23), "familiar spirit" (Leviticus 20:27), "spirit of jealousy" (Numbers 5:30), "evil spirit" (Judges 9:23; 1 Samuel 16:14, 15), "perverse spirit" (Isaiah 19:14), "spirit of whoredoms" (Hosea 5:4), "unclean spirit" (Mark 1:23), "dumb spirit" (Mark 9:17), "spirit of infirmity" (Luke 13:11), "spirit of divination" (Acts 16:16), "evil spirit" (Acts 19:15, 16), "spirit of bondage" (Romans 8:15), and the spirit of "disobedience" (Ephesians 2:2).

Below, I have made an effort to identify different spirits and their unseen influences. Their presence is only visible when human beings play out, acting in concert with their inspiration or manipulation. It is like the effects of gravity and obvious only when something or someone is falling; or when the leaves or trees move in response to the effect of the wind. You cannot see the wind, but you can see its effect.

Evil spirits can also materialize just as the loyal angels of God can. One example is the biblical story of King Saul's demonic apparition, which has already been mentioned. Other examples include Satan speaking with Eve, and appearing to Christ in the wilderness of temptation. Today, many of the apparitions parading as the Virgin Mary, or other appearances, are nothing more than spirits attempting to continue to propagate the archenemy's lie that the living never really die. However, most of the time, they prefer to work incognito, undetected, and subtly. Following is a list of demonic characteristics tracing their evil presence, which is just as tangible as the effects of the wind on the leaves of a tree or the gale forces that take down a tree.

Strife:

Satan is ever ready to take advantage when any matter of variance arises, and by moving upon the objectionable, hereditary traits of character in husband or wife, he will try to cause the alienation of those who have united their interests in a solemn covenant before God. In the marriage vows they have promised to be as one, the wife covenanting to love and obey her husband, the husband promising to love and cherish his wife. If the law of God is obeyed, the demon of strife will be kept out of the family, and no separation of interests will take place, no alienation of affection will be permitted.[107]

Intemperance:

Intemperance still continues its ravages. Iniquity in every form stands like a mighty barrier to prevent the progress of truth and righteousness. Social wrongs, born of ignorance and vice, are still causing untold misery and casting their baleful shadow upon both the church and the world. Depravity among the youth is increasing instead of decreasing. Nothing but earnest, continual effort will avail to remove this desolating curse. The conflict with interest and appetite, with evil habits and unholy passions, will be fierce and deadly; only those who shall move from principle can gain the victory in this warfare.

Intemperance is on the increase, in spite of the efforts made to control it. We cannot be too earnest in seeking to hinder its progress, to raise the fallen and shield the weak from temptation. With our feeble human hands we can do but little, but we have an unfailing Helper. We must not forget that the arm of Christ can reach to the very depths of human woe and degradation. He can give us help to conquer even this terrible demon of intemperance.[108]

It is a most difficult matter to unlearn the habits, which have been indulged through life. The demon of intemperance is of giant strength, and is not easily conquered. But let parents begin the crusade against it at their own firesides, in their own families, in the principles they teach their children from their very infancy, and then they may hope for success.[109]

In dealing with the victim of intemperance we must remember that we are not dealing with sane men, but with those who for the time being are under the power of a demon. Be patient and forbearing. Think not of the repulsive, forbidding appearance, but of the precious life that Christ died to redeem.[110]

107   E. G. White, *The Adventist Home*, 106.
108   E. G. White, *Child Guidance*, 401.
109   Ibid., 408.
110   E. G. White, *The Ministry of Healing*, 173.

Selfishness:

> The Saviour read the heart of Judas; He knew the depths of iniquity to which, unless delivered by the grace of God, Judas would sink. In connecting this man with Himself, He placed him where he might, day by day, be brought in contact with the outflowing of His own selfish love. If he would open his heart to Christ, divine grace would banish the demon of selfishness, and even Judas might become a subject of the kingdom of God."[111]

Greed:

> Mercy's pleading resisted, the impulse of evil bore final sway. Judas, angered at an implied rebuke and made desperate by the disappointment of his ambitious dreams, surrendered his soul to the demon of greed and determined upon the betrayal of his Master. From the Passover chamber, the joy of Christ's presence, and the light of immortal hope, he went forth to his evil work—into the outer darkness, where hope was not.[112]

Delusion:

> Christ came to a people who were deceived and deluded by the demon of ambition. At that time they were under the Roman yoke, but they expected One to come who would establish a kingdom from which would be excluded every other people on the earth. He was to break the heathen yoke, to lift up His people, and set them with princes. All nations were to be summoned to appear before the One sent by God, and there called upon to surrender themselves or be consumed.[113]

Passion:

> To every soul things will come to provoke, to stir up anger, and if you are not under the full control of God, you will be provoked when these things come. But the meekness of Christ calms the ruffled spirit, controls the tongue, and brings the whole being into subjection to God. Thus we learn how to bear with the censure of others. We shall be misjudged, but the precious ornament of a meek and quiet spirit teaches us how to bear, how to have pity for those who utter hasty, unadvised words. Any unpleasant spirit displayed is sure to arouse the demon of passion in unguarded hearts. Unholy anger need not to be strengthened, but bridled. It is a spark which will set on fire untamed human nature. Avoid speaking words which will stir up strife. Rather suffer wrong than do wrong. God requires every one of His fol-

111   E. G. White, *Conflict and Couraage*, 285.
112   E. G. White, *Education*, 92.
113   E. G. White, *Lift Him Up*, 135.

lowers, as far as is possible, to live peaceably with all men.[114]

After the death of Samuel, David was left in peace for a few months. Again he repaired to the solitude of the Ziphites; but these enemies, hoping to secure the favor of the king, informed him of David's hiding place. This intelligence aroused the demon of passion that had been slumbering in Saul's breast. Once more he summoned his men of arms and led them out in pursuit of David. But friendly spies brought tidings to the son of Jesse that Saul was again pursuing him; and with a few of his men, David started out to learn the location of his enemy. It was night when, cautiously advancing, they came upon the encampment, and saw before them the tents of the king and his attendants. They were unobserved, for the camp was quiet in slumber. David called upon his friends to go with him into the very midst of the foe. In answer to his question, "Who will go down with me to Saul to the camp?" Abishai promptly responded, "I will go down with thee."[115]

Jealousy:

Saul, however, did not long remain friendly to David. When Saul and David were returning from battle with the Philistines, "the women came out of all cities of Israel, singing and dancing, to meet King Saul, with tabrets, with joy, and with instruments of music." One company sang, "Saul hath slain his thousands," while another company took up the strain, and responded, "And David his ten thousands." The demon of jealousy entered the heart of the king. He was angry because David was exalted above himself in the song of the women of Israel. In place of subduing these envious feelings, he displayed the weakness of his character, and exclaimed. "They have ascribed unto David ten thousands, and to me they have ascribed but thousands: and what can he have more but the kingdom?"[116]

One great defect in the character of Saul was his love of approbation. This trait had had a controlling influence over his actions and thoughts; everything was marked by his desire for praise and self-exaltation. His standard of right and wrong was the low standard of popular applause. No man is safe who lives that he may please men, and does not seek first for the approbation of God. It was the ambition of Saul to be first in the estimation of men; and when this song of praise was sung, a settled conviction entered the mind of the king that David would obtain the hearts of the people and reign in his stead.[117]

114   E. G. White, *Our High Calling*, 274.
115   *Patriarchs and Prophets*, 668.
116   Ibid., p. 650.
117   Ibid.

Unkindness:

> When a man professes to be sanctified, and yet in words and works may be represented by the impure fountain sending forth its bitter waters, we may safely say, That man is deceived. He needs to learn the very alphabet of what constitutes the life of a Christian. Some who profess to be servants of Christ have so long cherished the *demon of unkindness* that they seem to love the unhallowed element and to take pleasure in speaking words that displease and irritate. These men must be converted before Christ will acknowledge them as His children.[118]

Darkness:

> A great work of saving souls remains yet to be done. Every angel in glory is engaged in this work, while every demon of darkness is opposing it. Christ has demonstrated to us the great value of souls in that He came to the world with the hoarded love of eternity in His heart, offering to make man heir to all His wealth. He unveils before us the love of the Father for the guilty race and presents Him as just and the justifier of him that believeth.[119]

Hysterics:

> However earnestly her husband may endeavor to pursue a straightforward course to serve God, she will be his evil angel, seeking to lead him away from righteousness. In her own estimation she is the idol he must worship; in fact, she is Satan's agent, seeking to occupy the place where God should be. She has followed the impulses of her own unconsecrated heart until Satan has almost complete control of her.
>
> Unless there is a change, a time will come soon when this lower nature in the wife, controlled by a will as strong as steel, will bring down the strong will of the husband to her own low level. . . . In this case it is not the woman whom Brother D is dealing with, but a desperate, satanic spirit. The Lord has a work for Brother D to do; but if he is overcome by these outbursts on the part of his wife, he is a lost man, and she is not saved by the sacrifice. . . . His best course with this child-wife, so overbearing, so unyielding, and so uncontrollable, is to take her home, and leave her with the mother who has made her what she is. Though it must be painful, this is the only thing for him to do, if he would not be ruined spiritually, sacrificed to the demon of hysterics and satanic imaginings. Satan takes entire control of her temper and will, and uses them like desolating hail to beat down every obstruction. Her husband can do her no good, but is doing himself in-

118   E. G. White, *The Sanctified Life*, 16, emphasis added.
119   E. G. White, *Sons and Daughters of God*, 278.

calculable harm, and robbing God of the talents and influence He has given. . . .

> Sister D is determined to rule or ruin. I was shown that she has so thoroughly yielded herself into Satan's hands that her husband fears for her reason, but he will make one of the gravest mistakes of his life if he permits himself to be controlled by Satan through the device of his wife. I tell you plainly, she is controlled by demons, and if these evil spirits have their way, your liberty, Brother D, your manhood, is gone; you are a slave to her caprices. . . . She is just as much possessed by a demon as was the man who tore and cut himself when Jesus cast out the devils. . . . Brother D must let Satan rage, and not allow himself to be cut off from religious privileges because his wife desires it.[120]

Heresy:

> Jesus is rich in grace. Draw, constantly draw from Him, for you may have rich supplies. The *demon of heresy* has mapped out the world, and has resolved to possess it as his kingdom. Those who are in his army are numerous. They are disguised, and are subtle and persevering. They resist every divine influence, and employ every instrumentality in order to compass the ruin of even one soul. They possess a zeal, tact, and ability that is marvelous, and press their way into every new opening where the standard of truth is uplifted.[121]

Of Appetite:

God sees that sin has debased and degraded man, but he looks upon him with pity and compassion; for he sees that Satan has him in his power. The demon of appetite in the intoxicating cup has robbed thousands of their reason. Still the Lord draws, draws, draws.

Quite a little number came forward. Among them were two very interesting cases—a man and his wife, still quite young. He was a master workman and overseer of hands who were engaged in building. He was intemperate—often drunk for days together. He had a good, noble-looking countenance, but this was his great weakness—he had formed the habit of intemperance and the demon of appetite controlled him, and his moral power seemed too feeble to overcome this appetite. His wife was a proud, worldly-loving woman. Both were convinced of the truth but neither knew what experimental religion was.[122]

Ambition:

> Christ came to a people who were deceived and deluded by the demon of ambition.[123]

120   E. G. White, *Testimonies on Sexual Behavior, Adultery, and Divorce*, 76, 77.
121   E. G. White, *The Upward Look*, 275, emphasis added.
122   *Manuscript Releases*, vol. 2, 140.
123   E. G. White, *Lift Him Up*, 135.

LINKS BY STEALTH

The means by which Satan seeks access or control of humans are sly. Silently, he waits for opportunities to insert his hellish control. For Christians, he recognizes the formidable barrier in Christ. Hence, he works at distancing them from Christ. The devil's mode of operation is like the scientific experiment of the frog whose water is heated up ever so slowly until it boils in its comfort, or the mosquito that first numbs before he bites.

Satan's work is not abrupt; it is not, to start with, sudden and startling. He will never appear and say, "I am the devil, and I have come to tempt you." Rather he sneaks in like the fowler setting a snare for the unsuspecting bird. He begins by secretly undermining the citadel of principle. He leads poor souls to neglect being true and loyal to God, and he seeks to accomplish this by starting on apparently what some consider to be small matters. Then, by arousing unholy desires, he aims to separate these individuals away from God, the only Source of divine strength. First, it begins with starting down the slippery slope of carelessness. Ultimately, they are left barren, futilely trying to satisfy the longings of their hearts with worldly enterprises, excitement, or temporary immediate gratifications.

Right from the start of man's creation, Satan, like a modern drug-pusher, portrayed the benefits to be gained by imbibing the supposed pleasantries of sin. This approach was successful in seducing mighty angels and, likewise, perfect man. Sad to say, his method is still effective in leading multitudes away from God. The perfect picture of an alluring utopia enticing would-be tourists to a pristine, harmless, and wholesome place still draws thousands. So it is with Satan's allurements. The way of disobedience is made to appear desirable; "but the end thereof are the ways of death" (Proverbs 14:12). Full well do the Scriptures plainly state, "the way of the transgressors is hard" (Proverbs 13:15). Conversely, joyful are they who, having fallen in Satan's trap, learn how bitter the fruits of sin are, and turn from it before it is too late. The Divine admonition is:

> Let the wicked forsake his way, and the unrighteous man his thoughts: and let him return unto the Lord, and he will have mercy upon him; and to our God, for he will abundantly par-

don. For my thoughts are not your thoughts, neither are your ways my ways, saith the Lord. For as the heavens are higher than the earth, so are my ways higher than your ways, and my thoughts than your thoughts. (Isaiah 55:7–9)

Oftentimes Satan appeals to pride and ambition. This weakness prompted King David to number Israel. "The numbering of the people would show the contrast between the weakness of the kingdom" prior to his ascending the throne, and the greatness achieved. The great contrast would tend "to foster the already too great self-confidence of both the king and the people. The Scripture says, 'Satan stood up against Israel, and provoked David to number Israel' [1 Chronicles 21:1]. The prosperity of Israel under David had been due to the blessing of God rather than the ability of her king or the strength of her armies."[124] The result of following this worldly policy was devastating to Israel. The incident is one of arrogance, the proud overstepping of bounds.

Satan's bullish attacks and delusions are strong and subtle, yet the Lord watches over the weak, struggling suppliant who declares his allegiance to Him. Though the affliction may be great, and the battle appears to be more than one can bear, Jesus will not abandon them. If the people persevere, the trials will purify and bring them forth as "gold is tried" (Zechariah 13:9) in the fire. The hazy image of Christ in them will become clearer and clearer until at last it will crystallize into the perfect likeness of the Savior.

When Satan bears down with his temptations, God does not abandon the tried to defeat. He will give needed help to those who call upon Him. His grace will be provided to all who sincerely repent, and especially to those who are seeking to emulate the likeness to His Son.

---

124   *Patriarchs and Prophets*, 746, with author's paraphrase.

THE DEVIL MADE ME DO IT

Because (as stated in the chapter "Deliverance Ministry") there is a tendency to see a demon in every wrong human decision or divergent activity, there is an attempt to try and find a "scapegoat." Taking responsibility for one's own misspoken words or inappropriate actions does not contribute to building the ego or self esteem. It is always easier to shirk the blame or cast it on something or someone else. Hence the charge: "The devil made me do it."

Biblically speaking there is no question that there is either a direct or indirect link between human misdeeds, evil speaking, or evil actions and the devil. The Lord stated unequivocally, when speaking to the religious leaders of His day:

> Ye are of your father the devil, and the lusts of your father ye will do. He was a murderer from the beginning, and abode not in the truth, because there is no truth in him. When he speaketh a lie, he speaketh of his own: for he is a liar, and the father of it. (John 8:44)

When a person commits evil, he or she may be carrying out the promptings of the enemy. However, Satan and his evil angels are not always directly accountable for every human deviation to do evil.

Some people become or are evil by nature and thrive in malicious activity. Of note in Europe's recent history are those who perpetrated the heinous atrocities of the Holocaust. In Africa, in the civil war between the Hutus and the Tutsis in Rwanda, more than 200,000 people were murdered (no doubt instigated by the archenemy); people thirsting for the blood of their rivals carried out this crime. That people would become hardened in evil pursuits is clear from the Scriptures.

> That which cometh out of the man [Jesus said], that defileth the man. For from within, out of the heart of men, proceed evil thoughts, adulteries, fornications, murders, thefts, covetousness, wickedness, deceit, lasciviousness, an evil eye, blasphemy, pride, foolishness: all these evil things come from within, and defile the man. (Mark 7:20–23)
>
> Because iniquity shall abound, the love of many shall wax cold. (Matthew 24:11)

The apostle Paul reiterated a list of past recurrent evils to exist in our day.

Being filled with all unrighteousness, fornication, wickedness, covetousness, maliciousness; full of envy, murder, debate, deceit, malignity; whisperers, backbiters, haters of God, despiteful, proud, boasters, inventors of evil things, disobedient to parents, without understanding, covenant breakers, without natural affection, implacable, unmerciful: who knowing the judgment of God, that they which commit such things are worthy of death, not only do the same, but have pleasure in them that do them. (Romans 1:29–32)

Now the Spirit speaketh expressly, that in the latter times some shall depart from the faith, giving heed to seducing spirits, and doctrines of devils; ²Speaking lies in hypocrisy; having their conscience seared with a hot iron. (1 Timothy 4:1, 2)

Again, he was inspired to write:

This know also, that in the last days perilous times shall come. For men shall be lovers of their own selves, covetous, boasters, proud, blasphemers, disobedient to parents, unthankful, unholy, without natural affection, trucebreakers, false accusers, incontinent, fierce, despisers of those that are good, traitors, heady, highminded, lovers of pleasures more than lovers of God; having a form of godliness, but denying the power thereof: from such turn away. (2 Timothy 3:1–5)

Several years ago a man and woman attended a seminar I was presenting. They were passing by when they saw the tent. Their curiosity led them to park and walk in. They stayed through the presentation and, as soon as I was finished, they made a quick exit and disappeared. The following night they returned and continued to for the following nights.

Then the night came when I made an appeal for anyone who wanted to turn to God and find peace in Him to come to the altar. The man and his wife responded. With tears streaming down his face, he requested a private audience with me. After I was able to dismiss the rest of the attendees, we sat down to talk.

"Can God forgive me?" This was his first question.

"Of course, God can forgive you!" I stated.

"How do you know? You do not know who I am, or what I have done."

"That is true," I said. "I do not know who you are, or what you have done. But I know who God is, and what He can do." Then I asked, "What do you think you have done that you do not think God can forgive you?"

"I have killed 3,500 people," he stated, wringing his hands.

"How did you kill 3,500 people?" I questioned.

"Well," he started. When I was growing up, my father was an atheist and a hired killer. Every time he killed someone, he was always hiding. I hated that. So I determined that I was going to figure out a way to kill people without having to hide. It was then that I began to body-build until I could beat up every kid on the block. However, I couldn't bring myself to kill anyone. When I was seventeen, I joined the U.S. Army. I then became a helicopter pilot and went to Viet Nam. There, I volunteered for every search-and-destroy mission. Then, placing bets against the other pilots that I could kill more people than they, I would go on the missions.

"I am now terribly sorry that I counted 3,500 lives that I snuffed out. At that time, I loved every moment of it. As an atheist, I had no regard for God or religion; neither did I have a conscience. When we came here the first night, it was with the intent to stir up trouble. We always loved to go to bars and needle someone, hoping to get somebody angry enough to want to fight with me. That gave me the opportunity I wanted to take their faces and twist them. Now, I am sorry for all that I have done. Can God forgive me?" Fortunately, the Lord was able to turn him from his wicked ways.

This man is one frightful example of the many that have accepted evil as a way of life. People, though of bright intellect—as was the case of this man, who was a nuclear physicist—use their keen minds to commit malicious acts. There is no doubt that these kinds of predispositions toward evil are tractable to the originator of evil. However, by their relishing evil the devil need not take credit, for they have become like him in nature. Satan must gloat over the fact that mankind reflects his character rather than their Creator's. He need not worry about them nor spend time trying to persuade them into evil deeds; they do it without him having to bend efforts upon them.

The recent Aurora, Colorado, massacre allegedly committed by James Eagan Holmes, highlights the reality that man is bent on evil. Other examples include shooting sprees in United States schools, such as at Columbine High School in Littleton, Colorado, on April 20, 1999. Another case of pure wickedness was that of John Allan Muhammad and Lee Boyd Malvo and their Beltway sniper attacks in October 2002 in Washington, D.C., Maryland, and Virginia. They drove from place to place, randomly killing ten innocent people, just to do it, which tells us that we are living, as the Bible puts it, in "perilous times" (2 Timothy 3:1). The air seems to be charged with a spirit of violence. The uprisings in the Middle East, where people are mercilessly murdered, the genocides of former Yugoslavia, and other situations give clear evidence that mankind is plagued with a maliciousness bent to evil.

Men's own doings have contributed to this human aberration. Human nature created to reflect the Divine has in its very makeup the potential to also degenerate into the extremes of evil. The mechanisms designed to reach higher than the human thought can reach can become instruments of the worst cruelty and violence. The constant bombardments of the media industry encouraging self-gratification, pleasure seeking, and portraying violence as exciting and even enviable contribute to the forming of characters with an antithesis against all righteousness; a character that is like a magnet pulling all to itself. Thus, man becomes perverted in nature and devoid of conscience converting him into an agent of evil. Once this level is reached, Satan need not lend his influence to encourage evil.

> About 200 traits are transmitted from generation to generation in humans. These are called hereditary traits. These include dominant as well as recessive traits. Many human traits are transmitted in a simple Mendelian manner [Gregor Mendel was a monk who believed that "heredity was particulate, not acquired, and that the inheritance patterns of many traits could be explained through simple rules and ratios."[125]], while many others follow a non-Mendelian pattern shown when there is co-dominance, polygenes and sex-linked genes.[126]

Some traits are good, but can also be bad. If they are maladies that are passed on, the individual has no choice; they are inherent. Yet, others are self inflicted and often perpetuated; for example, self abuse. The lists of consequences brought about by these secret vices are many: the intellect becomes dimmed; there is a mental and physical dwarfing; children are made idiotic; brain paralysis may occur; the conscience hardens by deadening of mental sensibilities; memory deficiency is caused by the destruction of nerve power; and others. This is one vice among many that people get involved with to the detriment of physical, mental, and spiritual health.

I remember a young man whom I visited in a mental institution. His eyes were covered with bandages. When I asked the reason for the bandages, I was told that he had taken Lysergic acid diethylamide (LSD), a hallucinogenic drug. He began to have bizarre visions. He wanted to stop them, but he could not. When he couldn't, there came into his memory a verse of Scripture that said, "If thy right eye offend thee, pluck it out, and cast it from thee" (Matthew 5:29). Sadly, that is what he attempted to do. While it is probably true that the devil instigated this tragedy, the reality is that the young man chose to take the drug, and the results were simply an outworking of his choice. Though he might claim "the devil made me do it," the reality is that the devil did not place the drugs in his mouth and make him swallow.

Though self-induced maladies need to be taken care of, the cooperation or acknowledgement of the sufferer must be in place for he or she to have a successful outcome. People are not always willing to change their habits

---

125   "Genetics," Wikipedia: The Free Encyclopedia, http://en.wikipedia.org/wiki/Genetics (accessed October 11, 2012).
126   "Human Hereditary Traits," TutorVista.com, http://www.tutorvista.com/content/biology/biology-iii/human-genetics/human-hereditary-traits.php (accessed October 11, 2012).

irrespective of the consequences. For example, a lady who smoked wanted to quit because of health issues. She wanted delivery. However, when I suggested that, in order to quit, she also needed to give up coffee, she refused. She loved her coffee, and determined not to stop irrespective of the consequences.

Some people want prayer for healing when what is needed is for that person to give up the habit causing the sickness. If an individual requests anointing of oil for the removal of a sickness, it should not be attempted without determining if the malady is self-inflicted. If so, then reforming the lifestyle or habit would be the remedy. It is so easy for some people who suffer sicknesses created by their own doing, to place the blame elsewhere—on the devil. To proceed invoking the blessing of God when the person is practicing a causative (ignorant or willful) sin will imply that God overlooks the infraction and confirms the lifestyle or practice as acceptable. This leads to a deception, which encourages the victim to continue the practice that brings about sickness and death.

Many bizarre and weird manmade occurrences take place. Nevertheless, this does not rule out the possibility of demonic interaction with people who are in violation of divine law for human wellness. Nor does it rule out the interplay of demonic influence with people who are doing the best they can with their lives. In other words, one cannot summarily assume that all is the devil or just nature. Each case must be decided on its own basis and dealt with by taking all factors into consideration.

A word of caution here: never allow or invite just anyone to assess someone's condition unless there is clear evidence that the invitee is reputable and credible. I have seen and have experienced well-meaning people who attempt to diagnose and prescribe a remedy based upon their assumption of the problem. My little daughter was sick with a terrible cough. We thought it would pass, but it got worse. A well-intentioned person suggested a mixture of herbs. When my wife gave the treatment to our daughter, she began heaving so badly that we became gravely concerned for her. There were those who supposed that the sickness was caused by the devil. We felt differently about it, however, so we got medical help.

Fortunately, there was a doctor in town who made the proper diagnosis. He gave the appropriate antibiotic, and our daughter recovered. For the sin sick soul there is also a physician who is willing and able to heal everyone who seeks it.

THE MIGTHY CONQUEROR

Because man is naturally inclined to follow Satan's suggestions, his innate ability to resist so terrible a foe is like a twig withstanding a hurricane. Fallen human nature is Satan's lawful captive. However, when Christ, the mighty Conqueror, comes to man's aid, replacing His power for the suppliant's weakness, strengthening the resolve, and guiding the desires—the tide is turned. That is why Jesus came on His mission—to save man from the power of his great enslaver. God alone can limit the power of the devil; Satan well knows this. For this reason he hides himself and seeks to undetectably approach the sinner, hoping not to arouse the victim to flee to his strong refuge.

The power of the enemy of souls is descriptively revealed in the metaphor of the lion. "Your adversary the devil, as a roaring lion, walketh about, seeking whom he may devour" (1 Peter 5:8). He is also called the "great dragon" (Revelation 12:9). Both beasts are voracious and have an overpowering strength over their victims. Man is not his equal. He makes claims to be the rightful ruler of the earth as he goes to and fro, walking up and down in it. Because mankind is Satan's claimed lawful prey, "he is not off his watch for a single moment, through fear of losing an opportunity to destroy souls."[127] However, when the humblest weakest petitioner entreats the mighty Conqueror for help, casting himself fully upon His help, Satan and his host tremble for they know that they can be successfully repulsed.

It is therefore imperative "that God's people understand this, that they may escape his [the devil's] snares. Satan is preparing his deceptions, that in his last campaign against the . . . ["very elect"] they may not understand that it is he."[128] The Bible in 2 Corinthians 11:14 forewarns, "No marvel; for Satan himself is transformed into an angel of light." Concurrently, at the point that those deceived are postulating his nonexistence, he is gleefully ensnaring them. Because he can give them the sense that they are free moral agents, he is able to employ them for his purposes. No one knows better than the devil the power that a faithful true believer can have over him when his or her strength is in Christ. The weakest believer, when relying firmly upon Christ, can effectively repulse the enemy and his entire host.

---

127   *Testimonies for the Church*, vol. 1, 341.
128   Ibid.

He knows too well that if he came openly and boldly with his temptations and sophistries, the somnolent (sleep-walking) Christian would awaken to his danger and flee to the all-powerful Succor. Instead, he stealthily and undetectably works by remote control through those who are already his, but who claim allegiance to Christ.

OUR ONLY SAFETY

Christ's declaration that there are two roads in life (Matthew 7:13, 14) crystallizes the veracity of the role that the mind plays in our eternal destiny. There is no middle-of-the-road safe haven. Either we are choosing life or, by default in not exercising our choice, death. Our only safeguard is to make Christ our all. For if by faith He is abiding in our hearts, He will be in all our thoughts. Our deepest affections will be for Him. Our innermost desires will center in Him. We will love to dwell in His pure atmosphere, and relish His companionship. Thus, He will inhabit all the chambers our minds. All our hopes and expectations will be linked with His. The thought of His soon appearing will well up in the heart the highest joy. Our trust in Him will evoke the sweetest sense of peace. As we train our minds "to delight in spiritual exercises" and accustom ourselves to dwell in heavenly places, we will "not be overwhelmed with the purity and transcendent glory of heaven."[129]

Whenever men reject the Savior's invitation, they are yielding themselves to Satan. Multitudes in every department in life, in the home, in business, and even in the church, are doing this today. It is because of this that violence and crime have overspread the earth, and moral darkness, like the pall of death, enshrouds the habitations of men. Through his specious temptations Satan leads men to worse and worse evils, till utter depravity and ruin are the result. The only safeguard against his power is found in the presence of Jesus. Before men and angels Satan has been revealed as man's enemy and destroyer; whereas, Christ has shown that He is man's friend and deliverer. His Spirit will develop in man all that will ennoble the character and dignify the nature. It will build man up for the glory of God in body, soul, and spirit. "God hath not given us the spirit of fear; but of power, and of love, and of a sound mind" (2 Timothy 1:7). He has called us "to the obtaining of the glory [character] of our Lord Jesus Christ" has called us to be "conformed to the image of His Son" (2 Thessalonians 2:14; Romans 8:29).

And just as there are spirits that lead to the commission of sin, contrariwise "sin can be resisted and overcome only through the [mighty] agency of the Third Person of the Godhead, who would come with no modified energy, but in the fullness of divine power. It is the Holy Spirit that makes effectual what . . . the world's Redeemer" has worked out for our deliverance and uplifting. Through the inner workings of the Spirit the heart is made pure which enables the believer to become "a partaker of the divine nature." He comes with divine power to overcome all hereditary and cultivated tendencies to evil and to impress His own character upon" all who believe.[130]

Baldy, in the introductory story, was totally oblivious and ignorant of his possessor, as were the rest of us gang members. We carried on with thoughts and acts of violence, thinking ourselves to be the pilots of our own course and volition. How deluded we were. If you have read this book, you have no doubt become cognizant that there is a battle for your mind. On the one hand, there is the villain stealthily and arduously laboring to take possession of the unwary or the willing. While we should be keenly aware of our exposure to the assaults of unseen and invisible foes, we are to be sure that they cannot harm us without gaining our consent. Ever keep in mind that unseen agencies are at work to take the control of the mind. They act with unseen yet effectual power. They are continually laboring to accomplish our destruction.

> The power and malice of Satan and his host might justly alarm us, were it not that we may find shelter and deliverance in the superior power of our Redeemer. We carefully secure our houses with bolts and locks to protect our property and our lives from evil men; but we seldom think of the evil angels who are constantly seeking access to us, and against whose attacks we have, in our own strength, no method of defense. If permitted, they can distract our minds, disorder, torment our bodies, and destroy our possessions and our lives. Their only delight is in misery and destruction. Fearful is the condition of those who resist the divine claims, and yield to Satan's temptations, until God gives them up to the control of evil spirits. But those who follow Christ are ever safe under his watch care. Angels that excel in strength are sent from Heaven to protect them. The wicked one cannot break through the guard, which God has stationed about his people.[131]

We have a great Advocate vigilantly and actively working to keep His own from being deceived and controlled. Moreover, He will shed light on those already in grave danger to lead them to the One who not only can set them free but also keep them free. Obviously, the struggle is in not only realizing the danger, but also desiring to be set free from it. However, being set free comes with a price. That price is the willingness to surrender self, and it does not come without pain. An addict (unless there is supernatural deliverance) must go

130   *The Desire of Ages*, 671, with author's paraphrase.
131   *The Great Controversy*, 1888 ed., 517.

through an excruciatingly painful withdrawal. To the proud and boastful, giving up on self may be deemed as cringe-making humiliation. To the licentious, it may be translated as being plunged into celibacy. To the glutton, abstemiousness may appear like torture. To the reveler, liberty from the addiction of incessant excitement may be viewed as entering into a monastic lifestyle.

All of these fears are consequences of demonic influences seeking to induce resistance to the Spirit of God. Satan takes advantage of our ignorance and lack of knowledge of God and His ways. I remember when I was sensing a need to forgo my music career as bass player with Bill Haley and the Comets. The thought that struck me was, "If I become a Christian, I can no longer have any fun." Whenever I ask audiences if that is true or false, the response is almost an overwhelming "false!" However, the answer is actually "true."

The correct answer has to be viewed from the person's perspective. You see, the only familiar activities that I associated with the feeling of having "fun" were drinking, womanizing, partying, drugs, and the like. Because I had no knowledge or experience with the clean fun of a Christian, as far as I was concerned, it was no fun becoming one. A true Christian would never find pleasure in the sinful practices of the world. Consequently, becoming a believer was tantamount to lying down and dying, or living a very boring, meaningless existence and life.

After I decided to accept by faith what God was requesting—to take a leap into the unknown, trusting that I would be better off living God's way and willing to forgo the temporary pleasures for the deferred joys—I found deliverance and victory in my life. In fact, it was not until after I became a Christian that I became aware of how real Satan really was. I then realized how much control he previously had over me, and to a limited extent, continued to keep his tentacles on me. This was the case until through the study of God's Word, I could discern the difference, and in the powerful, efficacious name of Christ I gained the victory.

So my appeal is to encourage you: if you have not yet yielded your heart, do not hesitate to give your life over to God. If you find yourself harassed by the enemy, flee to Jesus. He is your only safeguard. If, perchance, you discover either willingly or ignorantly that you, or someone you know, has been associated with the devil through activities, a system of beliefs, or practices, yet want to be free, then turn to Jesus Christ.

Remember! "If the Son therefore shall make you free, shall be freed indeed" (John 8:36).

BIBLICAL PROMISES

PROMISES FOR FORGIVENESS

1 John 1:9	If we confess, He will forgive.
Romans 8:1	No condemnation when in Jesus.
1 John 1:7	Blood of Christ cleanses from all sin.
Isaiah 1:18	Your sins shall be as white as snow.
Isaiah 38:17	He casts our sins behind His back.
Isaiah 43:25	He will not remember our sins.
Isaiah 44:22	He has blotted out our transgressions.
Micah 7:19	Casts our sins into the depths of the sea.

PROMISES FOR HOLY SPIRIT

Luke 11:13	Will be given the Holy Spirit upon asking.
John 14:26	Teach and bring things to our remembrance.
John 14:16	He shall abide with us forever.
John 14:17	He shall dwell in us.
Ephesians 3:16	Will strengthen us.

PROMISES FOR EVERYDAY LIFE

Psalm 32:8	God will instruct, teach, and guide.
John 14:13, 14	Ask in His name and it shall be given.
2 Chronicles 20:20	Believe in God and His prophets and you will be established and prosper.
Exodus 33:14	His presence will go with us and give us rest.
James 1:5	Ask for wisdom.
Philippians 4:19	God will supply all our needs.
Philippians 4:13	We can do all things through Christ who strengthens us.
Matthew 6:33 Luke 12:31	Seek the kingdom first and all these things shall be added to you.
2 Corinthians 9:6	He that soweth bountifully shall reap bountifully.

2 Corinthians 6:17, 18 He will be our Father, and we shall be His sons and daughters.

Philippians 1:6   God will continue the work He has started in us.

James 5:15   The prayers of faith shall save the sick.

1 Corinthians 15:58 Be steadfast, your labor is not in vain in the Lord.

Psalm 27:10   When parents forsake you, the Lord will take you up.

Psalm 34:17   The Lord delivers the righteous from trouble when He hears their cry.

Psalm 34:18   The Lord is near the brokenhearted.

Isaiah 40:28–31   Strength and power to those that wait upon Him.

Philippians 4:7   The peace of God shall keep your hearts.

Psalm 34:8   Those who trust shall be given every blessing.

Psalm 37:34   Be patient, the Lord will honor you.

Psalm 27:14   Wait on the Lord and He will help you.

Jeremiah 33:3   Secrets shall be revealed.

Psalm 138:3   He answers and strengthens.

2 Corinthians 8:15 We will have no lack.

2 Timothy 1:7   The Lord has given us the spirit of power, of love and of a sound mind.

Romans 8:31, 32   If God is for us, who can be against us. He will freely give us all things.

Matthew 18:20   Where two or three meet, He will be with them.

Jude 24   He is able to keep you from falling.

Psalms 55:22   He shall sustain you.

Proverbs 16:3   Your thoughts shall be established.

Psalm 119:165   Great peace to those who love the law.

Proverbs 3:6   He shall direct your paths.

Isaiah 26:3   He will keep us in perfect peace.

Matthew 11:28-30 I will give you rest.

Isaiah 58:11   He will guide you and satisfy your soul.

Proverbs 18:24   We have a friend who sticks closer than even a brother.

2 Peter 3:9   God is patient with us.

2 Peter 2:9   The Lord will rescue us from our trials.

Ezekiel 36:26, 27   A new heart and spirit.

James 4:7   Resist the devil and he will flee from you.

2 Corinthians 10:4, 5 Victory over evil thoughts.

Isaiah 41:10   Overcome fear because God will help us.

BLANK CHECK PROMISES

Psalm 34:10	Those who seek the Lord will never lack any good thing.
Psalm 37:5	Trust Him to help you and He will.
Ephesians 3:20	He is able to do more than we ask or think.
Mark 10:27	With God all things are possible.
Mark 9:23	All things are possible to him who believes.
Psalm 21:2; 37:4	Gives your heart's desire.
Luke 1:37	There is nothing God can't do.
John 15:16	Anything you ask in Jesus' name may be given.
John 16:24	Ask and you will receive.
Luke 11:9; Matthew 7:7	Ask and receive; seek and find.
Mark 11:24	What you desire, believe, and you shall have them.
Psalm 84:11	No good thing will He withhold.
John 15:7	Abide in God, and what we ask will be done.
Romans 8:28	All things work together for good.

PROMISES FOR THE LAST DAYS

James 1:12	Blessed are they who endure, for they shall receive a crown of life.
Revelation 3:10	He will keep us in the hour of temptation.
Psalm 91:15	He will be with us in trouble and deliver us.
Joshua 1:5	He will not forsake us.
Matthew 5:11, 12	When men shall revile you, the reward is great.
Jeremiah 30:5-7	We shall be saved out of the time of Jacob's trouble.
Daniel 12:1	We shall be delivered from the time of trouble.
Psalm 46:1–3	God is our help in trouble.
Matthew 24:13	Those who endure shall be saved.
Psalm 34:19	The Lord will deliver us from all afflictions.
Romans 5:3-5	Tribulation produces patience.
2 Corinthians 1:3, 4	He comforts in all tribulation.
Luke 21:36	Escape the things that shall come to pass.
John 14:18	I will not leave you comfortless.
Matthew 28:20	I am with you always.
John 16:33	We shall have tribulation in the world, but Christ has overcome.